THE VICTORY GARDEN COMPANION

THE VICTORY GARDEN

COMPANION

America's Most Popular Gardening Series Offers
Expert Advice for Creating a Beautiful Landscape for Your Home

Michael Weishan and Laurie Donnelly

Collins

An Imprint of HarperCollinsPublishers

HarperCollins books may be purchased for
educational, business, or sales promotional use.
For information, please write: Special Markets
Department, HarperCollins Publishers,
10 East 53rd Street, New York, NY 10022.

FIRST EDITION

Designed by Chalkley Calderwood Pratt

Library of Congress Cataloging-in-Publication Data
has been applied for.

ISBN-10: 0-06-059977-4
ISBN-13: 978-0-06-059977-5

06 07 08 09 10 WBC/TP 10 9 8 7 6 5 4 3 2 1

To Laurie Donnelly, friend, coauthor, and executive producer
extraordinaire, whose kind and nurturing nature
cultivates people, programs, and plants with equal aplomb.

MW

Contents

ACKNOWLEDGMENTS • xiii   PREFACE • xvi

CHAPTER ONE:

2 Values, Views, and Vantage Points

Empowerment • 4

Begin with the Beginning—The House • 5

Historical House and Garden Styles • 6

Into the Garden • 11

Step by Step: Making Your Own Landscape Plan, Part I • 12

Weekend Project: Charting the Lay of Your Land • 14

Garden Basics: A Landscape Design Checklist • 18

Fencing • 19

Digging Deeper: Fencing Styles • 20

Hedges and Screen Planting • 22

Choosing the Perfect Plant for Hedging • 24

Ask Michael: Zone Maps • 27

Inspired Gardens: Taliesin • 30

CHAPTER TWO:

34 Braving the Elements— Sun, Wind, Soil, and Rain

Let There Be Light • 37

Believe What You Read • 39

It's an Ill Wind . . . • 41

Step by Step: Making Your Own Landscape Plan, Part II • 44

In the Beginning, There Was Soil • 46

What Is Soil, Anyway? • 47

Garden Basics: Of Sand Dunes and Pottery Barns— Improving Clayey or Extremely Sandy Soils • 48

Digging Deeper: Winning the War of the Worms • 49

Weekend Project: Composting the Victory Garden Way • 50

Compost Contents • 51

Ask Michael: Fertilizer 101 • 52

Inspired Gardens: Les Jardins de Métis • 54

CHAPTER THREE:

58 Entrances and Exits— Designing the Front Yard

The Importance of Streetscapes • 60

Driveways to Success • 63

Some Paving Options for Modern Drives • 63

Design Basics: Alternative Driveway Schemes for Today's Living • 66

Walk the Walk • 68

On an Even Keel • 68

Size Matters • 70

To Curve or Not to Curve • 71

Garden Basics: Eye versus Paper • 71

Foundering Foundations • 72

Tough Choices • 75

Milwaukee Makeover • 78

Step by Step: How to Plant Foundation Shrubs • 82

Best Bets for Foundation Plants • 85

Digging Deeper: The Mysteries of Outdoor Scale • 88

Ask Michael: Olmsted's Magic Formula
for Step Design • 89

Inspired Gardens: Colonial Williamsburg • 90

CHAPTER FOUR:

94 Backyard Fixtures and Features

Easy Livin' Outdoors • 96

Choosing the Right Design • 96

Paving Considerations • 99

Step by Step: Laying Your Own Brick or
Stone Terrace • 104

Never Too Big • 106

Water, Water Everywhere • 107

Step by Step: Installing a Flexible Pond Liner • 110

Planning and Planting for the Future
in the Backyard • 112

Using Trees in the Landscape • 113

Using Shrubs in the Landscape • 115

Best Bets for Backyard Trees and Shrubs • 118

Garden Basics: Forcing Branches Indoors • 121

Best Bets for Forcing Branches • 122

Ask Michael: Ponds and Wildlife • 124

Digging Deeper: The Garden Conservancy • 125

Inspired Gardens: The Backyard of Thomas Hobbs,
Vancouver, British Columbia • 126

CHAPTER FIVE:

130 The Great American Lawn

The Green, Green Grass of Home • 132

Digging Deeper: A Little Lawn History • 133

How Much Is Enough? • 133

Assessing What You Have • 134

Starting a New Lawn • 134

Leveling the Field • 135

Seed versus Sod • 136

Choosing the Right Grass • 137

Selecting Grass Seed • 137

Step by Step: Planting a New Lawn from Seed • 140

Weekend Project: Laying Sod • 142

Know When to Hold 'em, Know When
to Roll 'em • 145

Lawn Maintenance • 145

Common Lawn Problems • 148

Alternatives to Lawns • 152

Inspired Gardens: Edith Wharton's The Mount • 154

CHAPTER SIX:

158 Flower Power

The Perennial Border • 163

Design Basics: The Color Wheel • 164

Sine Qua Non • 168

Choosing Plant Material for Perennial Borders • 169

Best Bets: Perennials for Partial Shade • 169

Best Bets: Perennials for Full Sun • 169

Garden Basics: Perennial Maintenance • 172

Ask Michael: Best Time to Plant or Transplant
Perennials? • 173

An Annual Affair • 173

Using Flowers in the General Landscape • 175

Best Bets: Annuals • 175

Creating a Massed Tulip Display • 178

Weekend Project: Growing Annuals from Seed • 180

Step by Step: Preparing a New Flower Bed • 182

Inspired Gardens: The Boerner Botanical Gardens,
Milwaukee, Wisconsin • 184

CHAPTER SEVEN:

188 The Edible Garden

Why Grow Your Own? • 190

Selecting the Site • 190

Preparing the Soil • 191

Organic versus Inorganic at the Victory Garden • 192

Design Basics: Laying Out a Vegetable Garden • 192

Ready, Set, Seed • 193

Step by Step: Building a Cold Frame • 196

Weekend Project: Vertical Gardening • 198

Planning to Get the Most from Your Garden • 200

The Victory Garden Vegetables • 201

Growing Culinary Herbs in the Vegetable Garden • 207

Maintenance • 208

Of Pests and Pestilence • 209

Mammalian Marauders • 212

Quick Tips: Autumn Soil Enhancement for Better Spring Harvests • 212

Digging Deeper: The Trouble with Heirlooms • 213

Best Bets: Top Tools for Vegetable Gardening • 214

Ask Michael: Top Tomatoes • 215

Inspired Gardens: The Vegetable Garden of Thomas Jefferson • 216

CHAPTER EIGHT:

220 A Berry Extravaganza

Raspberries • 222

Step by Step: Building a Raspberry Trellis • 226

Best Bets: Selected Raspberries • 228

Strawberries • 229

Weekend Project: Growing Strawberries in a Jar • 230

The Strawberry Clan • 232

Planting Times for Strawberries • 233

Best Bets: Selected Strawberries • 234

Blueberries • 235

Best Bets: Selected Blueberries • 236

Gooseberries and Currants: The "Other" Berries • 239

Digging Deeper: The Genus *Rubus*, or Berries by Every Other Name • 240

Ask Michael: The Missing Orchard • 240

Inspired Gardens: The Redland Fruit and Spice Park • 242

CHAPTER NINE:

246 The Urban Garden

Nowhere to Hide • 248

Inside Out • 248

Other Issues • 251

The Urban Environment • 252

The Dirty Truth About Urban Soil • 252

Best Bets: Trees for Urban Spaces • 254

Best Bets: Urban Perennials • 255

Best Bets: Shrubs for Urban Gardeners • 256

Alternative Urban Lifestyles: Raised Beds • 258

Container Gardening on Decks, Balconies, and Roofs • 259

Choosing Containers • 261

Step by Step: Repotting a Plant • 262

Garden Basics: Choosing the Right Pot • 264

Garden Basics: Planting the Perfect Window Box • 265

Digging Deeper: Behind Trompe l'Oeil • 266

Weekend Project: Creating a Small Water Feature in a Galvanized Tub • 268

Ask Michael: Succulent Gardens • 270

Urban Makeover • 272

Inspired Gardens: The Swinnen Garden in Sint-Niklaas, Belgium • 276

ART CREDITS • 279   RESOURCES • 283   INDEX • 285

Acknowledgments

There would be no *Victory Garden Companion* were it not for "The Victory Garden" television series. For more than thirty years we've had the privilege of sharing with our viewers the world's finest gardens, the best gardening practices, and the passion of countless individuals who have found joy in cultivating the earth and making gardens grow. To our millions of loyal fans, we give our heartfelt thanks.

It is with deepest gratitude that we also wish to acknowledge those highly skilled individuals who are responsible for bringing "The Victory Garden" series to life, both on the screen and off. Kudos go out to all the members of our ensemble cast, but most particularly to gardener Kip Anderson, without whose sage advice and sound practical knowledge major portions of both show and book simply wouldn't have been possible. Thanks also go to the country's finest production team— producer Hilary Finkel Buxton (who was also of major help researching portions of the manuscript), editor Harlan Reiniger, production coordinator Deborah Hurley, director of photography Joel Coblenz and principal sound engineer Gilles Morin. Praise is due as well to all the people in the various departments at WGBH who have worked tirelessly behind the scenes to ensure that "The Victory Garden" remains the best gardening program on television, and who generously aided us in the daunting task of translating the vital essence of the show to these pages.

Finally, a tip of the gardening hat must also go to the senior management at WGBH—Henry Becton, Jon Abbott, and Margaret Drain, as well as to our sponsors: Scotts and Subaru, without whose continued support there simply would be no Victory Garden to talk about.

To all of you—as well as to our families, whose patience and support made writing this book possible—we again say "thank you!"

Michael Weishan
Laurie Donnelly

WGBH

WGBH would also like to thank its intrepid, savvy, and wise literary agent, Doe Coover, who brought *The Victory Garden Companion* to the talented people at Collins to begin with. Estimable editor Kathy Huck and her invaluable colleague, Ryu Spaeth, have lent their editorial wisdom, guidance, patience, and flexibility to this complicated book; Chalkley Calderwood Pratt has worked design magic on it. The original photography of the Victory Garden by Jeff Dunn adds a wonderful sense of place to the book. And a big debt of gratitude is due Terry Hackford, who masterfully managed the art program, and photo researcher Toby Greenberg, who pulled out all the stops to get the book the images it needed. Thanks go to WGBHers David Bernstein, Stephanie Coyle, Mary Cahill Farella, Jeff Garmel, Julie Gomes, Betsy Groban, Charles McEnerney, Julie Reber, Abby Stevens, and Jennifer Welsh, who have contributed in their own way to the success of this book. At Collins, we would also like to thank Jean Marie Kelly, Shelby Meizlik, and Andrea Rosen, who have done so much to shine light on the Victory Garden. Last, but not least, we would like to thank Russell Morash, creator of "The Victory Garden," for creating a lasting television legacy.

Preface

Several years ago, when the folks at WGBH asked me if I would be interested in writing a new addition to the venerable *Victory Garden* book series, I was flattered, but flummoxed. While it had been more than a decade since the appearance of the last volume, quite frankly, I wasn't necessarily convinced that the world needed another general gardening book, even from a program as popular as "The Victory Garden." A quick visit to the burgeoning shelves of the gardening section at my local bookstore more than confirmed that suspicion: dozens of books, some quite good, have appeared over the last few years that would seem to have completely covered every aspect of the modern American landscape.

That is, every aspect except one: for I discovered in my search through these books that while there were hundreds of guides that listed, say, specific requirements for perennials and annuals, and many more that gave great technical information about laying a stone wall, building a garden seat, or starting a perennial bed, none told you in a clear, concise, and friendly voice *how* to integrate those perennials and annuals into your backyard, *how* to decide whether you even *wanted* a wall or not, or *where* to put that bench once you finally *did* build it. What was required, it seemed, was not necessarily more information but rather a triage of the data already out there, to help you, the amateur gardener, to decide what's good and what's bad,

what you need and what you don't, what works and what won't—all with the goal of creating the best landscape possible in your yard. That's what this book is all about: it's a sampler, if you will, of good gardening practice.

The following pages are designed to help you assess the overall condition of your current landscape, to identify assets and issues, to create a viable landscape plan that you can implement over a number of years, and to address individual sections of your landscape in an orderly, logical way. We'll talk about flowers, shrubs, and trees; grass and ground covers in their myriad forms; growing in containers, raising vegetables, and the trials and rewards of gardening in the city. We have tips on building water features, terraces, and decks. We'll even tell you how to plant a hedge. But best of all, you can be certain that whatever we tell you, the information we relate is tried and true, collected from over 30 years of actual gardening experience on America's oldest and most popular gardening show. You may not always agree with our conclusions, but at least you'll have the assurance of knowing that we're talking from personal experience, and you can use the information we relate to make your own informed choices. That's what distinguishes this book from all the rest, and why I think it forms a valuable addition to the American gardening library.

I hope you'll agree.

Michael Weishan

■ If this is the kind of garden you've dreamed of creating for your home, read on, because you can make it a reality! Equally lovely landscapes are achievable even for the beginner—if you follow the steps we lay out in the upcoming chapters.

Chapter 1
Values, Views, and Vantage Points

Plans should be made on the ground to fit the place, and not the place made to suit some plan out of a book.

WILLIAM ROBINSON
The Garden Beautiful, 1907

Empowerment

FOR YEARS I WAS CONTINUALLY AMAZED AT HOW THE mere mention of the term "landscape design" could intimidate otherwise totally confident people. Men and women who had adeptly mastered difficult professions—many well beyond my ken—told me again and again that they felt a sense of utter dread and doom when confronted with the task of "doing something about the yard." Adventurous souls who didn't think twice about ripping out and replacing a window, replastering walls, or doing their own electrical wiring or plumbing—tasks far more complicated than I would ever, even on my most ambitious day, imagine undertaking—related to me that they felt completely stymied by the great outdoors. How could this be? After almost 35 years of being in and around horticulture, I was baffled. Surely, learning to garden will take time and skill, but it couldn't be all that more difficult than flying a plane, building a bridge, or healing the sick!

Then, the answer occurred to me. The problem lay, as many do, in a simple matter of translation: Quite a number of people (and perhaps you include yourself in this group) simply fail to realize that for all practical purposes, design challenges indoors require the exact same skills as outdoor design challenges. If you can do one, you can do the other. It's just that simple.

Think about it this way: Unless you live on a 1,000-acre farm or rolling estate, you deal daily with an outdoor space that has precise visual boundaries—exactly the same kind of boundaries your house possesses, only with a different terminology. Outside, the walls are your property boundaries, the floor is the ground, and the roof is the sky. Views out to distant points are the windows, and the small interior sections of the yard with specific functions are the individual rooms of your outdoor house, otherwise known as your yard. To carry the metaphor further, outside, your grass is the rug, the vines are the drapes, the trees and shrubs are the furniture, and the flowers are the bibelots, books, or other decorative items scattered around your house. And on it goes.

So then it stands to reason that if you can put paint and fabric together, if you can match a couch and rug, if you can

■ In this small tropical garden, it's easy to see how the principles of interior design and landscape design are closely related. Here, the fence line forms a "wall," the pavers the "floor," and the framed view between the columns a "window." Translate your good sense inside to the outdoors, and you're halfway to a great garden.

lay out your home office in a functional way, then you too can have a beautiful garden. Whether you're starting from a completely blank slate or have inherited an outdoor space that no longer pleases or that functions poorly, all it takes to transform your yard from problem to perfect is to translate the design knowledge *you already have* to a slightly different outdoor medium. Once there, all you need to do is educate yourself a bit on how your new building materials—stone, soil, bricks, pots, plants—function in the exterior home environment. Now, granted, you may never fully master the intricacies of cross-pollination, or become an expert on historic garden styles—or even want to—but the truth is you *can* create your own beautiful garden without an ounce of fear or frustration.

How to begin?

Begin with the Beginning—The House

BEFORE YOU MOVE A SHOVELFUL OF SOIL, BEFORE YOU plant a single plant, before you prune the first branch or even pull a weed, I recommend that you pull up a yard chair, have a seat, and look at your garden's most dominant feature. And I'm not talking about the trees, bushes, or paving. Believe it or not, *the most important part of your garden is your house.*

This notion becomes easier to grasp if you consider how most of us use our outdoor spaces—as play, living, or entertainment areas. Your garden, then, really functions as an extension of your home, and as such, your landscape needs to be closely tied to your house, both in feeling and design. In order to achieve this unity, you first need to understand a bit about your home's architectural style. What type of house do you have? Modern? Colonial? Victorian? Or something in between?

One of the easiest ways to define the character of your home is by its building date. There are exceptions to this rule, such as a modern home built in the Colonial style, but by and large the age of your home will help you to determine what type of house you have.

Once you've determined your home's architectural style, take a closer look at its detailing. Does your home make extensive use of wood or brick? And if so, what color? Is the architectural style very ornamental, or is it streamlined? Are the elements of the facade symmetrical, or are they completely random? Familiarizing yourself with your home's most distinctive characteristics is important, because it is this same type of detailing or "feel" that you'll want to extend out into your landscape.

COMING TO TERMS

{garden vs. landscape} Although in the United States the word "garden" is often used to refer just to a flower garden, a vegetable garden, or other cultivated beds, in this book we will be using the term more as the English do, referring to the home landscape as a whole. Thus for our purposes, yard, garden, and landscape are all synonymous.

MAGAZINES: A GREAT SOURCE OF IDEAS

If the thought of drawing up your own garden plan seems overwhelming at first, why not ease into the process by creating your own garden album? It's fun, it's simple to do, and it will help you decide what elements to include in your new landscape once the planning phase begins.

Begin by clipping out any and all images from glossy gardening magazines, catalogs, or newspapers that you find appealing. Maybe it's an interwoven pattern of boxwood parterre that catches your eye, or a long perennial bed with a bold color palette that strikes your fancy, or an old farmers' stone wall that would go perfectly with your house. The trick here is not to overthink this process—go with your gut reactions, collect images that appeal to you, and place them in a folder with a quick note or two to jar your memory when the time to start planning arrives.

Another source of inspiration can come from other people's gardens that have distinct elements you like—just snap a picture or two and add them to your album. And don't forget to take the camera to regional flower shows, which can also be a great source for ideas.

When you're ready to think about a garden plan, mount these images on a bulletin board and study your selections. Is there a dominant color theme to your collection? Are there textures to which you seem drawn? Is there a certain style of garden that you particularly like? Or are you drawn to unique elements— a pond, a garden bench, a meditative walk? Make note of these preferences, and when the time comes to begin planning, you'll be well ahead of the game.

Historical House and Garden Styles

Style/Sub-Styles Date	Notable Architectural Elements	Common Characteristics of Corresponding Period Gardens
EARLY COLONIAL Before 1750 	Steeply pitched gabled roofs; small, multipaned windows; single, extremely large, central chimney.	**Overall garden style:** Small cultivated areas carved out of wilderness; vegetables and herbs raised in beds; large areas of copse and meadow. **Foundation plantings:** Few or none. **Lawn:** None; only pasture. **Drive materials:** Dirt. **Walk materials:** Compacted dirt or clay. **Decorative elements:** Extremely simple handcrafted elements. **Fencing materials/style:** Split rail, simple picket fence.
GEORGIAN/ADAM/FEDERAL 1750–1820 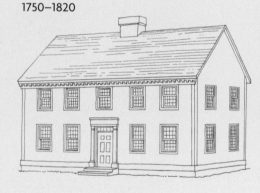	Symmetrical facades with paneled doors, multipaned windows and symmetrically placed chimneys; extensive borrowing of classical elements such as fluted columns, pediments, entablatures, or dentiled cornices.	**Overall garden style:** Depending on the opulence of the structure, informal to the extremely formal. Plant palette limited to those species commonly found during the period, i.e., biennials or European perennials; limited selection of trees and shrubs. **Foundation plantings:** Few or none. **Lawn:** Small, if any; extensive wild areas such as pasture and woodland. **Drive materials:** Dirt or gravel. **Walk materials:** Dirt, gravel, brick (rarely), stone. **Decorative elements:** Simple, handcrafted objects made primarily of local materials such as wood; occasional metal pieces such as sundials; summer houses; wooden benches; little or no sculpture. **Fencing materials/style:** Wooden fences, from simple split rail to elaborate picket styles.

Style/Sub-Styles Date	Notable Architectural Elements	Common Characteristics of Corresponding Period Gardens
EARLY REVIVAL STYLES: GREEK, TUDORESQUE, ITALIANATE 1820–1870 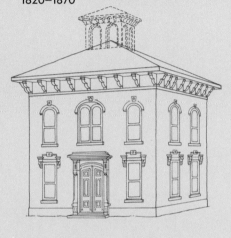	Generally symmetrical facades with ornamental elements borrowed from earlier historical styles.	**Overall garden style:** Similar to the previous period, but with expanding levels of ornamentation as general wealth increased and land areas became domesticated. **Foundation plantings:** Few or none. **Lawn:** Small, if any; extensive wild areas of pasture and woodland. **Drive materials:** Dirt or gravel. **Walk materials:** Dirt, gravel, brick (rarely), stone. **Decorative elements:** Increased use of commercially produced garden elements. **Fencing materials/style:** Wooden fences, with some use of cast iron.
VICTORIAN: QUEEN ANNE, SHINGLE, STICK, ROMANESQUE 1870–1910 	Asymmetrical massing; extremely detailed and ornamental facades, often with highly varied window/chimney shapes and styles designed to avoid flat and regular surfaces; eclectic use of wood, stone, and brick.	**Overall garden style:** Generally asymmetrical designs to match architecture, with emphasis on the bold and exotic. Broad plant palette, widespread use of annuals, especially bedding plants used in bold combinations. **Foundation plantings:** Houses "cloaked" in greenery, with extensive planting around the foundation. **Lawn:** Limited early in the period, becoming more extensive by the late 1800s. **Drive materials:** Gravel, cobble, brick, stone. **Walk materials:** Gravel, stone, cobble, brick. **Decorative elements:** Rustic garden ornaments in both wood and iron; intricately detailed gazebos, benches, tables, and sculptural pieces in metal and stone. **Fencing materials style:** Picket as well as turned wooden fence types; elaborate use of iron fencing in urban areas.

Style/Sub-Styles Date	Notable Architectural Elements	Common Characteristics of Corresponding Period Gardens
ARTS AND CRAFTS: CRAFTSMAN, PRAIRIE, BUNGALOW 1900–1930 	Low-pitched roofs cover single or 1½-storied structures; decorative beams under gables, large front porches with heavy, squared support columns.	**Overall garden style:** Less opulent than the preceding period, with a greater emphasis on more naturalistic plantings; fewer annuals, more perennials. **Foundation plantings:** Some, though generally low in keeping with the reduced scale of the facade. **Lawn:** More extensive as period progressed. **Drive materials:** Gravel, cobble, brick, stone, concrete, asphalt. **Walk materials:** Gravel, stone, cobble, brick, concrete. **Decorative elements:** Simple handmade pieces that matched the simple, unadorned lines of the house. **Fencing materials/style:** Simple wooden fences, both picket and panel, often with cut-out shapes.
COLONIAL/TUDOR REVIVAL 1920–1940 	Simplified versions of the earlier Georgian/Adam styles; symmetrical facades with windows often in adjacent pairs.	**Overall garden style:** Generally formal and symmetrical, meant to evoke "old-fashioned" gardens. **Foundation plantings:** Extensive. **Lawn:** Extensive. **Drive materials:** Gravel, cobble, brick, asphalt, concrete. **Walk materials:** Cobble, brick, asphalt, concrete. **Decorative elements:** Imitation pieces in the Colonial style, often far more elaborate than actual Colonial detailing. **Fencing materials/style:** Wooden, often imitating Colonial or old English fencing styles.

Style/Sub-Styles Date	Notable Architectural Elements	Common Characteristics of Corresponding Period Gardens
ECLECTIC STYLES: PUEBLO, MONTEREY, ITALIAN RENAISSANCE, TUDOR, AND OTHERS 1900–1940 	Highly varied styles based on regional/historical models.	**Overall garden style:** Generally formal and symmetrical. **Foundation plantings:** Extensive. **Lawn:** Extensive. **Drive materials:** Gravel, cobble, brick, asphalt, concrete. **Walk materials:** Cobble, brick, asphalt, concrete. **Decorative elements:** Pieces to match the housing style and evoke atmosphere. **Fencing materials/style:** Designed to closely match the individual style of the architecture.
MODERN RANCH, INTERNATIONAL, CONTEMPORARY 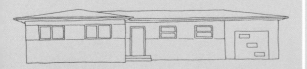	Few ornamental details; modern materials/methods evident in construction.	**Overall garden style:** Generally informal and asymmetrical. **Foundation plantings:** Extensive. **Lawn:** Extensive (though not necessarily required or wanted). **Drive materials:** Gravel, cobble, brick, asphalt, concrete, pre-formed pavers. **Walk materials:** Cobble, brick, asphalt, concrete, pre-formed pavers. **Decorative elements:** Minimal use of garden ornamentation; few outbuildings or secondary structures. **Fencing materials/style:** Large panel fences for privacy; revival of split rail and "country styles," especially for ranches.

Say, for instance, you have an Arts and Crafts bungalow and wish to construct an appropriate garden. You'll want to select major design elements such as paving, fencing, and garden ornaments that conform to the basic tenets of the Arts and Crafts style already reflected in your home, including the period's emphasis on simple, old-fashioned craftsmanship and the use of natural materials such as wood and stone. Thus, those modern-looking concrete pavers you may have been considering wouldn't be the best choice, nor would that cute Art Deco sundial you just bought at the nursery. Handcrafted bricks, on the other hand, would definitely be a great option, as would a simple wooden fence or rustic gazebo. The important lesson here is to allow your home's style to set the design parameters not only of the interior, but of the exterior as well, and then stick to these guidelines throughout the design and construction process.

If you own an older home, a safe bet is to choose a garden style and its concomitant elements that correspond historically to that of your home, and then carry that theme throughout the entire garden. A Colonial house, for example, could be surrounded with a Colonial-style garden using elements associated with that period: wooden fences, brick pavers, an herb or vegetable garden, and minimal use of foundation plantings. Another approach with older homes would be to mix and match elements from different styles to create a novel blend, with certain elements exactly matching the period of your house and others subtly contrasting with it. However, these combinations, sometimes termed "eclectic," are much harder to accomplish, and your success will largely depend on the level of your own design skills. If, however, like many of us you feel unable to dabble in multiple time streams at once, then it's best to stick to basics and choose a style that closely parallels the look and period of your home. Remember: garden

COMING TO TERMS

{symmetry vs. balance}. Two concepts that you'll hear a lot about in this book are symmetry and balance. Although both ideas are related, there are some important distinctions between them, as seen in the two pictures below. The top house is said to be symmetrical: the two sides are mirror images of each other. The bottom one

is balanced: while the gable and turret ends are quite different in appearance, the massing of each matches or "balances" the other. These concepts are equally important in garden design, since symmetry and balance are important tools in the creation of pleasing landscapes. While garden layouts don't have to be symmetrical (though they often are, especially in formal settings) in order to succeed visually, elements of the landscape *do* need to be balanced. For more on that, see Chapter Three.

■ Here's an ideal example of how house and garden should complement each other. This Federal-era structure, with its symmetrical lines and formal facade, is perfectly mated with an equally restrained and balanced landscape.

design is not static, and you can always experiment with additions later on.

And what if you have a modern home? Well, for modern structures designed with a heavy regional flavor, such as the thousands of Mission- or Mediterranean-style homes now springing up in the western and southwestern parts of the country, matching regional-style gardens can work quite well. An adobe-style dwelling, for instance, could be landscaped with a Southwestern-style garden, with a heavy use of succulents and other drought-resistant plants, very little lawn, and minimal ornamentation other than native wood or stone.

Those homes without any distinct style, such as modern box-style houses, can be a bit trickier, because you're essentially dealing with a blank slate. In these instances, sometimes a his-

torical perspective can still prove helpful. Many modern houses borrow their architectural vocabulary from previous design periods, and by selecting garden elements from corresponding historical garden styles you can achieve a pleasing synthesis.

Into the Garden

ONCE YOU'VE EXAMINED YOUR HOUSE, DETERMINED ITS style, and considered how you might extend that design orientation into the garden, the next step is to assess what you currently have to work with in your landscape, and what ultimately you would like to achieve. The easiest way to tackle this is by doing exactly what a professional landscape designer would do: draw up a plan of existing conditions.

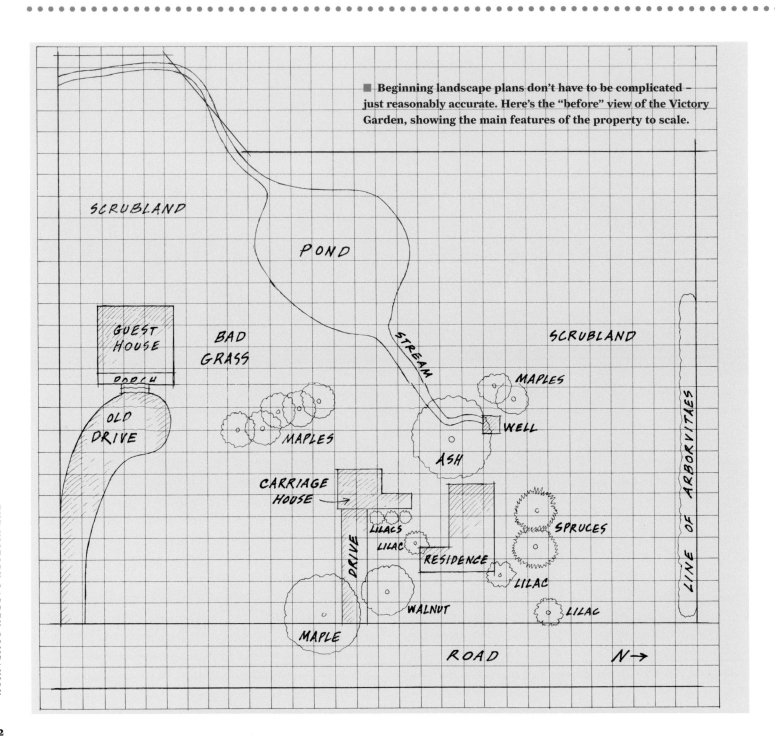

Beginning landscape plans don't have to be complicated – just reasonably accurate. Here's the "before" view of the Victory Garden, showing the main features of the property to scale.

SCRUBLAND

POND

GUEST HOUSE

BAD GRASS

PORCH

OLD DRIVE

MAPLES

STREAM

SCRUBLAND

MAPLES

WELL

ASH

CARRIAGE HOUSE →

DRIVE

LILACS

LILAC

RESIDENCE

SPRUCES

LILAC

WALNUT

LILAC

MAPLE

LINE OF ARBORVITAES

ROAD

N →

1 Many people hesitate to draw up a plan because they think it's too difficult, or not worth the energy, but the reality is that an accurate plan of your yard is probably the best gardening investment of time and money you'll ever make. The process is really quite simple. All you need is a sheet of graph paper, several measuring tapes (25' and 100', or one of the new electronic measures now commonly available), a pencil, and a compass. Start by drawing out the boundary lines of your lot. These measurements generally can be taken from your mortgage or building plot plan.

2 Next, measure your home's foundation line, called the footprint. Transfer these measurements to the graph paper, assigning one square for each foot, two feet, or three feet. (The exact scale you choose is up to you, depending on how large your property and your piece of graph paper are. Dividing the longest distance on your property by the greatest number of vertical or horizontal squares on your page will give you the largest scale possible for your situation.) Accurately note the location of all of your doors and windows, and then take a measurement from each of the four corners of your house to the property line. This will allow you to place your home accurately on its lot.

3 Next, make note of any of the existing features in your landscape that you intend to keep, such as large trees, bushes, sheds, or other outbuildings. These can be located accurately on your plan by a simple method called triangulation. To determine, say, a particular tree's location in your yard, take a measurement from a known fixed point, such as the corner of your house, then take a measurement from another known fixed point. Adjust your compass to reflect the correct scaled distance (for example, if your scale is 1 inch for every 10 feet, and your first measurement is 30 feet, adjust your compass to 3 inches) and lightly swing an arc from the first point on your plan. Next, adjust your compass to reflect the second distance you measured, and swing an arc from the second point. Where these two arcs meet is the exact location of your tree. This method can be used to fix the position of almost anything in your yard.

Charting the Lay of Your Land

WHEN DOING THE INITIAL PLANNING FOR THE GARDEN, it's often essential to know not only the horizontal distance from point to point, but the surface drop from one area to another. This is particularly critical when considering site drainage. Unless the ground around the foundation slopes away from the house, major problems can arise. The stagnant accumulation of water after a heavy rainfall can not only cause rot and other diseases in your foundation plants, but can also seep into the foundation and, ultimately, into your basement. Other potential construction projects, such as building garden stairs, terracing parts of your yard, or determining a fence line, also require you to know precisely how high or low particular areas are in relation to others. So how do you measure vertical rise and fall? Short of going out and renting surveying equipment, there's a very simple technique that was developed by the ancient Egyptians: the water level.

The theory behind a water level can best be understood if you take a flexible straw and bend it into a "U" shape. Then fill it almost completely with water and carefully move the two ends up and down. As you move the straw, notice that the water readjusts itself to exactly the same height on both sides. This ability of water to "find its own level" occurs because the pressure in the atmosphere is pushing down with the same force on both ends of the straw. This same principle can be used to measure vertical rise and fall in the garden. Here's how:

To begin, go to your local hardware store or garden center and buy transparent tubing. This tubing comes in rolls of various diameters. Any tubing smaller in diameter than a garden

THE VICTORY GARDEN COMPANION

■ **Kip Anderson holding one end of the water level. This simple tool provides a quick and easy way to measure the topography in various parts of your yard.**

hose will work fine, and generally 50 feet of length works well. (For very long distances you can also measure incrementally, so don't feel you need to purchase hundreds of feet.) You'll also need two tight-fitting corks. (You can cut your own to size from wine bottles if you prefer, which gives you a pleasant reason to enjoy a glass or two before you start!)

Next, enlist the help of an assistant. Fill the tubing with water. (Adding a bit of food coloring to the tube will make it easier to see the level of the water.) Cork both ends, and take one end of the hose to the first point to be measured. Your assistant should move to the second point. Hold the hose so that both ends are approximately at the same visual height. (Remember that once uncorked, the water will seek its own level, and if one side is much higher than the other, the water will come spurting out the lower end. In cases where the vertical rise and fall are great, you may need a ladder to accomplish this.)

Once both people are holding the hose at approximately the same height, uncork the ends. When the water settles, both individuals should measure the distance from the ground to the top of the water inside the tube at their respective ends. The difference in these two measurements is the difference in vertical rise or fall between the two positions. For example, if your measurement reads two feet off the ground, and your assistant's three feet, the ground under your assistant's feet is a foot lower than yours.

Once you have a rough drawing of your property, it's time to think about what needs to be changed, deleted, or added. The first step in this process is to delineate the future function of each individual area of your yard. By assigning each area a distinct identity, you can begin to decide what works for you and what doesn't in the current arrangement. You don't need to draw specifics at this point; just sketch out the

PLAN TWICE, CUT ONCE

When we started to build the current Victory Garden, there was a large blue spruce to the north of the house that I was itching to cut down. Without any companion plantings, the tree seemed to stand out in the landscape like a sore thumb. What had the person who planted this blue monster been thinking? I wondered. But I followed the advice I had given to others so many times before, and waited a full season before making any drastic changes such as removing large trees. Thank goodness I did, because what I failed to realize in the flush of early spring was that this tree not only formed an essential windbreak for the house during the winter, sheltering it

from cold northern blasts, but it also provided a home for a host of birds including several of my favorites—cardinals, blue jays, and finches. Whoever planted this tree had known *precisely* what they were doing!

The moral of the story? Wait an entire year before making any drastic changes to your existing landscape. Observe how the passage of the seasons and the work of your garden predecessors may affect your yard. Remember: what's done in a minute often can't be undone in a lifetime.

proposed use of each area and evaluate how well the existing garden matches what you want to do. Consider your lot as if it were a house, and divide it into various areas or "rooms" based on proposed future use. Mark the access pathway to the house as the "entry area." In that entry area, is there sufficient off-street parking for you and your guests? Do the walk and drive say welcome? In the "decorative area," do the plantings provide year-round interest, or are they merely an array of lackluster evergreens? In the backyard, are the outdoor living areas sufficient for entertaining or to accommodate the lifestyle of your family? Do you want a swimming pool or hot tub, or would you like a vegetable or cutting gar-

den? Where will you store tools and do your composting? Even if time and budget dictate that work on certain areas won't even be initiated for several years, carefully considering these questions now will save time and headaches later on.

One of the most important considerations in any landscape design is the question of sight lines—how you see the landscape from different vantage points inside the property, and how it is seen from the outside looking in. Interestingly, although most of us spend the majority of our time viewing our landscapes from the indoors, we rarely consider that factor when we lay out our gardens. While your yard is still in the

■ The rear entrance of the Victory Garden as it looked 15 years ago; a snapshot of the same view ten years later. My father hand-built the fence, gate, and arch for us several years ago to match a Victorian fencing pattern I had found in an old design manual.

planning stage, go to each of the principal windows in your house and take a look outside. What do you see? That flower border you were considering: will you be able to appreciate it from your home office, where you generally spend most of the day? That front planting: how well does it relate to the view from the living room? When you stand at the kitchen sink, will you be able to see anything of interest? Mark down on your plan these principal views from the house, and consider how you can arrange landscape elements to accommodate them.

Equally important to your planning are the things you *don't* want to see, especially those outside the property, like that neighbor's ugly garage, or the view of the road from the bathroom. Eliminating unsightly vistas and creating a sense of privacy is critical to the early part of the planning stage, because these considerations are often important enough to drive the entire design. Essentially, you have three main options—fences, hedges, and screen plantings. (A fourth does exist: tall brick or stone walls, though these are outside the budgets of all but the most elaborate of gardens.) While we'll be discussing the specifics of implementing these options later on in the book, let's take a quick look at the design considerations of each. That way, you'll get a better understanding of how well fences, hedges, or screen plantings might work in your yard.

■ **When planning your landscape, especially the areas nearest the house, don't forget that views from the inside looking out are just as important as views from without.**

PHOTOGRAPHS AS A TOOL FOR PLANTING

Working with actual photographs of your garden is another helpful technique for those who prefer a more three-dimensional approach to planning. This is a slightly more elaborate process than working from a flat plan, but it's also great fun. All you need is access to a digital camera, a photocopier, tracing paper, and some indelible markers. Here is how it works:

Purchase or borrow a digital camera and photograph your garden standing in the center and pivoting around 360 degrees. (You can also photograph each area of your garden and work on these areas one by one, rather than tackling the whole thing at once.) Then, enlarge those images with a photocopier, and cut and tape them together to form a panorama of the garden. Once you're done, photocopy the assembled image so you have several copies from which to work.

Next, take tracing paper the same size as your photo and lay it on top, securing the two with tape or clips. Using an indelible marker, start drawing in the shapes of the trees, plants, and shrubs you're considering, so you can visualize them against the landscape that already exists in your yard. It's amazing how effective this process can be in giving you a fairly accurate idea of the changes you're contemplating.

Garden Basics: A Landscape Design Checklist

Some questions to consider as you begin planning:

THE FRONT YARD

- **Do you have sufficient parking?**
  If not, driveway redesign may be in order.

- **Is the drive attractively surfaced and easy to navigate?** Badly surfaced driveways are an extreme detriment to a home's curb appeal as well as its resale potential.

- **Is the front entrance clearly defined, with good access from the drive and street?**
  Front doors should be easy to see and easy to reach.

- **What is the condition of the front walkway?**
  Is it sufficiently wide to accommodate two people walking side by side? Does the paving match the style and feel of the house? If not, changes are in order.

- **What is the condition of the foundation plantings?**
  Do they hide the house, or complement it? If they are large or overgrown, replanting probably will be necessary.

- **Is there sufficient screening of the house from a noisy road or tightly abutting neighbors?**
  Fencing, hedges, and screen plantings are all options in such cases.

THE SIDE AND BACK YARDS

- **Is there an easy way to navigate a wheelbarrow, mower, or other tools from the back to the side and front yards?** Good access to the entire yard is critical for easy maintenance.

- **Are the current outdoor living areas sufficient for your lifestyle? Do you have enough room to entertain?** A table for four requires a space 10' × 10', for example, and if too small, patios and terraces are inconvenient to use.

- **Do you want a pool, or a vegetable garden?**
  If so, both require the sunniest space possible—eight hours or more of direct sun a day.

- **Do you have children, or intend to? If so, where will they play?** Planning now for future needs will help prevent expensive redesign later on.

- **If there's a back lawn, what's its condition?**
  If marginal because of shade, should it be replanted with other ground covers or other materials?

GENERAL

- **Are you a gardener by nature? How much time do you spend per week working in your yard?**
  Unless paid maintenance is planned, design features should be tailored to the amount of time you realistically can expect to spend maintaining them.

- **Does your current landscape conform well to your climate, or does it require a lot of extra care?**
  If water restrictions are in the future, how will your current plantings fare? Will replanting be required?

- **How long do you plan to live in your current house?**
  Landscape alterations can be very costly, and some appreciate much more quickly than others. Front yard renovations to increase curb appeal generally yield very fast returns, for example, while alterations specific to a particular owner's taste, such as a swimming pool or greenhouse, will pay back their costs slowly, if at all.

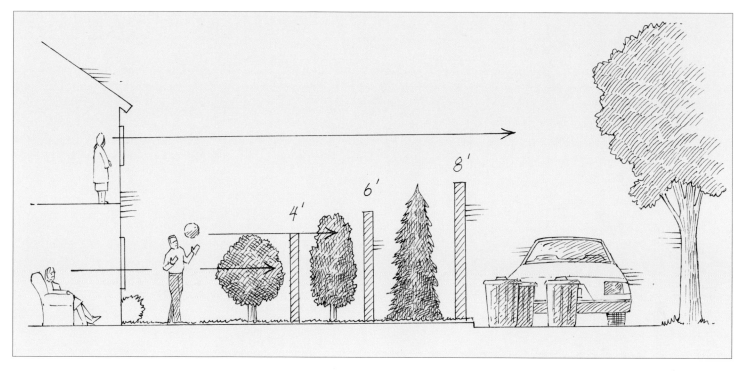

■ **When deciding on what kind of privacy barrier your yard might need, be sure to consider various vantage points. As this diagram clearly shows, the height required to block a particular view is largely dependent on where you're looking from.**

Fencing

OF THE THREE OPTIONS FOR BLOCKING UNWANTED views, fencing is the most difficult for the beginner to carry off successfully. The key to success is to remember that fencing was originally conceived either as a way to keep something in, such as livestock, or conversely to keep something out, such as roving animals or unwanted visitors. That meant that fences needed to start and end at some logical point in order to provide the desired containment—and fences still need to do so today, if they are to make any visual sense in our landscapes.

While this idea of a defined beginning and ending point may seem self-evident, you would be amazed how often this premise is forgotten these days. A quick tour of almost any neighborhood in the country will reveal instance after instance of the odd fence panel or two thrown up willy-nilly to block out a particular view, and left stranded in the middle of the landscape. Once you start looking around for these oddities, you'll find all sorts of bad examples: a fence that starts along the side of the drive and after a short run just ends, as if the builder had run out of lumber. Another arises from one side of a yard in wooden pickets, mysteriously changing to wooden panels halfway down the line and then back to pickets. And so it goes: thousands of fences on the road to nowhere.

Obviously something is wrong here, because to be effective in delineating a boundary or providing privacy, fences can't just start and stop at random. They must begin and end in a way that complements and corresponds to the rest of the landscape. If an isolated element is needed in the landscape to block a particular view, then some type of screen planting should be used instead (for more on that, see Chapter Four).

DIGGING DEEPER: FENCING STYLES

One of the quickest ways to go astray in garden design is to choose the wrong fence. To be successful, fences must match the look and feel of your home—if they don't, they will appear completely out of place in your landscape. Here are several examples of excellent fencing choices.

■ The grand sweep of this white wooden fence complements nicely the formal lines of this impressive brick home, and matches the trim color.

■ Rustic house, rustic fence.

■ Here, the turned spindles of the fence echo those on the porch, and share the same color as the window trim.

■ It's not always necessary to match fence colors or materials to those on your house; in this landscape, the black iron works with the home because both house and fence share the same ornate style.

■ This simple, cottage-style picket fence seamlessly matches the simple, cottage-style house.

The second important consideration when erecting a fence is to choose a fencing style that matches your home. A fence is, in essence, an extension of your home's architecture into the garden, and as such needs a similar look and feel. For example, if you have a rustic-style farmhouse, a picket or rail fence painted to match your home might be an excellent choice; or in the case of a more urban Victorian town house, you might opt for an intricate wooden or iron design; a modern urban dwelling would require a more streamlined design, and so on. Also keep in mind that historically, as architectural styles evolved, fencing styles developed along with them, so chances are there is a fencing type that pretty closely matches your home. While there is probably no single "right" choice for your house, there unfortunately can be numerous bad choices for any given home. The message here is that it pays to shop around and familiarize yourself with the various options. If you can't find just what you need, consider ordering a custom-built fence that echoes a particular architectural element found on the house or property, such as porch rail, bracket, or stair baluster.

Finally, don't buy cheap fencing. Good fences are expensive, but worth the price. Cheap fences don't last, and since a huge portion of the fence's cost comes from installation and maintenance, you will find yourself paying twice what you would have over the long run had you only installed a good fence in the first place. Excellent fencing options come in wood (naturally rot-resistant materials like cedar, or treated products), metal (iron and aluminum), and now even vinyl, which looks like wood, comes in several colors, and has the great advantage of never needing to be painted—ever. Here at the Victory Garden, we have used vinyl for a tall privacy fence running parallel to the street, as well as for the fence around the vegetable garden. Both have served their purpose beautifully.

■ Left: The low box hedge in this garden not only provides a pleasant frame for the walk, but also serves to direct the first-time visitor to the front door.

■ Right: Beech hedges give form and shape to a series of descending garden rooms in this long, narrow garden we visited in Belgium, providing a sense of mystery and expectation as you round each corner. Without these hedge divisions, the space would simply be one large blank square.

Hedges and Screen Planting

THE ALTERNATIVE TO BUILDING A FENCE IS TO USE TALL plant materials that will create a sense of privacy or block an ugly view. In these situations there are two good options. The first is to plant a straight row of a single species—a hedge—that will essentially act as a living fence. The other option is to plant a nonlinear grouping of different plant materials—a screen planting—that works in combination to form a barrier. Each has its advantages and disadvantages.

Hedges are ideal for situations where a narrow border is desired, either to shield a particular area from prying eyes or to delineate a space within the garden. Hedges have certain advantages over fences. First of all, their living nature makes their appearance much softer and less imposing than that of a fence, and they are often preferable where a more delicate ef-

fect is required. Also, hedges can reach heights far greater than any fence could in situations where a very tall border is needed.

While almost any kind of plant with an upright habit can be used to form a hedge, some plants work better than others. At its most basic, selecting the right hedge plant is a simple process of elimination using these three procedures: determine the maximum height and width available (finding a species that closely fits the site's parameters will save many hours of tedious pruning), then choose between evergreen and deciduous material, and finally decide between a formal (clipped) or informal (natural) look. Under most circumstances, your options within any given growing zone will be limited to three or four possibilities, which can then be selected on the basis of personal preference.

In terms of design parameters, probably the most important requirement for creating a successful hedge is to be realistic about how much ground space you have to devote, and how large the plants you choose will ultimately grow. Many people,

Choosing the Perfect Plant for Hedging

Following are some suggested plants for hedging purposes. (F) indicates formal; (I), informal; (sp.) indicates a number of different possible species. A shrub's evergreen ability sometimes varies by climate, so you should confirm a particular species's performance in your area with a local nursery.

Botanical Name	Common Name	Formal or Informal	Evergreen?	Zones
Berberis thunbergii	Japanese barberry	F or I	N	4–9*
Berberis x stenophylla	Rosemary barberry	F or I	Y	6–9
Buxus sempervirens	Boxwood	F	Y	6–9
Carpinus betulus	European hornbeam	F	N	5–9
Chamaecyparis lawsoniana	Lawson false cypress	F	Y	4–9
Corylus avellana	Hazel, European	I	N	4–8
Elaeagnus x ebbingei		F or I	Y	6–9
Escallonia (most species)	Escallonia	F or I	Y	8–10
Fagus sylvatica	European beech	F	N	5–8*
Forsythia sp.	Forsythia	I	N	4–9
Ilex (most species)	Holly	F or I	Y	5–8*
Juniperus sp.	Juniper	F	Y	4–9*
Laurus nobilis	Sweet bay	F	Y	8–11
Ligustrum sp.	Privet	F	Y/N	5–10*

looking at, say, a small yew or upright juniper in the garden center, will blissfully choose to disbelieve the label that reads "reaches 25 feet tall and wide." If you ignore such instructions, it will be at your peril; as sure as the sun rises each day, these shrubs will ultimately grow to their intended height, and at best you'll be confronted with a constant battle to keep these green giants in check. At worst, you'll be forced to begin the process all over again at great expense.

Also, be sure to keep in mind that hedges, just like fences,

need to start and end at logical points in the landscape—a straight row of shrubs floating in the middle of a lawn looks just as ridiculous as that stranded panel or two of fencing. This requirement for a coherent line, however, often conflicts with a demand of another kind: to do their best, hedges need light from both sides, as well as consistent light, water, and soil conditions over the full length of their run. If a portion of the hedge is subjected to different conditions than the rest, the result will be an extremely spotty and ineffectual barrier. Of-

Botanical Name	Common Name	Formal or Informal	Evergreen?	Zones
Osmanthus sp.	Osmanthus	I	Y	7–11*
Prunus cerasifera	Cherry plum	I	N	4–10
Prunus laurocerasus	Cherry laurel	F or I	Y	7–10
Prunus lusitanica	Portugal cherry laurel	F or I	Y	7–10
Rosa sp.	Shrub roses	I	N	4–10*
Spirea sp.	Spirea	I	N	4–11*
Taxus sp.	Yew	F	Y	4–10*

*will vary by species

And here are a few shrubs commonly used for hedging we suggest you *avoid*.

Botanical Name	Common Name	Reasons to Avoid
Elaeagnus sp.	Russian olive	Very fast-growing, but very short-lived and prone to winter damage; also invasive.
Philadelphus sp.	Mock orange	Becomes V-shaped at a very early age with no bottom growth.
Pinus sp.	Pines, especially white pines	Really trees, not shrubs; prone to dropping bottom branches after only a few years.
Syringa sp.	Lilacs	Becomes V-shaped at a very early age with no bottom growth.
Thuja sp.	Arborvitae	Some species, such as *Thuja occidentalis,* subject to severe snow damage in northern areas.
Tsuga sp.	Hemlocks	Really trees, not shrubs; prone to pests such as the wooly adelgid.

ten, design demands and hedge demands are impossible to reconcile, and in situations like this, fencing becomes the better option.

The final possibility for blocking unwanted views is a screen planting. Like hedges, screen plantings use woody plants to provide privacy and obscure ugly vistas, but unlike hedges, they are thick, multilayered compositions made up of a number of different species. Screen plantings generally aren't strictly linear either (though they *do* need to begin and end, like hedges and fences, at a logical place in the landscape). Instead, they vary considerably in depth (as well as height) from one end to the other, depending on the plant material used and the requirements of the design. This flexibility makes them ideal for tricky situations where growing conditions differ from one end of the planting to the other, and where a diversity of plant material would be an asset to the overall design.

The downside to screen plantings is that the incorpora-

■ **The conifers at the back of this garden form an ideal screen planting, almost entirely obliterating the view of the obtrusive building beyond.**

tion of multiple species requires significantly more space than a hedge would, and the resulting complexity of factors makes screen planting considerably more difficult than a hedge, especially for the beginner, to lay out and plant. But we're getting a bit ahead of ourselves here.

We'll talk more about these complicated creatures in Chapter Four. At the moment, there's more immediate work ahead—getting the full and final picture of the forces at work within your yard, a process we'll complete in the next chapter.

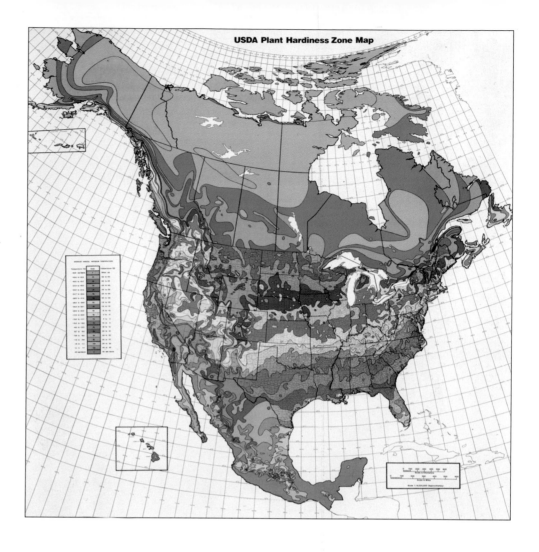

USDA Plant Hardiness Zone Map

Ask Michael:
Zone Maps

Dear Michael,

For years I've relied on the USDA hardiness zone ratings for selecting plants. Now I understand there is a new heat tolerance rating as well. Can you explain the difference between the two and tell me which measure I should use?

The U.S. Department of Agriculture's Plant Hardiness Zone Map was first developed in 1960, and revised in 1990. In essence, it organizes the United States into 20 different zones numbered 1 though 11 based on average minimum winter temperatures. Each zone is 10 degrees F (– 12 C) warmer or colder than its adjacent zone. Zones 2 through 10 are further subdivided into regions A and B, where the average minimum temperatures differ by 5 degrees F (– 15 degrees C). Hardiness zone ratings have always served as an indispensable tool for helping gardeners make plant

selections that match their location, telling them how well a particular plant will fare against the winter in their part of the world.

But the latest thinking is that we should really be looking at both cold *and* heat tolerance as a way of measuring the climate adaptability of a given plant, especially in regions where light frost is less of a consideration than scorchingly high temperatures. (Certain plants, for instance, aren't able to produce chlorophyll effectively in high heat, and go dormant.) So in 1997, the American Horticultural Society published a new plant heat-zone map that took into consideration a plant's ability to withstand heat. The new map divides the country into 12 heat zones based on the average number of days that reach 86 degrees F (30 degrees C) during the course of the year. A temperature above 86 degrees F is the point at which the AHS has determined a plant starts to experience physiological harm. In

reading the map, you can see that Zone 1 has an average of only one 86-degree day per year, while Zone 12 averages 210 days or more above 86 degrees each year.

This heat-zone map essentially helps take the guesswork out of knowing which plants will thrive in, or at least tolerate, the heat in your area. Eventually the majority of plants will be listed with both hot and cold ratings, but as the heat-zone ratings are still fairly new, you may have to consult the AHS website (ahs.org) for more information.

For those of you in the West, there's another type of map published by *Sunset* magazine that might be of interest. Taking into account not only heat and cold but humidity, seasonal winds, and precipitation as well, the highly detailed *Sunset* map and corresponding growing zones provide an excellent way to pinpoint climatic factors that can affect hardiness in your area. The information can be found at www.sunset.com.

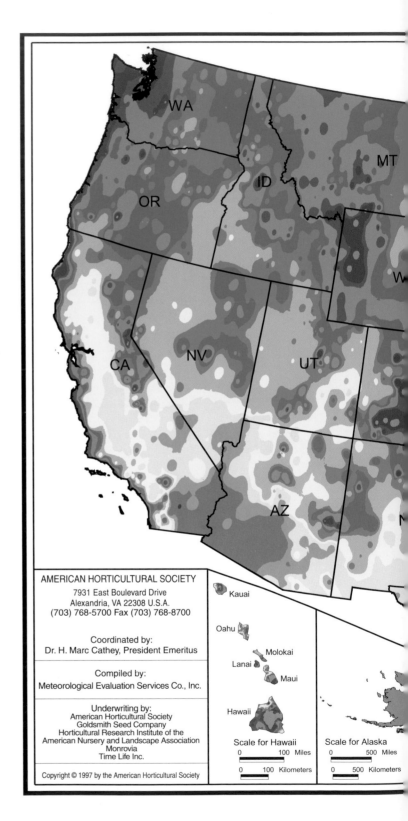

AMERICAN HORTICULTURAL SOCIETY
7931 East Boulevard Drive
Alexandria, VA 22308 U.S.A.
(703) 768-5700 Fax (703) 768-8700

Coordinated by:
Dr. H. Marc Cathey, President Emeritus

Compiled by:
Meteorological Evaluation Services Co., Inc.

Underwriting by:
American Horticultural Society
Goldsmith Seed Company
Horticultural Research Institute of the
American Nursery and Landscape Association
Monrovia
Time Life Inc.

Copyright © 1997 by the American Horticultural Society

Scale for Hawaii
0   100   Miles
0   100 Kilometers

Scale for Alaska
0   500   Miles
0   500 Kilometers

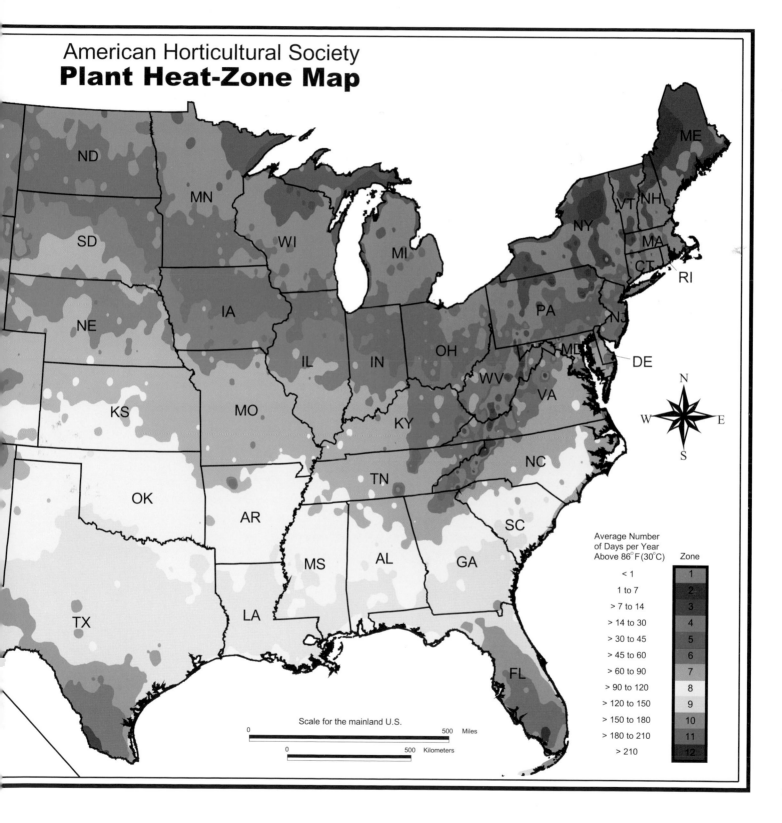

American Horticultural Society
Plant Heat-Zone Map

Average Number of Days per Year Above 86°F (30°C)	Zone
< 1	1
1 to 7	2
> 7 to 14	3
> 14 to 30	4
> 30 to 45	5
> 45 to 60	6
> 60 to 90	7
> 90 to 120	8
> 120 to 150	9
> 150 to 180	10
> 180 to 210	11
> 210	12

Scale for the mainland U.S.

0   500 Miles

0   500 Kilometers

N W E S

■ The back garden at Taliesin.

Inspired Gardens

Taliesin

FRANK LLOYD WRIGHT IS BEST KNOWN TO MOST AS AN architect—the daring creator of the Guggenheim Museum in New York and the groundbreaking Prairie houses in Oak Park, Illinois. But during his illustrious career Wright's talented hand touched not only the world of architecture, but also the world of landscape design. Wright was very much a believer that buildings and the surrounding land are inextricably linked, one flowing directly into the other, and that the man-made world should enhance, not smother, the land. These beliefs found expression in his own home, Taliesin.

Following a tumultuous divorce from his wife, Catherine, in 1911, Wright returned from Europe with his new companion Mamah Borthwick Cheney, the wife of a client for whom he'd designed a house in Oak Park, Illinois. Wright, looking to escape the past and start over, came with Mamah to the remote area of Spring Green, Wisconsin, he had known as a child, and there he set about designing a combination of country retreat, design studio, and working farm. This hilly region of southwestern Wisconsin, called by many "the Valley of the God-Almighty Joneses" (Wright's Welsh family were the Welsh Lloyd-Joneses), would ultimately become the site of the famed structure he named *Taliesin*—Welsh for "shining brow."

And a "shining brow" indeed it is: set on a high hill amidst 600 acres in some of America's most beautiful countryside, the house overlooks the rolling fields, pastures, and meadowlands along the banks of the broad Wisconsin River. The house that Wright designed is a natural extension of the landscape—it was built from the fieldstone, timber, and other existing natural materials he found on site. Even the cedar-shingled roof, with its distinctive long-and-low design, was meant to echo the lines of the surrounding countryside: "I knew . . . that no house should ever be on any hill or on anything," Wright once said. *"It should be of the hill, belonging to it, so hill and house could live together, each happier for the other."*

The gardens Wright conceived also flow naturally out of the house and into the broader environment. The doors of his home open onto exquisite flagstone terraces, which frame the views of the shimmering Wisconsin countryside below. There are also columns, paths, and low walls built of native stone, as well as a reservoir perched atop the hill that once fed both house and garden through the force of gravity.

Wright posited and planned every element of Taliesin's landscape. Orchards and vineyards spread out from the house and outbuildings, following the undulating lines of furrowed fields and mimicking the curves of the hills. They were designed not only to be practical but also to be pleasing to the eye. Just off the rear of the house, he installed an exquisite garden courtyard for his love, Mamah, complete with steps and walls carefully wrapped around several large oaks perched on top of the hill, the centerpiece of which is the famed Tea Circle Oak. Wright continued to emend and add to the house and landscape for the remainder of his nearly century-long life.

Today, Taliesin has become one of the enduring landmarks of Wright's genius, a symbol of what can be achieved when a human being dedicates every ounce of heart and soul to a particular project. (Not to mention every ounce of financial resources—Wright spent so freely on Taliesin that at one low point in his career he narrowly avoided losing his home to the bank!) Today, almost 50 years after his death, Taliesin continues not only as the home of the still thriving School of Architecture that Wright founded there, but also as a site of pilgrimage for anyone interested in understanding how perfectly landscape and architecture can be fused into a cohesive, working whole.

■ On the approach to Taliesin, Wright's skill at blending architecture and landscape is evident.

■ Light rain on *Veronicastrum* 'Fascination' in July at the Victory Garden.

Chapter 2
Braving the Elements—
Sun, Wind, Soil, and Rain

They have climate
in England; *we* have weather.

HELENA RUTHERFURD ELY
A Woman's Hardy Garden, 1903

■ Local conditions have a huge impact on your landscape. Take this Michigan garden, for example; although located in the northern part of the country not far from the Canadian border, the warming effects of the lake place this landscape in Zone 6B, while only a few miles inland, other gardens are much colder, dipping into Zone 5A.

Let There Be Light

BY THIS POINT, YOU'VE ALREADY MADE A GENERAL LAND-scape plan of your lot, thought about what to keep and what to change, considered the views from both within and without, as well as given a "room assignment" to the various areas of the property. So now it's time to begin digging, ripping out old shrubs, planting new trees, putting in those flower beds, building that terrace, and installing that long-coveted water feature, right? Well, not quite . . . There are a few more elements that need to be considered before work starts in the garden (don't worry, your dreamed-of garden will emerge soon enough!). First, however, if you'd like to save yourself a ton of aggravation, wasted time, and money, you need to consider the various environmental forces that shape the outdoor space around you—sun, wind, soil, and rain.

PERHAPS THE MOST DIFFICULT ELEMENT TO PREDICT when planning a garden is the interaction of sun and shade. At first glance, this would seem like a pretty easy thing to figure out. Most of us know that different plants need varying amounts of light to survive, and that different parts of a garden acquire various amounts of light. It would then be quite logical to conclude that you simply need to match the plants' requirements to what an area can supply, and *voilà*! Unfortunately, it's rarely that simple, for judging light conditions—especially for the beginner—is tricky business.

The most common mistake is to overlook the seasonal changes in sun and shade patterns—a fatal and invariably expensive error. To better understand this, take a look at the diagram below.

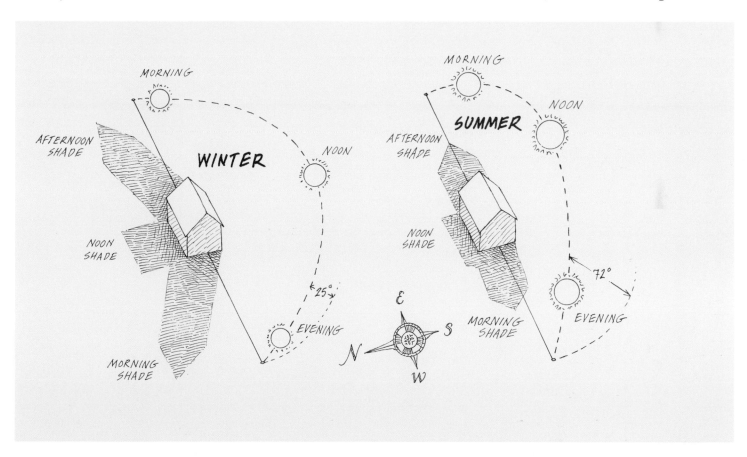

■ **Understanding the patterns of sun and shade are critical to your success in the garden. In the winter, the early spring, and again in the late fall (left), the sun is low in the sky and casts long shadows over the landscape. In the summer (right), with the sun high overhead, these areas are temporarily in the sun. Remember: partial sun for part of the year does not equal full sun!**

38 ■ **A veritable winter sonata: rain on crab apple (*Malus floribunda*) boughs at the Victory Garden in December.**

The right-hand side shows the position of the sun at noon on the summer solstice, June 22, the longest day of the year. Notice that the sun is directly overhead, and that the shadows on the north side of the house are limited to a very narrow band close to the foundation. Looking at the sun and shade patterns on that day, you might be tempted to think about putting your vegetable garden or sun-loving shrubs off the north side of the house. But hang on a minute (or in this case, a few months). Look at the left-hand side of the picture, which shows the exact same setting during the winter solstice. Notice how long the shadows are? The entire area to the north of the house is now in complete shade all day long. Spring and fall shadows will fall halfway between these two extremes, with the north side of the house still in shade for most of the day.

Knowing (or not knowing) this information would have a tremendous impact on your landscape plans. Had you located a pool there, for instance, the water would be very cold indeed, even on the hottest days of the year. A vegetable garden would fare equally poorly: the ground would be very slow to warm up in the spring, the plants would reach for light most of the season, and the harvest would be extremely meager. A border of sun-loving shrubs would have slowly but inevitably failed, completely wasting your time and effort. All these scenarios of horticultural doom are why I heartily recommend that you wait a full year before making any major changes to a new landscape. You simply need time to observe which areas receive full sun and which don't. It's a good idea to keep a journal and carefully mark and measure where the principal shadows fall in your yard at various points in the year—if you don't, it will be next to impossible to remember where the shadow patterns fell months before.

Believe What You Read

THE SECOND MOST COMMON MISTAKE WHEN ASSESSING sun and shade in the garden is to fail to believe printed advice about light conditions, both in gardening guides like this one and on the labels of individual plants purchased. People seem ashamed to admit that they have shade in their yard, perhaps from the mistaken belief that shade gardens are

■ In a protected corner of this yard, hydrangeas flourish. Just around the other side of the building, they fail. The moral? Familiarizing yourself with the various microclimates on your property is essential to succeeding with plants.

{microclimates} When discussing growing zones, you'll often hear people refer to microclimates, which are small areas of varying climatic conditions within your yard that can be either warmer or colder than the surrounding area. For instance, a south-facing terrace enclosed with a stone wall could be a half growing zone warmer than the rest of your yard. Similarly, the banks along a spring-fed stream will remain warmer than the surrounding area, thanks to the constant temperature of groundwater. At the opposite extreme, spots exposed to the full chilling force of the wind will often be a full growing zone colder than more protected areas. The lesson here is that it pays to familiarize yourself both with the growing-zone information for your specific locale and with all the mitigating factors within specific areas of your yard.

dull. The reality is that an area can't be called "sunny" if it receives, at most, one to two hours of direct sun a day. In the same spirit, an area that is plunged into the deepest of dark shade for the entire day should not be labeled as receiving "partial sun." Nothing is sadder than a shady area filled with sun-loving plants—these weakened, sickly plants, starved for light, will all ultimately fail, forcing you to rip out the dying mess and start all over again. While it's true that the palette of plant possibilities is larger in full sun, shade gardens, when properly designed, can be just as beautiful as sunny ones. For a successful shade garden, be realistic and don't try to finesse your assessment of the light conditions. To avoid any confusion, here are the guidelines:

FULL SUN means no less than seven hours of direct sun per day for the entire season, without break or obstruction.

PARTIAL SUN means four to six hours of direct sun a day for the entire season, as in an area that receives full or direct sunlight only in the morning or the evening and then is partially shaded for the rest of the day.

PARTIAL SHADE means no more than two to three hours of direct sun a day for the entire season, as in a spot that receives direct sun only in the early morning or late afternoon and then gets dappled sunlight or full shade for the remainder of the day.

FULL SHADE means no direct sun at all, ever, for the entire season, such as shade caused by the shadow of the house or other solid structure.

Please note the words "for the entire season" in the above descriptions. This phrase means exactly what it says: areas in your yard that receive full sun only in the middle of the summer and are partially shaded at other times of the year are not considered "full sun," and should be planted either with full-sun plants that live principally during the summer period, such as summer annuals, or with plants that prefer partial sun for the entire year. While there are some exceptions to the rule, in general it behooves you to err on the side of caution in areas of mixed light and shade, and choose materials that will thrive in the next-lower light category. In other words, *a plant is considerably more likely to tolerate more light than less light, and it pays to be conservative in your selections when you are just starting out.*

It's an Ill Wind . . .

WHILE LIGHT IS THE MOST OBVIOUS ENVIRONMENTAL factor in the garden, don't underestimate the power of the wind to wreak havoc on your plans and plants. Wind affects the garden in two fundamental ways. The first is by sheer, naked force, as I can attest from personal experience. Very early in my career, I was asked to design a garden near the seashore, and set about creating one of the finest gardens I had built up to that point. The only problem was that I had forgotten how strong even fairly mild winds can be, especially near the shore, where they race across open water without obstruction. As a result I neglected to secure some of the larger plantings, and during the first summer storm (tame compared to the winter storms, which pack an even bigger wallop) many of the large ornamental trees I had installed blew completely over. Some were so damaged they needed to be replaced, others had to be replanted, and all had to be securely staked—a costly affair, both in terms of my personal embarrassment for not having known better and financially, since the replacing, replanting, and securing of all those plants was done at my own expense.

After that debacle, I have never again forgotten to check prevailing wind conditions before laying out a garden, and neither should you. This is particularly true if your design calls for some type of flower border. While trees and shrubs can generally be protected from the effects of wind with stakes and supports, flowers are much more difficult to secure and totally at the winds' mercy. You would be appalled to see what even a fairly mild gust can do to a perennial border when it's in full bloom. Thus, if you are contemplating creating any type of flower bed on a particularly breezy site, consider installing some kind of windbreak such as a wall, fence, or hedge as protection for your plants.

Another way in which wind can dramatically affect the garden is by super-cooling exposed areas—the "windchill factor," which many people are surprised to learn impacts plants, though in a slightly different way than it does humans. Not only do cold, harsh winds lower ambient temperatures (sometimes enough to push a particular area into a lower growing zone; see page 27), but in the winter these winds have a terrific dehydrating effect, especially on evergreens. When the ground is frozen, evergreens are unable to transfer water from the roots to the leaves, and the cold, drying winds suck the available moisture out of the leaves, essentially freeze-drying them on the spot. This is the "winter kill" you hear so much about in gardening circles. So if you're planning to include broad-leaf evergreens in a cold-climate garden, make sure they receive sufficient protection from the wind (in terms of covers or antidessicant sprays) to avoid this chilling—and deadly—fate.

■ Sunshine highlighting one of the many Oriental lilies at the Victory Garden. As lilies like these prefer part sun, they must be carefully placed in order to thrive.

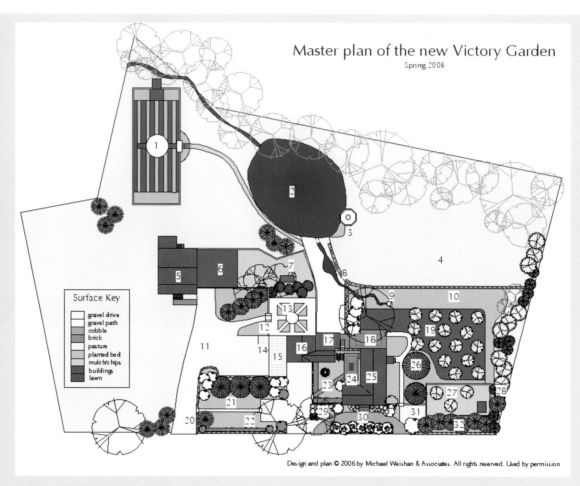

Master plan of the new Victory Garden
Spring 2006

Surface Key

gravel drive
gravel path
cobble
brick
pasture
planted bed
mulch/chips
buildings
lawn

■ **The Victory Garden today. Charting your property in plain view like this is critical to achieving a harmonious, cohesive landscape.**

1 Vegetable garden
2 Pond
3 Octagonal gazebo
4 Pasture
5 Guesthouse
6 Guesthouse lawn
7 Utility area
8 Stonewall
9 Old well

10 Long perennial border
11. Service drive
12 Double-seated arbor gate
13 Parterre garden
14 Cold frames
15 Greenhouse
16 Office
17 Stable
18 Lower terrace

19 Orchard
20 Front stonewall and arbor
21 Iris garden
22 Yew hedge
23 Entrance garden
24 Upper terrace
25 Main house
26 Shade garden
27 Chicken coop

28 Evergreen privacy
   screen
29 Front planting
30 Cobble drive
31 Aerial hedge of
   European hornbeam
   (*Carpinus betulus*)
32 Screen planting of
   white pine and yew

1 After you've made a scale drawing of your property, noted down the existing features, and made several copies of the base plan (or saved the base file on your computer), the next step is to note patterns of sun, wind, and rain that influence your land. Remember to be realistic here: while certain situations can be mitigated, such as by planting a windbreak, others, such as dense shade cast by a house, cannot. Being utterly realistic about your situation, despite wishes to the contrary, will provide you with a much better landscape in the long run.

2 Next, take a careful look at the property from the inside of the house, and jot down which views should be enhanced and which may need to be blocked or altered. Effective sight lines, both from inside the structure and across the landscape, are key to good landscape design.

3 The third step in the process is to decide which elements in the existing landscape work well and which you intend to change. If you own a new house with little or no landscaping, this may not be too difficult; if, however, you're renovating an older garden, you need to carefully assess the current situation. Remember, while it's very easy to cut down a tree, it takes decades to grow one, so don't rush your decisions. On the other hand, don't resist removing a feature such as an overgrown foundation planting simply because it's already there, especially if you've finally come to the decision that a particular element truly doesn't work in the landscape: each season you hesitate making a change is one less your new yard will have to grow and mature. Now is also the time to note how you move around the property, and whether or not you need to consider additional or expanded walks, drives, and parking areas.

4 With step four the fun begins. Finally you can start designing the garden of your dreams, and to do that, it helps to become familiar with the various symbols landscape designers use to indicate various features of the landscape.

These symbols serve as a common language among planners, allowing you to quickly and easily share your ideas with other gardeners, contractors, and landscape professionals. Here is a planner's palette of common landscape symbols.

Finally, never hesitate to make successive versions of your plan, by adding or deleting elements until you have just the right mix. Remember, careful and thoughtful planning now will save huge amounts of time and energy later, and it's much easier to change things on paper or on a computer than it will be once your plans are realized in the actual garden.

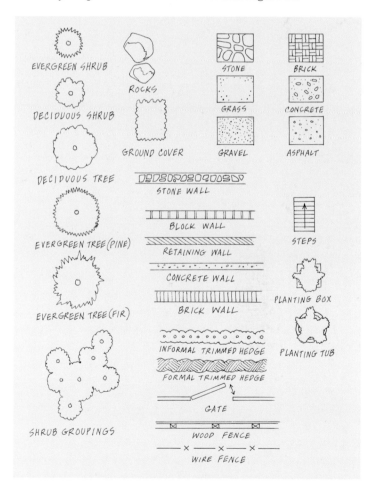

■ **Symbols commonly used by landscape and garden designers.**

In the Beginning, There Was Soil

TO BEST UNDERSTAND YOUR SOIL, GO OUT INTO YOUR yard and grab a handful of dirt and run it through your fingers. What does it feel like? Does it crumble easily into small, gritty grains? Or is it smooth, like talcum powder? Next, squeeze the soil into a ball and then open your fist. If the ball immediately falls apart, your soil is sandy. If it stays together until tapped, and then falls apart, you are the lucky possessor of loam (or "loom," as they say in some parts of the country),

that perfect mix of sand, humus, and clay so often aspired to in garden manuals. If the ball of soil stays together when tapped, then your soil has a large clay component.

This simple test is important, because it gives you a good idea of what your soil is made of—sand, clay, or something in between—and this is critical information you'll need before beginning any serious gardening.

■ **Left: A typical cross-section of unimproved soil: a thin layer of humus on top, a mixture of sand, humus, and clay in the middle, and pure clay beneath in the subsoil. Notice how most of the existing plant roots are limited to the upper humus layers. This soil would need considerable augmentation in order for heavy feeders like vegetables and annuals to thrive.**

■ **Right: Black gold for gardeners—compost!**

What Is Soil, Anyway?

SOIL ESSENTIALLY CONSISTS OF TWO INGREDIENTS: A small quantity of organic matter (generally about 3 to 5 percent) and a mixture of eroded rocks and minerals. These nonorganic components can be further divided into four distinct types according to size: rocks, sand, silt, and clay, the relative quantities of which can vary considerably from place to place and have a direct impact on how things grow in your garden. Not only do these elements determine the ability of water to drain through the soil, but they also affect the ability of soil to retain nutrients.

The rocks and stones we often dig up in the garden, though the biggest of all the soil components, surprisingly constitute the smallest percentage of soil's overall mass, despite whatever impressions you may have garnered from hauling away endless loads of rocks. These are generally removed from well-prepared beds where they are large enough to be a nuisance but have little overall effect on how plants perform.

Next in size is sand, whose individual granules range from 0.05 to 2 millimeters. The amount of sand particles in your soil is very important, because the gaps between granules allow water and nutrients to flow more easily through the ground. Too much sand, however, and all the water and nutrients run quickly through the soil without ever benefiting the plants.

The next particle down the list is silt, from 0.002 to 0.05 millimeters in size, which, although initially more difficult to wet, retains more water and nutrients than sand. Finally, there is clay, whose particles can't be seen without the aid of an electron microscope. Clay particles are so tiny and tightly bound that it takes a long time for water, even on the molecular level, to pass between them, and once there, it's equally difficult for the water molecules to detach themselves. This is precisely why clay soils are excellent for pottery, but not very good for gardening— it's nearly impossible for plants to absorb water and nutrients from their roots when surrounded by heavy clay soil.

So what do you do if you have clay or sandy soil? In all but the most extreme cases, the best thing is to enrich it with organic matter.

Organic matter is a catchall term used to describe plant and animal residues in various stages of decomposition. While organic matter may constitute only a small portion of the overall soil mass, its horticultural importance can't be overstated. In fact for the gardener, it's really black gold. Organic matter benefits the garden in two principal ways. First, it contains a considerable quantity of essential nutrients that are gradually released into the soil as the material decays, thereby increasing the soil's overall fertility. In the long term, however, its secondary effect is more important: adding organic matter to clay soils, for example, essentially isolates the clay into smaller lumps, allowing water and nutrients to penetrate the soil more freely. In sandy soil, it has the opposite effect: organic matter helps to retain water and keep nutrients from draining immediately through the soil.

Organic matter comes in many forms: manure and other animal waste; sawdust; peat products; and, of course, compost, which is the rotted vegetable waste from your table and garden. While differing slightly in results and ease of use, the form you choose will most likely be determined by cost and availability in your area, since you'll be needing a great deal of it for your garden. For instance, here at the Victory Garden, we don't make enough compost to entirely meet our needs, so

HOW MUCH IS ENOUGH?

Beginning gardeners often ask me how much manure/compost they should add to their soil. The answer is a great deal, though the precise amounts and timing will depend on whether or not you have sandy soil, clay soil, or loam. For sandy and loamy soils, add at least two inches of organic matter once a year in either the spring or fall. For clay soils, one inch is better, added in the fall. Using too much organic material at once can add to clay soil's inability to shed excess moisture. For new beds, dig or rototill the organic matter as deeply as you can, preferably to a depth of 10 inches or more. For existing beds, you can top-dress with manure. The action of worms and other soil creatures will eventually transport the organic matter down to the root level, though it will take much more time.

most of our additional organic matter comes from our official Supervisor of Turf and Pastures—otherwise known as my horse, Claudius. Short of getting your own four-legged composter, you'll probably have to supplement your organic material needs from time to time by purchasing it, either bagged at the nursery or in a bulk truck delivery from a local farm or garden supply center.

A quick word or two on manure. Almost any farm animal manure can be used in the garden: cow, horse, sheep, goat, pig, etc., as well as some of the more exotic manures such as bat guano harvested from caves, or cricket or earthworm castings, a byproduct of the fish-bait industry. One thing you want to stay away from, though, is dog or cat manure, both of which can carry parasites that are harmful to humans. It's also important to remember that unlike finished compost, which can be applied directly to garden beds at any time of the year, fresh manure can be applied only when the garden area in question is dormant and fallow, as with empty vegetable beds in the fall. Applying fresh manure directly to a growing area can "burn" the plants with excess nitrogen. If you acquire fresh manure during the active growing season, simply store it in a pile where it will partially decompose, and then add it directly to the garden in the fall or subsequent spring.

One final tip about improving your soil's structure: after you have spent all that time and energy amending your soil, by all means keep heavy machines and human traffic out of the garden. Soil compaction is a major problem for plants. Even the best soil, when compressed, will lose the essential spaces between particles that allow water and nutrients to penetrate, resulting in poor growth performance. When it comes to garden beds, that old Revolutionary War motto still rings true: "Don't Tread on Me!"

Garden Basics:
Of Sand Dunes and Pottery Barns— Improving Clayey or Extremely Sandy Soils

IF YOU LIVE IN A SPOT WITH CLAYEY OR EXTREMELY SANDY soil, the truth is that you are in for more work than those lucky people blessed with good loam in their garden. If you have sandy soil, your job is extremely simple: add well-rotted organic matter in the form of manure and compost, two to three inches per year, and the soil quality will gradually improve. If clay soil is your problem, adding organic matter is also the solution, but there are additional steps you'll need to take. Unfortunately,

■ The three main constituents of garden soil, from left to right: sand, humus, and clay.

these measures are much more labor intensive than simply adding compost, and will require extra time and care.

As common sense might dictate, it is possible to amend clay soil with sand. It has to be just the right amount of sand, however—adding too little will essentially create cement. In order to have a beneficial effect, you need to add at least one-quarter sand by total volume. In other words, to improve the top 10 inches of clay soil, you'll need to add almost 3 inches of sand. That's a lot of sand—6 cubic yards, or 18,000 pounds of sand, as a matter of fact, for a mere 25' × 25' plot—and you will still need to add organic matter!

Another way to improve clay soil is by adding gypsum. As it breaks down, gypsum releases calcium ions that cause the tiny clay particles to clump together, improving air and water circulation. Depending how much additional calcium your soil can tolerate (which can easily be determined by a simple soil test), dig into your garden between two to four pounds of gypsum per 100 square feet. This needs to be done twice a year until you notice your soil improving, at which time you can switch to organic matter. While this may seem like a very lengthy process, it's far better than the alternative sickly plants in sodden, clayey soil.

DIGGING DEEPER: WINNING THE WAR OF THE WORMS

AS BIZARRE AS IT SOUNDS, COUNTING EARTHWORMS IS A fairly accurate way to gauge how well you've succeeded in the battle for good dirt. Earthworms are attracted to decaying organic matter in the soil, which they digest and excrete, and the castings not only provide an extremely nutritious fertilizer but also aerate your soil in the process. Thus the more "soldiers" you have fighting in your army, the more likely you are to

achieve overall success in the garden campaign. To determine the number of available troops, all you have to do is excavate a one-square-foot site to the depth of six inches. Next, place the soil in a shallow plastic bin or wheelbarrow and gently move the earth bit by bit from one side of the container to the other, counting the worms as you go. If you find only a worm or two (or even worse, no worms!) you're losing the war, and your soil still needs a lot of organic matter. You should excavate the area and dig in four to six inches of additional organic matter.

More than two but less than ten worms indicates still more fighting ahead: for unplanted beds, dig in several inches of organic matter in the autumn; in planted areas, consider top-dressing with an inch or two of organic matter in the spring and fall. Finding more than ten worms means you're on the way to victory. But remember, organic matter decays in the soil and needs to be replaced continually, so annual top-dressing in the fall is always a good idea.

■ **Your new best friend: the earthworm.**

■ **The three-bin composting system we use at the Victory Garden. During the active gardening season, the bins are filled in succession from left to right to provide a steady stream of finished compost; in the fall, however, all three are loaded to capacity with leaves, manure, and garden residues in order to provide as much compost as possible come spring.**

Composting the Victory Garden Way

ALTHOUGH WHOLE BOOKS HAVE BEEN WRITTEN ON composting, there really isn't anything terribly mysterious about it. At its simplest, composting is nothing more than piling bits of organic matter—vegetable scraps from the table, pieces of sod, waste from the garden—into a single pile and waiting for them to rot. In the natural course of things and without any additional work, this material will be ready for use in the garden a year or so after being added to the pile. You'll know it's ready when the garden debris has been reduced to a dark brown soil-like consistency.

If you need your compost sooner, there are a number of methods to speed up the process: a weekly turning with a fork aerates the pile and promotes the growth of helpful microorganisms; adding activators such as fresh manure will supply food and additional bacteria to the pile; using a special tumbling compost bin can help mix and aerate the pile more thoroughly than if you did it by hand. Here at the Victory Garden, however, because of the large amount of material we have to compost, as well as the numerous constraints on our time from other quarters, we like to use a method that limits the amount of work we need to do while simultaneously providing the largest possible amount of compost. It's called the "triple bin" system.

As the name implies, this method requires the construction of three separate bins, built from rot-resistant timber and plastic-coated wire mesh. Each of our bins is 4' × 4' (though they could be built to almost any dimension to accommodate your space and projected composting needs). Each holds compost in a different stage of decomposition— fresh, partially rotted, and almost finished. The system works like this: we add organic matter to the first bin until it is full, at which point we toss the partially rotted material with a pitchfork into the second bin, thereby freeing up space in the first bin, as well as serving to mix up the compost and speed up decomposition. There the half-finished compost sits until the first bin is full again. When this occurs, the process repeats itself, though this time the contents of the second bin are moved into the third and the first into the second, again freeing up the first bin to receive fresh debris. Because of the fairly large size of the bins, it takes us about two or three months to completely fill one to capacity, and by the time this occurs, the older bin is sufficiently rotted to move on to the next stage. By using this method we need to turn the piles only twice, and we can generally accommodate most of the organic waste from the garden. Best of all, we are able to provide many large wheelbarrows-full of fresh compost for the garden beds every season.

Compost Contents

GARDEN WASTE FALLS INTO THREE GENERAL categories: "green" materials such as seaweed, new grass clippings, or fresh manure that supply large amounts of nitrogen; "brown" materials such as old leaves, cornstalks, or wood shavings, which are carbon rich; and "balanced" materials such as old sod and soil, rotted wood, or manure with bedding, which supply a bit of both nitrogen and carbon. To produce the best compost in the shortest amount of time, you'll want to add equal amounts of green and brown materials. (Adding imbalanced quantities of green or brown, by the way, won't hurt the process, it will just slow it down. Balanced materials can be added in any quantities.)

Here's a more extended list of common additions to many compost and their categories:

Greens	Browns	Balanced
• Fresh manure	• Leaves	• Manure with bedding
• Fresh grass clippings	• Straw and hay	• Vegetable peelings
• Seaweed	• Sawdust	• Sod and soil
• Crushed eggshells	• Wood shavings	• Well-aged manure
• Various meals (byproducts of factory production) such as blood, cottonseed, and soybean	• Shredded newspapers	

There are a few things you should never add to your compost pile, and why. They include:

What	Why
Weed debris with many seeds, or remnants of tenacious weeds like bindweed that will sprout from a bit of root.	While most compost piles will generate quite a bit of heat from decomposition, certain piles may not heat up enough to kill the weeds.
Human, dog, or cat waste.	These manures may carry dangerous parasites.
Diseased plants.	Again, the pile may not heat up enough to kill the pathogens.
Nonbiodegradable materials, or materials that degrade extremely slowly, like twigs and branches.	Yes, this sounds obvious, since nonbiodegradable materials by definition won't break down through decomposition, but you would be surprised how many materials like seaweed contain bits of plastic and other substances that are a pain to fish out of compost. On the other hand, materials that decompose too slowly, like wood, will have to be removed from the finished compost by hand.
Pesticide waste or residue.	Toxic chemicals may not break down and will poison the pile.
Meat, bones, cheese, fat, or other animal food waste.	These may attract pests and rodents.
Coal, coal dust, charcoal dust.	These may contain substances toxic to plants.

THE VICTORY GARDEN COMPANION

52

Ask Michael:
Fertilizer 101

Dear Michael,
The other day I went to the store to buy fertilizer and came back totally bewildered. All those types, all those numbers! Can you explain to me the difference between the various kinds, and when I need to apply what?

Fertilizer is, plain and simple, plant food, or what is sometimes referred to as plant nutrients. Although these nutrients can be found naturally in the earth's soil, they aren't always available in the exact proportions or in the amount that your plants need. Therefore the soil in your home garden often requires supplementation with a man-made fertilizer that contains the same ingredients found in nature.

There are three essential nutrients that contribute to a plant's health: nitrogen (N), phosphorus (P), and potassium (K). Nitrogen helps build new plant material and encourages leafy growth, something especially critical for plants that are mostly made up of leaves such as grass. Phosphorus is what promotes the development of strong roots and, by extension, a stronger plant. This is particularly critical if you're planting new trees, shrubs, or perennials, as it helps establish them quickly. The third ingredient, potassium, aids among other things a plant's ability to resist disease. While nitrogen, phosphorus, and potassium are the primary nutrients required for good growth, there are other important elements that contribute to a plant's overall health: sulfur (S), magnesium (Mg), calcium (Ca), and other trace elements such as iron (Fe) are critical to various biological processes and are sometimes added to commercial fertilizers.

If you look on the back of a fertilizer bag, you'll see that the N-P-K content is always listed in terms of three different numbers. These numbers indicate the percentage of each of the three elements immediately available in a given mixture. So, for example, 8-16-24 means that this particular fertilizer consists of 8 percent nitrogen, 16 percent phosphorus, and 24 per-

■ **One of the most common balanced fertilizer blends, 10-10-10.**

cent potassium ready and roaring to go. A mixture of 5-5-5, on the other hand, contains only 5 percent of each of the principal elements in immediately available form. Why choose a lower number when you can double the bang for your buck with a more concentrated mix? Fertilizers with higher numbers are more potent—providing a quick, concentrated dose—which sometimes is a good thing, but at other times detrimental. (Fertilizers with high concentrations can easily burn sensitive plants, for example.)

Fertilizers alter the respective percentage of the three primary nutrients based on their intended use. A fertilizer with a high proportion of potassium, for example, will help promote flowering and fruiting, and is great for vegetables whose edible parts are flowers or fruit. A more balanced fertilizer, on the other hand, with equal amounts of N, P, and K, is just what the doctor ordered for everyday general use. There are also specialty fertilizers that are designed specifically for lawns, roses, tomatoes, and container gardens. While these plant-specific varieties can be more expensive, they eliminate the guesswork from figuring out which element a particular plant most re-

quires. When in doubt, select a balanced middle-concentration fertilizer such as 10-10-10.

Once you've decided on a type, you can then select from two broad categories: organic, derived from either animal or vegetable sources; or inorganic, which indicates that the fertilizer is created from various chemical sources, some of which may actually occur naturally (such as mined minerals) and some of which are man-made. Which you use is a matter of personal choice. Within these two categories are two subdivisions: water soluble and nonsoluble. As the name implies, water-soluble fertilizers can be applied in solution, which makes them easy to use, especially after planting. Their very solubility, however, means that they are easily displaced from the soil where they are needed, by rain and erosion. Nonsoluble fertilizers remedy this deficiency. However, to be effective, nonsolubles need to be present down at the roots of the plant, which means they have to be well mixed in with the soil at the time of planting. Adding both types to your garden—nonsolubles at planting, and solubles later in the season—ensures that your plants will have the nutrients they need when they need them.

When to apply fertilizers depends on the type of fertilizer used and the plants to which it's applied. Although it's hard to formulate a generalization for all cases, it's usually safe to say that fertilizers can always be applied at planting time, and again throughout the active growing season (while plants are putting on new growth), according to the manufacturer's instructions.

■ Along a stream in a protected valley, a whole host of rare and exotic plants, among them the spectacular blue Himalayan poppy (*Meconopsis*), bloom well to the north of their normal range at the Jardins de Métis—a convincing testament both to the power of microclimates, as well as the ability of the gardener to push the boundaries of what can grow where.

Inspired Gardens

Les Jardins de Métis

THE REFORD GARDENS, OR TO CALL THEM
by their formal name, Les Jardins de Métis, are very much an
anomaly. Situated in Zone 4, far to the north of Quebec City,
this incredible collection of plants thrives where no garden of
this magnitude should be able to survive. The reason for its
existence hinges on an odd convergence of two powerful
forces—the amazing talents of an amateur gardener, and an
extremely peculiar microclimate.

The human element of this equation was first supplied by
Elsie Stephen Reford (1872–1967), who in the 1920s began landscaping the grounds around what was at the time a rather rustic summer estate. Over the next 30-odd summers she slowly
carved a series of garden rooms out of the spruce forests, until
her creation encompassed 40 landscaped acres that are home
to more than 3,000 species of exotic and native plants.

This was an extraordinary achievement for a woman who,
when she first set foot in the garden, was said not to have
known "the difference between a dandelion and a daisy," as
her great-grandson Alexander Reford recounts. Elsie gar-
dened from intuition, adding to her knowledge through trial
and error, and in the process created a landscape that integrated diverse species of plants in a flowing, naturalistic fashion. But the process wasn't easy. Elsie faced design challenges
unknown to most gardeners: the extreme northerly situation

THE VICTORY GARDEN COMPANION

55

■ **Crab apples in bloom.**

of her garden, for instance, meant that most deciduous trees wouldn't survive, requiring the exclusive use of a limited number of evergreen species for the overhead canopy. Nor did the soil cooperate. The thin, rocky ground grew little very well, and Elsie was forced to barter with the local farmers for the huge amounts of manure and compost her dream garden required.

To her aid, however, came a unique microclimate. Early on, Elsie realized that her land was unlike the rest of the surrounding area. Nestled close to the sea, and built around a flowing stream, her gardens benefited from a steady supply of moisture, as well as the slightly warmer temperatures the water provided. Also, in the winter a heavy blanket of snow (up to 11 feet!), which arrived as early as November and often lingered through May, provided her plants with a cozy insulating blanket against the worst of the Quebec winter and allowed Elsie to successfully grow numbers of exotic species such as rare alpines, blue Himalayan poppies, and the then-new Exbury azaleas—all species that were considered not hardy enough to survive in her Zone 4 landscape. (Gardeners in similarly snowy conditions, take note!) And while the gardening season at the Jardins de Métis ends up being considerably shorter than most, even that has its advantages. Explains Alexander Reford: "The plants quickly burst into life once the snow has melted and the cool summer nights help maintain the bloom."

Today Elsie's grounds are open to the public, enchanting garden connoisseurs with a series of spaces that include the Blue Poppy Glade, the Azalea Walk, the Moss Garden, the Stream Garden, and the Primula Glade. Great-grandson Alexander, who has taken on the mission of preserving and developing the gardens that Elsie built, notes the tremendous challenge in managing a historic garden such as this is, attempting, as he says, "to search for a happy balance between the legacy of the creator and the march of time." Clearly he is succeeding, for nowhere else will the visitor find a better illustration of what can be achieved when gardener and climate work as one.

Note: All quotes are from *Guides to the Gardens of Quebec*, "Reford Gardens," text by Alexander Reford, copyright © 2001, Éditions Fides.

■ **The Blue Poppy Glade.**

■ Who wouldn't want to come home to an inviting
landscape like this one? If your front yard doesn't say
"welcome," some changes are in order.

Chapter 3
Entrances and Exits—Designing the Front Yard

Large or small, [a garden] should look both orderly and rich. It should be well fenced from the outside world. It should by no means imitate either the willfulness or the wildness of nature, but it should look like a thing never to be seen except near a house. It should, in fact, look like part of the house.

WILLIAM MORRIS
Hopes and Fears for Art, 1882

■ In the Victorian era, the front garden was a place of pride, as this 1876 illustration reveals. The attention Victorians lavished on this part of the landscape created a beautiful parklike setting along many streets, a custom that stands in stark contrast to the plain front yards—and ugly streetscapes—often seen today.

The Importance of Streetscapes

TAKE A WALK DOWN ANY STREET IN AMERICA AND you'll soon realize that by and large, few of us concentrate our gardening efforts in the front yard. It's not that these front areas aren't well tended: row after row of clipped plantings file past foundations; walkways march from curb to front door; driveways parade to the garage—all very neat and tidy. But these spaces are boring and lifeless, similar to a guest room that's opened up only once or twice a year: presentable, but without personality. If this sounds too much like your front yard, then perhaps it's time for some changes.

It wasn't always this way. In the Victorian era, a hundred

years ago, when to see and be seen was a driving societal force, the *front* yard—especially with the advent of a new phenomenon, the suburb—was all that really mattered. At a time when homeowners generally came and went by their front doors, when guests always did, and passersby strolled on that other new innovation, the sidewalk, careful attention to the front landscape was critical. Meanwhile, the less scenic aspects of Victorian domestic life—the washing, stable areas, privies, produce gardens, and ash pits—were all relegated to the rear of the lot, well out of public view.

This Victorian emphasis on beautifying the front yard had the effect of producing a series of verdant, parklike streetscapes that haven't been seen since. All those scenes in the old movies of children playing in front of lovely homes set amidst lush lawns, towering trees, and ornamental landscapes weren't just figments of some screenwriter's imagination. They really existed—that is, until the rise of the automobile made the main access to our homes the garage, and traffic congestion forced us to seek solace in private gardens created from where the now long-departed servants' areas once stood.

Given this sea change in our lifestyle habits, you may be wondering why I'm suggesting that you even bother tending to your front yard. Chances are you hardly ever use it, except as a pass-through. But there are more than a few very good reasons why it pays to pay attention to your front landscape. The first is that unless you approach your house consistently from the rear, the front part of your lot is the area you probably see the most of on a day-to-day basis, and there is nothing more welcoming to a soul wearied by a long day at the office than a beautiful entranceway offering the solace of hearth and home.

The second good reason to pay attention to your front yard is that it does in fact present your public face to the world, and says much about who you are and what you care about. The third reason has to do with aiding the public good: beautiful front yards improve the overall appearance of the streetscape. Passing down a well-landscaped street gladdens the spirit of all those who journey back and forth on their daily errands, and is a priceless part of the urban and suburban experience. Finally, if none of these aesthetic or altruistic arguments sway you, the hard cold-cash fact of the matter is that your home's

■ One of the keys to designing the front landscape is to make sure the style of the garden matches that of the house. Here the wooden walks echo the wooden siding, and the simple, naturalistic plantings complement the minimalist design of the modern architecture.

■ These three photographs of the Victory Garden show the value of improving the front landscape. In the first snapshot, the house sits isolated and alone; the plantings are overgrown; there is nowhere for visitors to park, and no way to get to the front door. In the second, taken seven years later, a cobble drive provides both auto and pedestrian access to the main entrance; the stone wall and the line of European beech (*Carpinus betulus*) screen the house from the street, and the overgrown yews have been replaced with a fence and appropriately scaled plantings. The third photograph, taken 15 years later, shows the planting in the process of being refreshed in the summer of 2005. Changing conditions—in this case increased shade—often mean rethinking foundation plantings every 10–15 years.

"curb appeal" (in other words, its front yard) is a major factor in its resale price. Real estate studies have shown again and again that money spent on front yard improvements have a greater rate of return than any other landscape expenditure.

So let's begin by taking a look at the three main aspects of your front yard: the drive, the walk, and the plantings (including that bane of the modern American garden, the foundation planting), and see how each of these might be designed to make your home say "welcome" every time you return.

Driveways to Success

UNLESS YOU ARE ONE OF THOSE LUCKY PEOPLE WITH A garage accessed from the rear of your lot, chances are the dominant feature of your front yard is the driveway. Unfortunately, from a landscape design perspective, this can present quite a problem, because—let's face it—the average modern drive is pretty ugly. Normally constructed in a deadly monotone of concrete or asphalt with very little concern for aesthetics, these boring strips of paving overwhelm every other feature in the yard. But it doesn't have to be this way: your driveway could and should be an asset to your landscape, not a detriment.

The first step to improving the look of your front yard is to think beyond the asphalt-and-concrete box and consider a driveway paving material that is both practical and appropriate to the look and feel of your home. The good news is there are a host of paving possibilities out there that can provide the durable, practical surface you require in a driveway while simultaneously avoiding the appearance of a mall parking lot. Depending on the style of your home, your taste preferences, and your budget, gravel, brick, cobble, stone, and prefabricated pavers (or combinations thereof) are all options. And of course, if you are building a new home, or substantially renovating the landscape of an old one, putting in a good-looking driveway is fairly easy, at least from a construction perspective.

What happens, though, if you already have a worn-out concrete or asphalt drive and don't have the option—for budgetary or other reasons—of installing the whole thing anew? Well, with badly damaged concrete you are unfortunately stuck until you're able to replace the surface, since old, broken concrete

Some Paving Options for Modern Drives

Material	Assets	Liabilities
BRICK	Relatively easy to put down; can be laid in interesting, decorative patterns; comes in various colors; combines easily with other materials; has a natural look that goes well with a large number of housing styles.	Expensive; can buckle under heavy traffic if laid improperly; will grow weeds if unused; harder to snowplow than asphalt.
COBBLE	Elegant, natural appearance; can be laid in interesting decorative patterns; combines well with a variety of other materials and housing styles.	Very expensive; difficult to lay; will grow weeds if unused; harder to snowplow than asphalt; generally too rough for games.
GRAVEL AND OTHER AGGREGATE MATERIALS, SUCH AS OYSTER SHELLS	Natural, old-fashioned feel; easy to apply; relatively inexpensive; works well in a country setting.	Must be maintained on a yearly basis; will grow weeds if unused; harder to snowplow than asphalt; generally too uneven for games; must be edged to avoid splaying of gravel; can't be used on steep slopes; generally not suitable in the city.
CHIP-SEALED ASPHALT	Natural feel with the advantages of a hard surface; suitable for games; easy to plow; can be used on slopes.	More expensive than gravel, though less than other materials; must be recoated every five years or so.

can't be easily repaired. (In cases where the problems are less severe, concrete can be patched and then painted with a special concrete paint, which has the added benefit of converting cold-looking concrete into a much warmer-looking surface.)

With asphalt, however, you have other options. Modern technology has come to the rescue with some wonderful resurfacing possibilities that can substantially alter and improve the look of a beat-up old driveway. Called by a number of different proprietary names such as "chip seal," this technology essentially places a hot tar cap on your existing asphalt driveway, which can then be covered with a variety of different-colored aggregate materials. The final effect comes close to the look of an old-fashioned gravel driveway.

And speaking of gravel drives, I'd like to spend a moment in defense of this old standby. I'm often asked by homeowners worried about maintenance and plowing issues whether or not gravel driveways are a still a good idea in today's landscape. My answer is a resounding yes—there is nothing more pleasing to the ear than the sound of gravel crunching under foot or wheel as you approach the door on a well-designed gravel drive. In addition, gravel driveways are fairly easy to install, less expensive than other paving options, and provide a far less harsh appearance than hard pavement, especially where a large surface area is required.

There are, however, several caveats to gravel driveways of which you should be aware before you set about installing one. The first is that gravel drives, to my eye at least, very much possess a country air and don't seem particularly appropriate in the context of an urban setting. Therefore if you live in town, I would strongly recommend using hard paving instead.

Gravel should also be avoided if you have a drive with a steep slope, as the aggregate will continually migrate downhill, causing a maintenance nightmare. You should be aware as well that there will be some additional upkeep involved with a gravel drive. Weeds have a tendency to sprout in areas not heavily trafficked (a problem common to brick and cobble drives as well), and gravel can often be displaced a bit after a winter of heavy snowplowing (something that can be largely avoided by having your plower raise his or her blade an inch or so higher than normal). Here at the Victory Garden, where we have two large gravel drives, we take care of any weeds with a semiannual pass with a string trimmer; other options are to kill the weeds by applying a mild herbicide such as Roundup or to boil water with rock salt. As for displaced gravel, I simply rake shifted stones back into place after the last snows have passed. That's really about all the work a gravel drive requires—and to my mind, it's well worth the effort for the soothing appearance it lends the landscape in return.

The other major concern when designing driveways—regardless of material—is their shape, size, and direction. There is a common tendency, especially when drives are constructed by inexperienced contractors intent only on the bottom line, to run the smallest possible strip straight to the garage door. And while it's true that as a designer I spend a lot of time trying to minimize a driveway's visual impact on the front landscape, a drive that is too narrow, or that has an inadequate number of parking spaces, serves no purpose whatsoever. The average car with its doors open requires an amazing 12 feet of paving space to allow passengers to disembark dry-shod and safe, and even more width if you wish to have enough space to drive past parked cars in the driveway. Careful attention to your parking needs, in terms of both the number and frequency of parked cars you anticipate on an average daily basis, is critical to designing a good driveway.

Also, if you are planning the course of a new drive or redesigning an old one, think about ways that your driveway can simultaneously access both the garage *and* the front door. This can often be accomplished by creating a circular or U-shaped drive. Too frequently today you'll see a drive pulled straight down the side of a lot leading directly to the garage, which then forces the creation of a long walkway to the front door. Of course, this design works perfectly well if you consistently enter your home directly from the garage. However, if your poor guests wish to get indoors they are condemned to either a long march to the front door through all kinds of inclement weather or to snaking their way through the minefield of parked cars, bicycles, trash cans, and other domestic impediments. Neither option is ideal.

Additionally, creating such long walks from drive to door inevitably leads to a series of unpleasant design consequences for the front landscape, especially in terms of symmetry and balance. In such a drive and walkway scheme, the side of the lot with all that paving is visually heavy, making it virtually impossible to create a balanced front planting. All sorts of design solutions are contrived to get around this problem—curving the front walk, creating flanking beds, installing offset plantings—none of which is particularly successful. Far better, if you have the budget and space, is to design a circular or semicircular drive that gives equal and ample access to both house and garage.

■ **These three diagrams show minimum dimensions for three commonly used front drive schemes. Most people are surprised when they learn how much room an average car needs just to safely unload goods and passengers, and novice designers have a tendency to drastically underestimate the space required for parking. If you are redesigning a driveway and have any doubts on the matter, pull your car in for a "test park" before you commit your ideas to brick and mortar.**

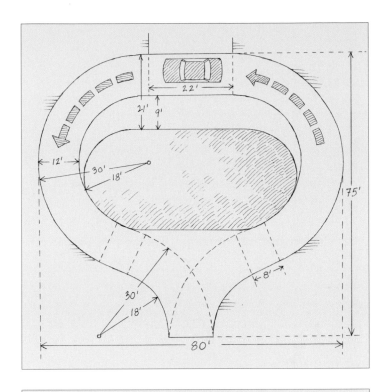

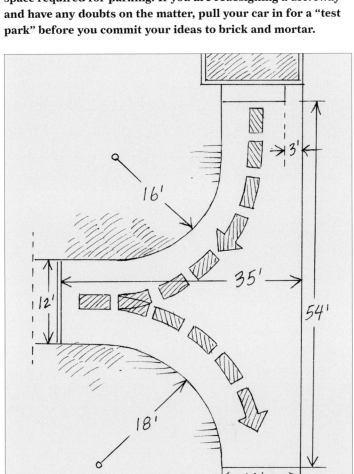

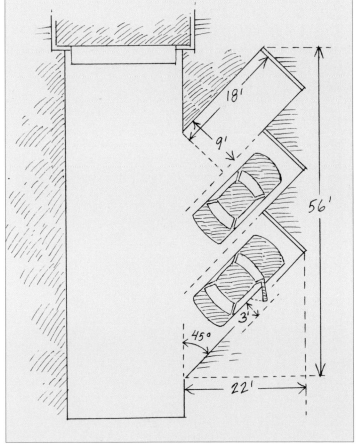

Design Basics:
ALTERNATE DRIVEWAY SCHEMES FOR TODAY'S LIVING

■ **TOP LEFT:** This driveway is composed of concrete pavers with a bricklike finish.

■ **TOP RIGHT:** Here, an edging of granite cobblestones and a flanking stone wall at the entrance add distinction to an asphalt driveway.

■ **BOTTOM RIGHT:** This gently curving pea-gravel driveway is edged in cobbles, which can prevent the gravel from migrating to the lawn.

■ **THIS PAGE:** Hard paving adds up fast in the landscape, and often large driveways can take on a monolithic appearance. To avoid this heavy visual effect, one common trick is to use a combination of soft and hard paving options, like the grass and brick used here. Another possible choice would have been cobble and gravel.

Walk the Walk

AFTER THE DRIVEWAY, THE NEXT MOST IMPORTANT aspect of the front landscape is the walkway leading to your front door. It is, in a manner of speaking, the entrance to your world, and the first impression that guests receive of you and your home. Too often, however, modern American front walkways suffer the same problems as our driveways: poor design implemented with boring materials. Take a moment to assess your own front walk. Is the surfacing material harmonious with the look and feel of your house? Does it offer interest throughout the year? Is the walkway wide enough for two people to walk comfortably side by side? Does it get people to the front door in an efficient manner, without unnecessary curves and detours? Is the walkway entrance easy for strangers to find, and does it clearly delineate the way to the front door? If the answer to any of these questions is no, changes are in order.

On an Even Keel

IN TERMS OF SURFACE OPTIONS, WALKWAYS ARE VERY much like driveways—they should be made from materials that match the look and feel of your home. But because people traverse walkways on foot rather than from the inside of a car, there are certain additional design considerations of which you need to be aware. The principal one is ease of use in all weather conditions. Whereas you might happily construct a driveway from gravel or cobbles, neither choice would be the best option for a front walkway, especially one that receives heavy traffic. Gravel, for example, has the unpleasant tendency of scratching expensive leather footwear, and in dry weather can cover shoes with loads of dust that will then track right into the house. Cobbles, on the other hand, have a nasty habit of eating high heels (they get stuck in the cracks) and are also difficult to navigate on foot for anyone with balance or mobility problems.

The bottom line? When choosing walkway materials, consider not only aesthetically pleasing options that provide a uniform and even surface, but ones that will be easy to navigate on foot in sun, rain, or snow. Also, remember that unlike driveways, which are frequently seen only in passing from the interior of a car, walkways are viewed directly and from close quarters, which provides opportunities to add interesting design details that will enhance the welcoming look and feel of your walk. Decorative patterns in brick, interesting edging materials such as cobbles, tiles, or stones, or unusual surface materials like pebbles pressed into concrete can all work to convert the prosaic path into a pleasing and practical asset to your landscape.

■ **An ample front walk and comfortable steps set a welcoming tone for this front landscape.**

■ This curving front walk of brick and stone lends a nonchalant air to this flower-filled front garden.

Size Matters

WHEN IT COMES TO WALKWAYS, SIZE DOES MATTER. Being forced off the pavement and into the mud by your companion in an attempt to reach the front door defeats the purpose of the walkway. The minimum width for any front walk is four feet—enough for two people to walk comfortably abreast to the door dry-shod and unmolested by passing greenery. (Note: Garden or other secondary pathways can be as little as three feet wide, just enough to get a mower or wheelbarrow through.) Often, though, especially with particularly tall or massive houses that possess grand front entrances, a four-foot-wide walk will seem too narrow and out of scale with such a large structure. In these cases, walks five, six, or even seven feet wide are quite appropriate. When judging what width is best, I often try to align the dimensions of a new walkway with some existing feature, such as the sides of the front steps or the edges of the door sidelights, keeping in mind that in no case should the front walk be narrower than four feet. Also, while we are on the subject of front steps, if your steps

■ Here, a straight path to the front door was the best option; this clean design is set handsomely in brick.

are old, crumbling, have unequal risers, don't match the walk-way, or are too small to allow someone to stand on the top plat-form when opening the door, consider replacing them along with your front walk. Although front steps aren't cheap, espe-cially when built from quality materials such as stone or brick, there is very little sense spending the time and effort to con-struct a lovely new, expansive front walkway only to have it end with a set of constrictive, worn-out steps.

To Curve or Not to Curve

FOR THE AMATEUR GARDENER OR DO-IT-YOURSELF designer, perhaps the hardest part of laying out a new front walk is to decide exactly from where and in what direction it should run. The terminus is obvious—the front door. But how to get there? Directly, in a straight shot, or with a meandering set of curves? And from where should the walk run? Exclu-sively from the sidewalk, or from the driveway, or a combina-tion of the two? Of course in many cases, simple site constraints will dictate a single route. But in other situations there is no one right answer, and here is where problems start to arise.

For some reason in current landscape design, given the equal opportunity to run either a straight or curved pathway, there is an aversion to running a walk in a straight line from point A to point B. The direct path seems too prosaic, and in-stead a series of curves is randomly introduced to lead the vis-itor down the proverbial garden path to the front door. You would never attempt this indoors—imagine having to run a fixed circuitous route every time you needed to go to the bath-room or get to the oven!—but outdoors this is an inexplicably acceptable practice. The fact of the matter is that a straight walk *is* often the best option. Why force your guests to point-lessly meander amidst the shrubberies to get to the front door? Design your front walk based on two things: the style and feeling of the house, and the normal day-to-day traffic patterns in your yard. Both are quite easy to assess. If your home is geometric in style, with a fairly symmetrical facade that contains many sharp 90-degree corners and angles, then chances are a front walkway with similar straight lines is a good bet. Conversely, if your home is asymmetrical, with lots of different nooks and crannies, a curved walkway may be just the thing. In either case, let your home be your guide. As for determining traffic patterns, simply watch how people come and go across your space. Does the mailman continually cut across the grass to get to your front door? Have the chil-dren, or your dog, or your spouse, beaten a dirt path to your front entryway with their shortcuts? Do guests park in the street or the drive when paying you a call? Answering these kinds of questions will show you how to lay a path to your front door.

Garden Basics: Eye versus Paper

NO MATTER HOW ADVANCED YOUR DRAFTING SKILLS OR initial design concept may be, there is always a considerable difference between what looks good on paper and what looks good on the ground. One of the best ways to get over this trans-lational difficulty, especially when installing a new walk, is to lay out your planned route using a common garden hose.

Simply take two lengths of hose (it helps to make the hose supple by warming it in the sun first) and use one hose to plot the edge of your proposed walk. U-shaped pins, made from old wire coat hangers, will help keep the hose in place. Then use the second hose to lay out the other side. It's amazing how this simple graphic illustration helps you to see exactly where and how the walkway should go, and how well its planned scale re-lates to the rest of the landscape.

This method is especially useful when planning a curved path, as the flexible nature of the hose makes it very easy to see whether or not the curves flow together properly, and whether the intended path looks right. If you have any doubts about your creation, readjust the hose line until you are completely satisfied.

If you have the time, it helps to leave the hose in place for a few days, giving you the opportunity to view the planned path from all angles, especially from both ends, and from inside the

■ **What to avoid in foundation plantings: a lot of heavily pruned evergreen shrubs that require constant maintenance to be kept in check.**

house. Also, don't forget to walk your intended pathway—this helps to make sure you've incorporated the correct route into your design. Nothing causes more chagrin than building a new walkway only to find that friends and family use an easier shortcut on their daily comings and goings.

Once you are happy with the route, use some fluorescent landscaper's spray paint (available at most hardware stores) to more permanently mark the layout until construction begins. If you don't, inevitably someone will decide to pick up and use the hose, forcing you to lay out the walk all over again!

Foundering Foundations

THE FINAL MAJOR ELEMENT OF THE MODERN FRONT yard, the foundation planting, is perhaps the most abused aspect of American landscape design. It's not that a foundation planting is terribly difficult from a horticultural standpoint, other than having to follow some fairly strict plant selection criteria. Indeed, creating a successful foundation planting involves no more skill than developing a successful vegetable plot or perennial border. The problem lies more in a century-old tradition that dictates the only acceptable method of planting the front of the house is to line up a single file of overused evergreens (many of them

■ **This simple cottage-style planting perfectly complements the simple cottage-style house. Note the extensive use of perennials and other deciduous material. When thinking about foundation plantings, it's important to break out of the evergreen-only box.**

actually large trees in the wild) that quickly grow out of scale and in turn overwhelm your house. This misguided approach has been aided and abetted in part by the landscape contracting business. Despite all the best design advice of the last 50 years, these companies continue to perpetuate this kind of planting scheme because (1) it's easy, fast, and profitable to install, and (2) it requires tremendously expensive upkeep just to keep these giant plants in check (generously supplied, it's no surprise, by these same contractors, again at a large profit!). Surely there must be a better way to plant the front of our houses than

committing money and resources to a titanic battle we are fated to lose? Fortunately, there is.

The key to understanding why modern foundation plantings commonly go awry is to know something about how these types of plantings arose in the first place. Despite their now ubiquitous presence, foundation plantings are a relatively recent phenomenon, cropping up only over the last century and a half. Before that time, houses had little or nothing around them in terms of landscaping. In fact, surrounding the house with plantings was considered to be unhealthy. The disease theory of the day believed that most illnesses were

73

■ **This shot clearly demonstrates another important aspect of foundation plantings—adequate depth. To be effective, and to avoid a rigid, linear effect, foundation plantings need sufficient room to allow for three rows of material: high plants at the back, mid-sized plants in the center, and low material at the front.**

caused by bad air, and that good health could be achieved only with good air circulation. Dark, moist spaces were thought to breed disease, and any house worth its salt sat clearly and markedly distant from any surrounding woods or forest. The architectural taste of the period also mandated little or no foundation plantings for two reasons: aesthetically, the form of the structure was meant to be appreciated from afar without obstruction, and second, building methods of the time called for running wooden clapboards almost to ground level,

meaning that any plantings up against structures quickly induced rot.

It wasn't until the mid-1800s and the rise of Victorian houses, characterized by high masonry foundations that sat several feet or more above the ground, that the idea occurred to the newly minted profession of landscape designers to "cloak" the foundation with a low ring of plantings. Frank Scott, one of the greatest of all Victorian landscape gurus, put it extremely well: the theory was to "nest the house . . . with plantings that seem to spring out of the nooks and corners with something of the freedom that characterizes similar vegetation springing naturally along stone walls and fences." Note that the emphasis here was on *low* plantings, which would "nest" the house and reach no higher than the bottom of the first-floor windows. Unfortunately, this period also coincided with the introduction of thousands of new plant species recently discovered in the Near and Far East. Victorian plantsmen, faced with these unknown varieties, had no way of knowing how large many of the plants would grow, and innocently included species that ended up as giants in foundation plantings. Faced with the prospect of ripping out these plants and starting over, most people simply decided to put up with the oversized specimens. The result of all this was that slowly but surely, as the original concept of "decorating" a high foundation was forgotten, people became accustomed to the idea of masking a house—even a low one—behind a cloak of heavy evergreen shrubs.

It's high time for change. Unless you firmly believe your house is an eyesore, no decent structure should be condemned to cower behind a veil of shrubbery. Why not restore the original idea of foundation plantings—that is, using select greenery as a decorative element to ornament your home? Foundation plantings can and should be an enhancement to your house, making the structure look as if it's part of the surrounding garden. To achieve this natural effect, though, you need to select the right plant material and position it wisely.

Tough Choices

CHOOSING PLANT MATERIAL FOR THE FOUNDATION IS basically a process of finding specimens that will fill a rather specific set of criteria. The first of these is that the plants need to be pretty tough. The space immediately surrounding your foundation is in essence one of those microclimates we discussed in the last chapter (see page 40)—and a fairly difficult one at that. If you have any doubt of this, go stand near a southerly or westerly foundation wall on a sunny day, even in the middle of winter, and feel how warm the area is. Con-

versely, if the foundation area is facing north, you'll probably feel a distinct chill. Your home, in fact, acts as a large heat trap, and depending on its positioning either blocks or enhances the power of the sun, greatly limiting the choice of plants that will thrive near the house.

Another factor that heavily influences the selection of plant material is the foundation itself. Most foundations these days are made out of concrete, and because of all the lime used in the manufacture of cement, they generally leach a considerable amount of alkalines into the surrounding soil, which in turn can have a significant effect on pH levels. If you have a concrete foundation, it's wise to select shrubs that are tolerant of alkaline soils.

You should also carefully consider the amount of space you have to donate to a foundation planting, both vertically and horizontally. It's essential that you choose plants that won't outgrow their location. Remember that the idea here is to enhance, not hide, your home, and unless you want to be constantly out front pruning, it behooves you to select species that won't grow larger than the area allotted them. While particular sites might call for the occasional large upright or small tree, in general, most homes will be better served by

WHEN TO CALL FOR HELP

Although we've already talked a lot about the need to carefully plot out your landscape before you plant a single plant, at no time is this principle more important than when planning a foundation planting. To be successful, foundation plantings need specimens that are carefully chosen to enhance your home's look and feel. This is often a difficult task for the beginning gardener to achieve. If you are very much the do-it-yourselfer but feel incapable of such intricate planning, consider hiring a professional to design the space for you, and then prepare and plant it yourself. That way you get the best of both worlds—a successful planting that will enhance your home, and the satisfaction of watching your own handiwork grow.

■ Another great aspect of using a mix of evergreen and deciduous material in the front yard is the seasonal diversity and interest it produces, as these spring (above) and summer (opposite page) shots clearly show. Note, too, how the planting isn't just lined up along the foundation wall, but rather is pulled away from the structure, making the house seem as if it were set down magically in the middle of a garden—which is exactly your goal.

compact selections that will grow less than five feet tall and five wide.

When choosing plantings, I encourage you to break out of the evergreen-only trap and move beyond the same old species of yews, rhododendrons, azaleas, and camellias that you see surrounding countless other foundations. While it's certainly important to include some nondeciduous material in founda-

tion plantings for year-round interest, it's a mistake to think that foundation plants need to keep their leaves year round in order to be effective. Think of your foundation planting as a garden, and include plants with interesting bark, variegated leaves, colorful flowers, berries, or twig forms. And don't forget that foundation plantings need not consist entirely of shrubs: perennials and annuals make excellent

additions to the foundation, especially when used in masses to dress the front of taller plantings. Not only do flowers supply a dash of color, but their yearly rise and disappearance will add a touch of welcome variety to any facade.

Finally, avoid the most common mistake people make when laying out a foundation planting—positioning the shrubbery in a single row across the front of the house. The result, without exception, does nothing to help the structure settle into the landscape. Instead, draw up a plan on paper that includes deep beds with several tiers of plantings. (The taller the house, the deeper the bed should be; 10 to 15 feet is not exces-

sive for the average two-story house.) Carefully place the tallest specimens at the rear of your plan, graduating to smaller material at the front. Use a limited plant palette— three to five different species in repeated groupings of threes, fives, and sevens, with an occasional single specimen for accent. Also, don't simply run the bed straight across the front of the house, ending precisely where the structure ends. Instead, pull the lines of the foundation planting around the facade to link up with beds and borders at the sides of the house or at the edges of the property. Properly done, your foundation planting should seem a natural extension of the yard around it.

Before

Milwaukee

■ This is the front yard of the house we redid during our
29th filming season. Here you see a typical ranch-style
home with a typical suburban landscape: lots of grass, and a
monotonous planting of overgrown evergreens in front. (In
fact, many had already been removed when this picture was
taken!) In short, a boring field of green.

78

Makeover

■ The "after" shot—what a difference three days make! Next year, in phase two of the renovations, the homeowner plans to transform the front drive with a "chip seal" coating that will give the black asphalt the appearance of tan-colored gravel—the perfect complement to this stone-fronted home.

■ **Left:** In this view out the living-room windows, you can see how extending the planting away from the house and into the front yard creates an extremely pleasing effect. This shot also illustrates the importance of planning your landscape not only from the outside looking in, but the inside looking out.

■ **Below:** Here's the plan that landscape architect Dennis Buettner developed for us; note that unlike most traditional American front gardens where the shrubbery is plastered right up against the house, this planting consists of three distinct areas: the foreground near the foundation; the middle ground near the drive; and a third background layer near the street.

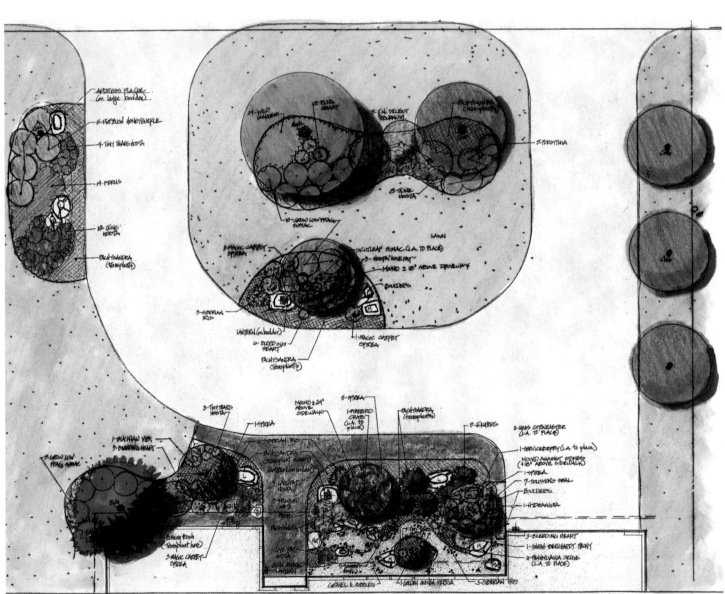

In this close-up shot of the planting (above), you can appreciate one element of the design scheme that's not obvious on the plan: the slight berm or rise that provides the house with a bit of added protection from the drive. The large boulders strewn about the landscape are comprised of the same stone used in the home's foundation—a great touch. This second picture (right) shows the back of the same berm—the part nearest the house—where the designer has cleverly installed a dry stream bed of river-washed stones that adds year-round interest near the foundation, and insures good drainage in wet weather.

Prepare the soil

Always follow *The Victory Garden*'s golden rule: don't plant anything before adequately preparing the soil. Think of it this way: your shrubs will (one hopes) be around for a long time, so they'll need a well-prepared bed full of nutrients that will literally last them a lifetime. Start by turning over and weeding the site, just as you would a flower or vegetable bed. Next, make sure the soil structure is the best it can be—include adequate amounts of organic matter and nutrients, and dig them in well.

Place your plants before you dig

Using your plan, place your plants in their approximate positions, and adjust as necessary. The difference between how things look on the plan and how they look in the real world is fairly great, and it's best to use your eye to make the final adjustments.

1. Dig the hole

Don't skimp on the hole: make sure you have dug it deep enough to allow sufficient room around the root mass so you can adequately pack in soil, and that the top of the root ball sits slightly (about one inch) above the current ground level. See illustration 1.

2. Remove the plant from the container and untie the ball

If you are removing the plant from a container, tip it over, keeping a firm hand on the top of the soil to prevent any of it from falling out. (Occasionally plants will stick in their pots; generally a few good thumps on the pot sides and bottom will release the root ball.) If you have a burlapped plant, put the specimen in the hole, untie the ball, and then loosen the burlap sack surrounding it. See illustration 2. You do not need to remove the burlap, as it will decay. Be sure to tuck the burlap

well beneath the soil surface so that it can't wick moisture out of the soil before it decays. (Plastic "burlap" occasionally found on shrubs must be removed entirely.)

3. Adjust the soil level as necessary, and then backfill

Once the plant has been placed squarely and firmly in the hole, fill in with soil, tamping down firmly to remove any air pockets, and making sure the soil level on the top of the plant is even with the surrounding soil.

4. Water, water

To get your plants off to a good start, it's generally best to create a several-inch-high temporary ring of soil around each plant. See illustration 4. This prevents water from running off too quickly, and ensures whatever moisture the plant receives will seep directly into the roots, where it desperately needs to go. Once the saucer is completed, water thoroughly with a hose, counting a very slow "15" over each plant to ensure sufficient moisture reaches the lower roots. Then, make sure the new planting receives two inches of water per week throughout its first season.

Mulch

Finally, add a layer of mulch, such as pine bark or buckwheat hulls, after you plant, both for water conservation and to keep your newly planted plants protected from winter cold (an especially important step if you are planting in the fall).

{botanical nomenclature}

Most plants have two sets of names: a common name, and a proper horticultural name. Though using the common name is sometimes easier, it can quickly lead to confusion. Common names aren't necessarily specific to a single species; for instance, several completely different plants have been called "cedars" over the years. Say "cedar," and which are you talking about? That's why, in general, it's best to familiarize yourself with correct botanical nomenclature.

Proper plant names are governed by a very specific set of rules. Although at first glance the system looks a bit complicated, is really isn't; in fact, using the correct plant name not only makes sure everyone is on the same page horticulturally, it also allows you to see precisely where a particular specimen fits in the family tree of plants. Plant names generally are divided into two or three parts. Take, for instance, *Boltonia asteroides* 'Snowbank': *Boltonia* (always in italics and capitalized) is the *genus* name, telling us that this particular plant is a member of the Boltonia clan; *asteroides* (in italics but not capitalized) is the species name, and tells us that this plant belongs to the further subdivision of *asteroides*, which means "aster-like"; and then, as here, there sometimes occurs a final name in single quotes, capitalized, in regular type. This last is called the cultivar (from "*culti*vated *var*iety"), which is a synonym for the more common term "variety name." So in this case, 'Snowbank' is a cultivated variety of the *asteroides* species, which is a subdivision of the *Boltonia* genus. There are some variations to these rules, of course, but knowing the basics will help you chart your way much more easily in the world of plants.

■ *Cotoneaster.*

Best Bets for Foundation Plants

The list of candidates is huge: any compact plant with interesting shape, foliage, or flower is a possible candidate. Here are some of our favorites:

Species/Variety	Common Name	Deciduous or Evergreen	Hardiness Zone	Comment
Berberis thunbergii var. *atropurpurea* 'Crimson Pygmy'	Dwarf red barberry	D	4–9	Red foliage.
Buxus microphylla	Little leaf box	E	5–6	Compact evergreen, hardier than *Buxus sempervirens*.
Buxus microphylla Koreana varieties	Korean box	E	4–6	'Wintergreen' is the best of *koreana* cultivars for winter foliage.
Cephalotaxus harringtonia cultivars	Japanese plum yew	E	6–10	Family varies widely, so be sure to choose dwarf cultivars like 'Prostrata.'
Chamaecyparis lawsoniana 'Minima Glauca,' 'Minima Aurea'	Dwarf Lawson false cypress	E	4–9	Other dwarf cultivars available.
Chamaecyparis obtusa 'Spiralis' 'Nana'	Dwarf Hinoki false cypress	E	5–10	Many other dwarf cultivars such as 'Aurea' and 'Coralliformis' are available.
Chamaecyparis pisifera filifera 'Aurea Nana'	Dwarf golden Sawara false cypress	E	5–10	Genus varies widely, so be sure to choose dwarf cultivars.
Clethra alnifolia 'Hummingbird'	Dwarf summer sweet	D	4–9	This cultivar is more compact than species.
Cotoneaster salicifolius 'Repense'	Willowleaf cotoneaster	E	6–10	Other excellent cultivars available, such as 'Autumn Fire' and 'Exburyensis.'
Cotoneaster adpressus 'Tom Thumb'	Creeping cotoneaster	D	4–9	Interesting dwarf cultivar.
Cotoneaster horizontalis	Rockspray cotoneaster	D	4–9	Prostrate form.
Daphne cneorum 'Ruby Glow'	Garland flower	E	4–9	Interesting foliage; other excellent cultivars available.
Daphne odora	Winter daphne	E	8–10	The most fragrant of the daphnes.

Species/Variety	Common Name	Deciduous or Evergreen	Hardiness Zone	Comment
Deutzia gracilis 'Nikko'	Dwarf slender deutzia	D	5–9	Genus varies widely and other deutzias are worth investigating.
Fothergilla gardenii cultivars	Dwarf fothergilla	D	5–9	Fragrant white flowers; 'Blue Mist' comes with bluish foliage.
Hebe spp.	Hebe	E	7–10	Genus varies widely, and many hebes are worth investigating.
Hydrangea macrophylla cultivars	Bigleaf hydrangea	D	5–11	Huge genus with many valuable cultivars.
Ilex cornuta 'Burfordii Nana'	Dwarf Chinese holly	E	6–10	Free-fruiting form with red berries.
Ilex crenata cultivars	Japanese holly	E	6–10	Excellent evergreen foliage; many interesting cultivars such as 'Helleri' and 'Golden Gem.'
Ilex x meserveae cultivars	Blue holly	E	6–10	Huge genus with many valuable cultivars.
Itea virginica 'Henry's Garnet'	Virginia sweetspire	D	5–9	Honey-scented flowers and excellent fall color; other dwarf cultivars available.
Jasminium nudiflorum	Winter jasmine	D	7–9	Sprawling shrub/vine with fragrant flowers in late winter; other jasmine species also merit investigation.
Juniperus communis cultivars	Common juniper	E	2–8	Interesting needle-like foliage; seek out dwarf cultivars such as 'Compressa,' 'Depressa Aurea,' 'Nana,' and 'Pendula.'
Juniperus conferta	Shore juniper	E	5–9	Low-growing groundcover, excellent for seaside conditions.
Juniperus procumbens 'Nana'	Dwarf Japanese garden juniper	E	4–9	Prostrate groundcover; interesting habit.
Juniperus scopulorum 'Horizontalis'	Rocky Mountain juniper	E	5–9	Both upright and prostrate cultivars exist.
Lespedeza thunbergii 'Alba,' 'Edo Shindori,' 'Gilbraltar'	Bush clover	D	4–9	Often semi-evergreen in warmer climates with profuse pealike flowers in late summer.

Species/Variety	Common Name	Deciduous or Evergreen	Hardiness Zone	Comment
Pieris japonica cultivars	Japanese pieris	E	6–10	Numerous cultivars vary in foliage and flower color.
Pinus mugo var 'pumilo'	Dwarf mugo pine	E	2–8	Dwarf cultivar; very low and slow growing.
Pittosporum tobira cultivars	Dwarf Japanese pittosporum	E	9–11	'Wheeler's Dwarf' and 'Nana' are excellent cultivars.
Potentilla fruticosa cultivars	Shrubby cinquefoil	D	3–9	Hundreds of cultivars in various leaf shades and flower colors.
Prunus laurocerasus 'Zabeliana'	Dwarf cherry laurel	E	7–10	Dwarf cultivar to 3 feet.
Raphiolepsis indica cultivars	Indian hawthorn	E	8–11	Can be invasive in temperate climates; 'Ballerina' with pink flowers; 'Monme' with bronzy new growth.
Rhododendron spp. (dwarf types)	Rhododendron	E	5/6–9	Many excellent dwarf cultivars.
Skimmia japonica 'Snow Dwarf'	Japanese skimmia	E	7–10	Prostrate form with white flowers.
Spiraea japonica cultivars	Spirea	D	3–10	Many interesting cultivars; in particular, 'Anthony Waterer' with purple-red flowers.
Spiraea nipponica 'Snowmound'	Nippon spirea	D	5–10	Leaves with bluish hue and white flowers.
Stephanandra incisa 'Crispa'	Cutleaf stephanandra	D	4–10	Deeply serrated foliage; excellent in shade.
Syringa meyeri	Dwarf Korean lilac	D	4–9	'Palibin' with pink/lavender flowers; 'Superba' deep pink.
Taxus baccata cultivars	Dwarf spreading English yew	E	5–10	For foundations, seek out dwarf cultivars such as 'Repandens,' 'Nutans,' and 'Dwarf White.'
Taxus cuspidata cultivars	Dwarf Japanese yew	E	4–9	For foundations, seek out dwarf cultivars such as 'Densa,' 'Densiformis,' and var. *nana*.
Weigela florida cultivars	Weigela	D	5–10	'Alexandra' with purple foliage and red flowers.

DIGGING DEEPER: THE MYSTERIES OF OUTDOOR SCALE

BACK IN THE FIRST CHAPTER WE DISCUSSED HOW INDOOR and outdoor design were in many ways the same, and how we could translate the walls, doors, and windows of the inside to the boundaries, gateways, and vistas of the outdoors. There is one major difference between inside and out, however, and that is relative scale. Inside, a typical room might measure 12' × 12' with 8-to-10-foot ceilings. Outdoors, however, our spaces are much larger—a typical garden "room" might measure 50' × 50', with a ceiling height higher than the clouds in the sky. In this much larger space, objects such as walks, stairs, paved areas, and even garden furniture and decorative objects need to be much bigger than their indoor equivalents to make a suitable visual impression. To prove this to yourself, take a card table or some other moveable piece of furniture and place it in the center of the largest room in your house. Then, take this same table outside, and set it down in the backyard. See how small it appears by comparison? It clearly looks too insubstantial to be at home in the larger landscape. The lesson is simple: outdoors, think big.

This rule applies equally to the square footage of the outdoor areas themselves. Keep in mind that outside activities often require a substantial amount of space—far more than their inside equivalents. (Anyone who has ever had 30 barbecue party guests forced inside by a sudden thunderstorm, or any parents who have caught their children playing football inside the house, will know exactly what I mean.) Thus, when planning your landscape, avoid the common mistake of making landscape spaces and their features too small. Dinky planting beds, narrow walkways, tiny terraces, and too-small driveways are the common creations of the beginning gardener—well intended, but totally ineffective. To head these problems off at the pass, why not do what professional designers do? Make a mock-up and see how they appear in real life. Lay out a revised walkway with a hose;

■ **If this stairway were located indoors, it would seem overly massive. Outside, the scale is just right. Remember: outside, bigger is often better.**

mark out the path of a proposed driveway with stakes and twine; position scaled cardboard squares the size of your furniture on a planned terrace; use ground limestone to mark the borders of a new garden bed—in essence, do whatever it takes to give you a clear impression of what your plans will look like and how they will function outdoors. This way you leave nothing to the imagination, and nine times out of ten you'll find that the areas that seemed so large on paper really translate into very small spaces outdoors and may well need to be enlarged. Conversely, you may occasionally discover that your plans are too large for the proposed space and need to be adjusted accordingly. Either way, a few hours spent now in mastering the mysteries of outdoor scale will save countless headaches—not to mention considerable expense—down the road.

Olmsted's Magic Formula for Step Design

Dear Michael,

I thought I once remembered reading that there was a famous "magic formula" for figuring out how to lay out garden steps. I can't recall what it was, only that someone named Olmsted invented it. Who was Olmsted, and what's the equation?

Yes, you remembered correctly. Determining the appropriate width of the treads and the height of the risers can be quite a task for the amateur gardener, but fortunately, one of the founders of American landscape architecture, Frederick Law Olmsted, came to our rescue over a century ago by popularizing an easy-to-use formula for perfect outdoor steps.

Frederick Law Olmsted (1822–1903) was something of a Renaissance man, only coming to his final career—landscape architecture (it was he, in fact, who first coined the term)—relatively late in life after sampling an amazing variety of jobs. Olmsted was, at various times in his life, a merchant seaman, a newspaper correspondent, a magazine columnist, a gold mine manager, the administrative head of the United States Sanitary Commission (an early version of the Red Cross), and the superintendent for the construction of New York's Central Park. It was here, under the guidance of landscape designer Calvert Vaux, that he learned the trade that would make his name famous throughout America. So successful was he on this project, his most famous creation, that Olmsted went on to shape landscapes all over the United States. In addition to hundreds of private commissions, Olmsted designed the parks of Boston's Emerald Necklace; the grounds of the U.S. Capitol; the Niagara Reservation at Niagara Falls; Buffalo, New York's Park System; Prospect Park in Brooklyn; Riverside Park in Manhattan; Lake Park in Milwaukee; and the grounds of the 1893 World's Fair in Chicago.

Although the number of lessons that could be drawn from such a huge body of work are almost endless, one of the more useful for our purposes was the development of the perfect formula for creating garden steps—what is commonly referred to as "the ratio of riser to tread." Anyone who has ever attempted to design a set of outdoor steps knows that this was an important achievement, indeed.

While your site will mandate a set overall height and length for your proposed stairway, the way those measurements are divided among the number of steps, the horizontal surface (the tread), and the vertical surface (the riser) is much more flexible.

Take, for example, a set of projected stairs that needs to rise four feet in height and can be no more than four feet long. Any number of potential sets of steps could be envisioned: a set of four steps with foot-long treads and foot-high risers, for instance. Or eight steps with six-inch treads and six-inch risers. Or six steps with eight-inch treads and eight-inch risers. The list goes on and on.

Which version you choose, however, is critical to the success of your design. Deep and shallow steps, for example, will force you to slow down the pace at which you move about the garden. This is sometimes a good thing in casual settings, but if overdone can make steps more difficult to traverse as your mind continually anticipates a riser that doesn't come, forcing you to watch your feet to see when to step up. Very steep steps, on the other hand, are uncomfortable to climb and can be quite dangerous, especially in bad weather. (Risers of more than eight inches are also illegal in many localities.)

After much trial and error, Olmsted determined that to make a set of steps comfortable, ***twice the riser plus the tread should equal no more than 26 inches***—an extremely simple formula indeed, but one that was the product of genius.

■ As you can see from these two Williamsburg examples, the Lightfoot House (left) and the Finnie House (pages 92–93), less was certainly more when it came to front plantings in the Colonial era. The simple, symmetrical arrangements make the real star of the landscape—the house—shine.

Inspired Gardens

Colonial Williamsburg

IT DOESN'T TAKE MUCH MORE THAN A FEW MINUTES walking the shaded streets and winding lanes of Colonial Williamsburg to feel right at home, and one of the principal reasons for this is the understated elegance of the era's front gardens. Not only do these landscapes provide insight into the garden trends of the past, but they also provide important design lessons for the front yards of today.

According to Kent Brinkley, longtime landscape architect for Williamsburg and co-author of *The Gardens of Colonial Williamsburg*, the modern-day visitor is often struck by how welcoming these 18th-century streetscapes are, despite their very simple design: "If you ambled down the main street, called Duke of Gloucester, for example, you would be struck by the fact that the front yard of each of these houses was positioned almost directly on the road. The reason for this is that as originally constructed the houses had a 99-foot right of way with only a six-foot setback from the street, that didn't leave much room for front gardening."

These main-street homeowners dealt with their small patch of land by erecting a picket fence, a little grass, and a brick gutter at ground level that wrapped its way around each of the houses. It wasn't much, but it worked perfectly to link the house to the front yard and provide an easy transition from the street, thus creating a welcome place of entry. "Colonial front yards were designed to make people feel drawn in, while at the same time allowing separation from the public spaces. People liked those distinctions and could relate to them on a visceral level," according to Brinkley.

While simplicity prevailed throughout the town, the houses located on the side and back streets of Williamsburg had a bit more opportunity for planting. These more elaborate front yards typically had some kinds of trees for shade, which were usually positioned symmetrically along either side of the front entryway to match the house's architectural symmetry. In addition to echoing the house, these trees provided welcome shade in a part of the country where summers were notoriously brutal. The species used varied quite a bit, but native species of oak, maple, some linden trees, and smaller-scale Carolina hornbeam trees were commonly planted.

Garden beds were often constructed with geometric lines and patterns that usually consisted of multiples of rectangles and squares. This style didn't originate in the colonial era; its use, in fact, dates back to ancient Rome. According to Brinkley, "these are tried and true methods of design that can be adapted to any size space. You can use a smaller grid, and narrower paths when developing a smaller yard, and larger geometric modules, and wider paths when working in a bigger one." From a practical standpoint, these geometric forms were also easy to build, especially important since the technology and ability to implement wavy or circular designs didn't come into its own until the 19th century. In the 18th, linear geometry reigned supreme in the landscape.

Compared to today's often overplanted front gardens, 18th-century yards might at first seem a bit stark. Ornamental plantings were few, and if there were flowers you would usually see something very simple, such as hollyhocks or day lilies along the front fence. Inhabitants of the colonial era believed you shouldn't hide your houses behind obtrusive shrubbery. Instead, the focus was placed on the house's architectural detailing, or on elements of the hardscape, such as the intricate and lovely bond or basket-weave patterns found running up the brick pathways.

THE VICTORY GARDEN COMPANION

■ The backyard is essentially
the living room of the
outdoors. It should be
comfortable, easily accessible,
and aesthetically pleasing.

Chapter 4
Backyard Fixtures and Features

I never had any other desire so strong, and so like to covetousness, as that one which I have had always, that I might be master at last of a small house and a large Garden.

ABRAHAM CROWLEY
The Garden, 1666

Easy Livin' Outdoors

FROM A DESIGN PERSPECTIVE, THE BACKYARD AND THE front yard are two completely different animals. While the front generally has a number of mandatory features such as a driveway, a walk to the front door, and some plantings around the foundation, the backyard has no such specific requirements. It's a blank slate, waiting for the imprint of the owner to bring it alive. For the home gardener, this nebulous state can be both a benefit and a bane: while you're not forced to accommodate any one specific feature, you do face an overwhelming amount of possibilities. What should your backyard contain?

The answer depends entirely on you, your family, and what kind of outdoor activities you enjoy. Once you've assessed these needs, the requirements demanded of various areas will begin to drive your design. For example, if you've decided you'd like a swimming pool, you'll need to locate it in the sunniest area you possess to maximize its potential; games and other sport activities will require a large amount of lawn space; and if you plan to entertain a lot, a spacious terrace will need to be located near the house. And since by now you have *surely* followed the advice we offered earlier in the book, and made a detailed plan of your site, carefully assessed your recreational/horticultural needs, and sketched out a general drawing of what you intend to do in the back, in this chapter we're free to discuss various elements common to backyards and how best to accommodate them into your overall design.

To my way of thinking, a relaxing, well-designed outdoor living area is the most important feature of the entire backyard. It's here, after all, that you get to reap the rewards of all that hard labor—the hours spent weeding, mulching, and planting come to fruition when you sit down in a comfortable chair with a cool beverage, survey your domain, and drink in the pleasures of a job well done.

It's surprising, then, how few properties actually have welcoming spaces like these! Granted, many yards have a paved area for a chair or two, or perhaps a grill tucked into a spare corner, or a small deck that juts out from the rear of the house, but by and large these spaces are devoid of character and not terribly comfortable for spending any considerable amount of time. In order to be successful, an outdoor living area requires several important qualities: first and foremost it needs to be well designed (and built of quality materials sympathetic with those used on the house); second, it has to have an ample amount of space; and third, it needs to possess sufficient décor, in terms of plants, pots, furniture, and other paraphernalia, in order to make the space a place where you'll want to spend time.

Choosing the Right Design

THE KEY FEATURE OF MOST OUTDOOR LIVING AREAS IS some type of hard surface to accommodate all the accoutrements we now find necessary for modern outdoor life, such as the chaise longue, deck chairs, the grill, a collection of planters, and cocktail tables. While it is certainly possible to position these items on the grass (and up until the early 1950s people in this country often did just that), it's no longer really practical—the bevy of domestic servants required to periodically reposition all that furniture has long since disappeared. That means if you want some kind of space that's useful for day-to-day living, you'll need to plan for some kind of patio or deck.

I have to admit that I almost always prefer terraces over decking, owing largely to the overuse and misuse of decking in modern American landscapes. To understand this bias, it helps to know a little bit about the history of decks in America, and what they were originally intended to do—and more important, not to do.

Wooden decking first became popular in the United States during the 1960s, at the same time that Americans became interested in what is commonly referred to today as "outdoor living." This trend, which we now take for granted as part of everyday life, would have been viewed as highly curious by people back in the 18th and 19th centuries, who spent considerable time and effort trying to escape the uncomfortable extremes of the great outdoors. By the 1960s, however, civilization had progressed to the point that spending time outside not only seemed attractive, but having some type of outdoor living space had become downright fashionable.

■ **Backyards don't have to be big to be successful; they do, however, need to be well planned and organized.**

Designers of the 1960s rose to the challenge and borrowed an element from the Far East to accommodate this trend: they adapted the wooden walkways that had historically linked the Asian house and landscape together and created the first decks. These Eastern-inspired decks had one crucial feature that the inventors of this style took for granted, but was forgotten in later interpretations: *these early decks were extremely low, standing not more than a foot or so off the ground*. This low profile not only made them fairly unobtrusive in the garden, but also meant that they were easy to access from any point in the landscape—a single step up and you were on the deck, a single

{ patio vs. terrace} You might be wondering if there is a difference between a patio and a terrace, and the answer is yes, etymologically speaking. However, *patio* is the Spanish word and *terrace* the French word for the same thing, and they are used in this book interchangeably.

■ **This type of traditional Asian walkway is the precursor of the decking now so ubiquitous in the United States.**

step down and you were in the garden—a critical factor in terms of practicality and aesthetics.

Unfortunately, this feature was rapidly forgotten in subsequent iterations, and through the 1970s, 1980s, and 1990s, larger decks were constructed higher and higher off the ground, which in turn required an intricate system of multiple steps, stairs, and railings. What had begun as a simple land-based structure now became a massive sky element, hanging high off the backs of houses and dominating the landscape. Instead of keeping an easy entrance and egress—and more important, allowing overflow when larger crowds were present—these huge modern decks held people captive a story or more off the ground, buffeted by every breeze, blasted by every ray of sun, and subject to every prying gaze of their neighbors. Of even greater concern from a landscape design perspective was the fact that these decks were a disaster when viewed from the garden. The overall impression was not unlike a large, spindly-legged spider attached to the side of the house—ugly and impossible to blend into the landscape. To add insult to injury, the areas underneath these monstrosities formed a veritable dead zone: completely dark and parched, where even the nearly indestructible, stalwart ivy couldn't survive.

Fortunately, this trend for mammoth decks has slowly be-

■ **Top: Here's an example of great decking. The rustic style of the deck corresponds to that of the house, the deck is low to the ground, the sides are planted to settle the structure into the landscape, and the floor space is sufficiently ample for both relaxation and entertaining.**

■ **Bottom: An example of a poor decking scheme: an overly complicated, multilayered deck squeezed into a small backyard area. This is not the way to merge indoors and outdoors effectively.**

■ Bricks are among the most adaptable of all pavers. They can be laid in a wide variety of patterns, as in this terrace of old Flemish brick. Changing brick color and pattern has a dramatic effect on the final look and feel of a surface, so it pays to experiment a bit before committing to one option or another.

gun to moderate, due both to their extreme cost and to the pleas of designers forced to try to integrate these unsightly behemoths into the landscape.

This having been said, there *are* certain cases where decking—*low* decking—might still be appropriate, and the choice between a wooden surface that's raised off the ground versus some type of ground-level patio should be based on what better suits your style of house. For example, if your home is fairly streamlined and made mostly of wood, then a deck based on this same modern, minimalist style would be completely appropriate. If, however, you live in a brick Georgian with a very formal garden, a wooden deck probably isn't the best choice.

Paving Considerations

ONE IMPORTANT FACTOR TO KEEP IN MIND WHEN constructing any kind of hard paving is the need to make the final surface look as attractive as possible. That means paying

■ **For the back terrace at the Victory Garden, I designed a decorative central element of brick, granite, and bluestone that indicates the four cardinal points of the compass. Even when the large planters are empty and the growing season is over, the terrace still retains year-round visual interest.**

attention both to your choice of materials and the way in which you use them. Very few people would be content to have unfinished plywood floors in their living room, but all too often today you see the outdoor equivalent: a patio that's been shoddily laid with ugly brick in a simple running bond, or even worse, plain concrete pavers just plunked down right into the dirt. If you're building a terrace, apply the same practices you would use inside your house: choose quality materials that enhance the overall look and feel of your space. Here are some design tips to keep in mind for the various materials commonly used for paving outdoor living areas:

Brick

It's a safe bet to assume that most people think all bricks are pretty much created equal—that is, until they need to buy them, when they discover that bricks come in a bewildering array of shapes, colors, qualities, and costs. There are two basic types of brick: molded and wire-cut. Wire-cut bricks are uniform, and because of their regularity are easier to lay, especially when creating complicated patterns. Molded bricks are much more randomly shaped, and often vary in width and length by over a half-inch. While such bricks are more difficult to install (especially in complicated patterns such as herringbone), their handmade look is much more appealing in traditional applications.

Both molded and wire-cut bricks come in a wide variety of colors, ranging from light cream, through orange, to every shade of red and even brown. The color you choose will have a major impact on the final look of your project, in much the same way that changing the color of carpeting will drastically alter a room's appearance. If you're unsure about what hue is best, obtain some sample bricks from your supplier and try them out in your yard—just as you would swatches of fabric or rug indoors. Also, be sure when choosing bricks that you purchase those specifically designed as pavers. Wall bricks, or reused bricks from unknown applications, may not be sufficiently durable, and will often disintegrate when exposed to weather extremes.

In the same way that a brick's color can change the look of your garden space, pattern will have an equally significant effect. Certain patterns, like running bond, have the tendency to enlarge a space, while others, such as basket weave,

■ Rough, irregular flagstones
are perfect for an occasional-
use walkway like this, but are
murder on your feet and
chairs when used on a sitting
terrace!

■ This bluestone terrace uses different-sized pieces to form an interlocking pattern of stone that provides a much more pleasant surface than you would achieve by using only one size of paver.

will make an area look more compact. It pays to experiment with different patterns or combinations of patterns when laying out your brick surfaces. Properly designed and laid, a brick terrace or walkway can not only assume the grace of an Oriental rug, but also add year-round beauty and interest to the landscape.

Stone

Paving stones are essentially divided into two distinct types: flagstones and cut stone. Flagstones are flat, irregular pieces of stone of varying width that are pieced together to form a more-or-less contiguous surface. The actual kind of stone used varies greatly by locale, but it's often some type of granite or slate. Cut stone, as the name implies, consists of pieces of stone that have been cut into regular geometric shapes. Though bluestone is most often used for cut stone, you'll occasionally see sandstone, limestone, slate, or granite as well.

As you can imagine, the difference in final appearance between cut stones and flagstones is immense. Flagstone gives an irregular, more natural effect to paved areas, while cut stone provides a polished urban feel. While you'll find both used in outdoor living areas, to my mind, flagstones are best reserved for rustic walks and pathways, and should not be used for expansive seating areas. Anyone who has ever tried to push back a chair while seated on a flagstone surface will quickly understand why: the irregular surface of the stone makes for very rough going, not to mention the deleterious effect on expensive shoes! Conversely, you should also avoid using very smooth types of stone, such as slate, in areas that will be traversed in wet weather. Very few combinations are more treacherous than damp slate and leather soles!

Again when choosing stone, don't forget to pay attention to color. As is the case with brick, varied hues will make an immense difference in the overall look and feel of your living area. It therefore pays to bring home a few samples from the stone yard to see exactly how the pieces blend with the materials already in your yard and on your house. Pattern also plays an important role in stone surfaces, but unless you're using blocks of exactly the same size (a practice that's generally not recommended because of the monotonous effect it often pro-

duces), determining the pattern for a stone patio or terrace is a complicated affair best left to professionals. Most stone yards offer a free design service; if you provide them with the exact dimensions of your space, they'll come up with a combination of different-sized stone pieces that's pleasingly random and varied. You can then either install the stone yourself or have a professional do it for you.

■ **If you plan only occasional light duties for your outdoor sitting area, gravel can be a cost-effective choice in lieu of hard paving.**

Step by Step: Laying Your Own Brick or Stone Terrace

BUILDING A TERRACE FROM BRICK OR STONE DOESN'T require a particularly specialized set of skills. Anyone who's reasonably fit with a back strong enough to move heavy brick and stone can finish an average-size terrace in a weekend or two. Surprisingly, the real trick to successful masonry work lies not so much in laying the brick or stone correctly (that part of the process is actually rather automatic), but rather in properly preparing the base—something many beginners fail to do, with much detriment to the final product. If you want a professional-looking result that will last for decades, a firm, level foundation is essential. Here's how to get started:

1. Mark out your area

Do this with string or landscaper's paint, and excavate to a depth of six inches. (If you have room, the soil you remove can be stockpiled for later use. Otherwise it will need to be hauled off site.) Next, fill the area with three inches of 3/8-inch crushed stone and three inches of stone dust. While many recipes for preparing the base call for using masonry sand, we prefer stone dust, which unlike sand has an adhesive quality that helps hold brick and stone. Both of these materials can be ordered from a stone yard or masonry supply store; if you give them the square footage, the folks there can tell you precisely how much you'll

need. Also, be sure to order a bit of extra stone dust for filling in the cracks between the bricks or stones at the end of the project.

Thoroughly compact the base with a mechanical compactor (available at most landscape equipment rental outlets). While many guides claim that the base can be compacted manually, we've found that to be true for only the smallest of spaces; anything larger than 5' × 5' should be compacted by machine. After the first pass, water the base thoroughly and compact again. It's also advisable to let the base sit for a week before laying the brick to ensure complete compaction.

2. Adjust the grade

To drain properly in wet weather, patios should slope a minimum of one inch for every ten feet, keeping in mind that if you're working adjacent to the house, your terrace should always slope *away* from the structure. Using a water level or a transit, determine the position and relative height of each of the four corners, and mark the points with a stake. Run a taut string line down two of the sides from the highest to lowest corners, and adjust your base materials to match this slope. Some people, myself included, insert an additional step at this juncture, especially if working with a straight-edged geometric design, building a wooden frame from 1" × 8' inexpensive spruce boards around the edges secured to stakes with screws. Although not absolutely necessary, I find that this step simplifies the process of finishing off the edges and corners, and also has the advantage of providing rigidity. Leveling strings have a tendency to sag; boards never do, and it's much easier to follow a clearly defined slope with boards installed. When you're finished, compact again, water, and fine-tune the level with a rake. You're now ready to lay the pavers.

3. Lay the stone or brick

If you've chosen randomly cut stone pieces, the remaining work is reasonably simple. Following the pattern plan given to you by the stone yard, begin laying out the pieces, starting with those closest to the house and working outward. (You may need to add or subtract a bit of stone dust under individual slabs to accommodate slight variances in width.) Use a hand level to check that each piece is following the correct slope, and leave at least one-eighth of an inch between slabs to allow for expansion. Although most random-patterned stone pieces are sufficiently large to stay in place without an edging material, edgers, such as cobbles, do provide a nice finishing touch.

If you are working with brick rather than stone, begin laying bricks at one of the corners nearest the house. Following your chosen pattern and keeping an eye on your slope guides, place each brick as tightly as possible next to its neighbor, and then tap it with a rubber mallet. (Don't use a regular hammer, or you'll crack the brick.) If you've firmed up your base properly, the work should proceed very quickly; however, if your base

isn't quite solid, you may need to slightly adjust the level of some bricks by adding or subtracting a bit of stone dust.

Laying brick is more complicated than laying stone in that bricks often require angle cutting. They can be cut with a simple masonry chisel or, if you are mechanically inclined, with a wet saw. While not difficult, both methods require some skill and should be practiced beforehand. Keep in mind when choosing brick that some patterns are far more complicated to cut than others: running bond or basket weave, for instance, only require cutting half bricks, something that can be easily done with a chisel. Herringbone, on the other hand, requires angle cuts, which need to be made with a saw.

4. Brush the surface with stone dust

Once the stones or bricks have been laid, brush stone dust over the entire surface to fill in any cracks and water it well. If you've used boards as a frame, now is the time to remove them. A brick patio or terrace will require some type of permanent edging to prevent splay, in the form of metal stripping or bricks set on end, either wide side to wide side (called soldiers) or narrow side to narrow side (called sailors). If you plan to use bricks as edgers, be sure to let your brick supplier know when you place your order, as this will significantly increase the number of bricks you'll need. (As will differences in pattern: running bond requires 10 percent extra for cutting and waste; more complicated patterns such as herringbone require 15 percent.)

■ It's easy to see how just a few pieces of furniture can quickly eat up space outdoors: this 25' × 25' terrace is pretty much filled by two outdoor settees and a table. The result, however, is an intimate, enclosed space that can be enjoyed well into the evening.

Never Too Big

A LANDSCAPE ARCHITECT FRIEND OF MINE IS FOND OF saying that outdoor living areas "can never be too big," and while I have found an exception or two to his dictum over the years, by and large it seems to be true. Most outdoor living areas built today are too small for their intended use, something that people generally don't discover until it's far too late and construction is long finished. Unfortunately, this is one arena of outdoor design where appearances can be extremely deceptive: when laid out solely as boundary lines, potential living areas such as terraces or decks always look huge, and the general inclination is to err on the side of discretion and plan for a smaller (not to mention less costly) space. Before you make final decisions on square footage, however, you should do a simple test:

Envision the social occasions you think will most often occur in your new space and calculate the number of people involved

SAMPLE SIZES

Outdoor furniture takes up a surprising amount of space. Here are sample dimensions for some commonly used pieces:

CHAISE LONGUE: **2.5' x 6'**

RECLINING CHAIR AND OTTOMAN: **3' x 6'**

CAFÉ TABLE WITH FOUR CAFÉ CHAIRS: **8.5' x 8.5'**

ROUND TABLE FOR FOUR WITH FOUR CHAIRS PUSHED BACK: **10' x 10'**

RECTANGULAR TABLE FOR SIX WITH SIX CHAIRS PUSHED BACK: **10' x 13'**

SQUARE TABLE FOR TWO WITH TWO CHAIRS: **5.5' x 9'**

ROUND TABLE FOR SIX WITH SIX CHAIRS PUSHED BACK: **11' x 11'** (barbecues for six, cocktail parties for twenty, romantic dinners for two). Next, place enough furniture (in a pinch, scaled cardboard cutouts will do; see the sidebar for sample sizes) to allow for everyone to be seated. Don't forget to locate a few large empty pots or planters in areas where they might be placed in the final design. Then, borrow a few live bodies in the form of friends or family members, and have them come and stand within the boundaries you've been contemplating. Chances are you'll find yourself with less leg room than an airline seat in coach. The lesson here? You undoubtedly need to add more square footage.

Water, Water Everywhere

WATER GARDENING HAS BECOME BY FAR THE FASTEST-growing aspect of American gardening, and with good reason. Ever since the Greeks first ascribed divine magic to flowing springs, man has been enchanted by moving water. The Romans employed water extensively in their landscapes, with running streams, atrium pools, and even fishponds. The an-

■ When laid out in the design stage, the terrace off this pool house probably seemed gigantic; now, however, it's just right for a table and several chaise longues. Another example of not being afraid to think big when it comes to outdoor living areas.

■ This is a perfect example of what to avoid when creating a water feature. Although the fountain itself is lovely and technically well done, it arises out of nowhere in the middle of the lawn, making the entire ensemble look somewhat fake. The naturalistic impression of the freeform pool is diminished by the collection of garden ornaments gathered around the water. The lesson here: don't try to "out-nature" Mother Nature.

cient Arabs also loved water—their gardens were never far from the sound of trickle and splash. Today, water still has that power to calm, soothe, and delight, and can be an important part of your backyard as well. The trick, though, is to use water features correctly; badly done, and all your effort will flow—pun intended—right down the drain.

I'm sure you've seen something similar on your garden travels: you enter a small suburban garden space and suddenly you spy a small, irregularly shaped pond plunked down right in the middle of the lawn. Perhaps it has a small stream trickling into it, arising from somewhere near the garage and flowing past the children's play set, debouching merrily over a series of small cascades before disappearing under a fence. The only thing missing are the gnomes. The entire feature,

which undoubtedly cost the hapless but well-intentioned owners several thousand dollars, sticks out like a sore thumb: with no relation to the house or surrounding landscape, the entire assemblage looks out of place.

The key to effectively incorporating a water feature into the landscape is to make sure that whatever kind you select matches the style, size, and shape of both your house and its surrounding landscape. And for many of you, especially those with small gardens in urban settings, that means avoiding all those free-form shapes that attempt to mimic water in the wild. Ask yourself what kind of water feature would look most "natural" in the context of an urban setting with buildings all around. By and large the answer to that question, for both urban and suburban gardens, is some type of geometric pond or fountain. While many people initially eschew this kind of rigid pool because they think that the final effect will be too harsh or formal, the fact is the overall look and feel of the pond will be determined not only by its shape, but how it's positioned and planted within the general landscape.

Here at the Victory Garden, for example, we have a 5' × 3' rectangular pool in the center of the entry courtyard. This pool, 24 inches deep, is formed with a rigid fiberglass liner. Depending on the effect we wanted to achieve, the pond could have had a very formal, minimalist appearance with no planting surrounding it. Some type of central fountain element that rose above the surface would have also heightened this feel, giving the whole ensemble a simple, clean, sculptural appearance. But in this instance, given the generally rustic feel of the actual garden, that kind of formality would have been inappropriate. Instead, we opted to use water lilies and papyrus to soften the edges of the bluestone-edged pool and provide a casual air of welcome. The addition of a single jet not only serves

■ **The upper terrace and fountain at the Victory Garden in July.**

{ rigid vs. lined pools}

Water features fall into two general categories: rigid pools made of fiberglass that are simply inserted into the ground, and pools that are excavated and then lined with butyl sheeting. Each method has its own preferred use: butyl-lined pools are better for large, naturally shaped applications, while rigid pools do well in smaller-scale settings where a distinct shape, such as a circle or square, is desired. Although rigid pools do in fact come in some fairly large irregular shapes, in the end, their very rigidity defeats any attempt to make them look natural, while butyl liners are almost impossible to conform to strict geometric shapes.

to aerate the pond, but the soft splashing sound it produces obviates the noise of the nearby road.

All this, however, is not to imply that if you possess a natural setting where a free-form, naturally shaped pool would be appropriate, you shouldn't install one. On the contrary, naturalistic water gardens in rustic settings are quite delightful. Just keep in mind that the hardest of all styles to imitate is that of Mother Nature, and one of the most difficult design challenges is to make something man-made look "real." If you're contemplating such a feature, it's a good idea to visit a few local streams and ponds in your area before you begin: notice how flowing water naturally sorts rocks by weight in a streambed (the heaviest are in the lees); note what types of stones and boulders occur naturally in your area; see what kinds of riparian grass and sedges inhabit the banks; and discover what types of plants live in the pond itself. Most important, when you go to position your feature, be sure to locate it where it might have occurred naturally—at the edge of a woodland, emerging from a rock outcropping, or incorporated into the edge of a meadow. Correct positioning will go a long way toward making your feature a valued part of your yard, rather than an expensive detraction.

Step by Step: Installing a Flexible Pond Liner

WATER FEATURES ARE AN INCREDIBLY SATISFYING PART of the backyard landscape. Besides providing a perfect focal point for the garden, they offer the profound pleasure of sitting by the edge of a small pond or running stream and listening to the soft gurgle of the water as reflected clouds race across its surface. Add to this the large amount of beneficial wildlife you find wherever there's water, and water features become one of the most desirable aspects of the backyard landscape.

Historically, unless Mother Nature had been kind enough to create a natural body of water on your property, making your own water feature was pretty much the exclusive province of the very rich. Complicated excavation and elaborate clay linings made creating a pond extremely expensive. Now, however, with the advent of flexible pond liners, as well as rigid fiberglass pools, small water features can be found in even the most modest gardens. Here's how to get started on your own water garden by installing a flexible pond liner, which can be adapted to almost any site.

Siting the pool

Where you place your pool is critical to your water feature's long-term success. Not only should it be located in a highly vis-

ible area, but the site should preferably be within easy earshot of outdoor activities as well so you can appreciate the soothing sound of moving water. If you're anticipating growing water lilies and other aquatic plants, you'll need a site in full sun; by all means avoid locating your pool under large overhanging trees that will drop leaves and debris into the water. Also, contrary to instinct, your water feature should not be located in a naturally low-lying area. Runoff can easily contaminate artificial water features with mud, debris, and chemical residues from fertilizers and pesticides.

1. Planning and excavation

Once you've chosen your location, the first step is to delineate the shape of your pond. You can do this by laying down a flexible hose or a rope, or by spraying the outline you desire with spray paint. To determine the amount of liner you'll need, figure out the proposed depth of the pond and add twice that amount to each dimension (height, length, depth), and then add another two feet. When you're ready to begin excavating, rough cut the liner to those dimensions and leave it in the sun to soften slightly for easier handling.

Before you lay shovel to soil, it's extremely important to be

sure that there are no electrical cables or utility pipes in the area you plan to dig out. Many states have "one-call" centers that will contact utilities for you to ensure that you dig safely. Once you've established that your excavation area is safe, dig out the hole to the depth you wish, making sure you provide room for an additional two inches of sand to be added. Providing a shelf about 12 inches down around the edge of the pond will give you a convenient place to site shallow-water plants; if you've planned on a deeper pool, you can even add a second shelf farther down to hold taller plants (see illustration). These "shelves" also ensure safety when emerging from the pool during maintenance. If you plan to edge with sizable stones or want your edging material flush with the ground, dig out the area around the edge to the thickness of your edging material to provide a professional "flush" look. When digging out the soil, transfer it into wheelbarrows for spreading elsewhere in the yard (or for disposal), and be sure to keep a wheelbarrow or two of soil on hand for backfilling once the pool is in place. Dig the deepest area first, and then the sides, creating a slope about 20 degrees from the vertical.

Now's a good time to take a good look at the bottom of your pool. If there are roots protruding, or rocks that might puncture the liner, be sure to remove them at this point. You want to have a smooth base. Also, check that the sides of the pool are reasonably even by using a level set on a piece of lumber, and taking measurements from several points. Any required adjustments can easily be made using some of the soil you've dug from excavation.

2. Adding sand

Add about a two-inch layer of clean sand to the excavated hole; dampening the sand in advance will make it easier to smooth and mold to the shape of the pond. If you wish, you can create a flat, smooth base by using a tamper, or you can smooth the sand with a piece of wood—a method that works very well along the contours of the pond.

3. Laying in the liner

Spread the liner over and down into the pond—find a friend, as this is a process best done with more than one person. Let the liner fit loosely at first. The excess liner around the edges should be secured with some heavy rocks or other weights. Stand in the pond and smooth out wrinkles in the liner by hand. The excess liner along the edge can be folded neatly into pleats and secured under the rocks. When the liner has been

smoothed into position, slowly begin adding water. As the pond fills, the liner will fit itself to the pond's shape that you've created. It's best to stay in the pond at this stage and observe the filling carefully, should you need to adjust the liner as it shifts into position.

4. Adding Edging

The pond is full when the water reaches about two inches from the top. At this point you should install any pump or filtration systems, or fountains. These connections can be concealed by the edging material later. When ready to edge the pond, trim the liner down to about one to two feet of excess around the perimeter of the pond. The amount of liner edge will depend on the size and nature of the edging material that you choose; you should have enough edging material to conceal the excess liner, and also to overhang the edge of the pool by an inch or so. Mortar can be used to stabilize the edging for safety, and to further hide the liner. A piece of one-inch PVC pipe set in the mortar under the edge will provide a place for electrical and other types of cords. If working with rounded stones as edging, you'll want a good supply of smaller rocks to work into the spaces between the larger stones in order to effectively hide the liner—this will also help give a more naturalistic feel to your pool.

One final tip: Wait at least 24 hours before installing any fish or aquatic plants. If mortar has been used in your finishing process, wait until it's completely dried, and flush the pool thoroughly to avoid contaminating the pond with lime that could be harmful to your fish. Now sit back, relax, and enjoy the beautiful sound of water in your garden.

Planning and Planting for the Future in the Backyard

DURING MY CHILDHOOD IN THE EARLY 1970S, MY grandfather's backyard was surrounded by a tall privacy hedge of lilac and honeysuckle and dotted with a variety of mature trees. Of particular interest to me were several large crab apples with low-branching limbs, which my grandfather had kindly pruned especially for climbing. As a kid I loved crawling up into trees, and I spent many long hours in those branches with my cousins, building a tree house and playing a game we called "tree tag," which was similar to the terrestrial version but involved a complicated series of rules to determine who was "it," and how and when others could be tagged. Today, I suppose, most parents would be horrified to have their children riotously chasing each other from high limb to high limb, but in those more innocent days no one thought anything of it, nor, it seemed, did anyone ever suffer more than the odd scrape or bruise.

The point of telling you this childhood tale is to make you aware of the remarkable magic that trees and shrubs, especially mature ones, lend to the home landscape. Whether your purpose is to create a shady spot for relaxing, or to add privacy to an open backyard space, or merely to provide interest and variety to your backyard planting, correctly choosing trees and shrubs is an important part of successful backyard design.

The problem, of course, lies in that simple word "correctly," for it's not always easy to choose from among the thousands of available options when selecting trees and shrubs. The solution lies in good planning: decide what effect you want to achieve, and how you want to achieve it, long before you ever move the first shovelful of earth.

Using Trees in the Landscape

BEFORE WE GET DOWN TO THE SPECIFICS OF recommending individual varieties (see the Best Bets section), let's talk a bit about how a professional might go about selecting trees for your landscape. Essentially, most designers use a simple process of elimination based on four important criteria: eventual size, eventual shape, intended use, and growing requirements. By employing this same formula, you easily make informed choices about which varieties will be best for your yard.

Of the four criteria, eventual size is perhaps the most obvious factor in choosing trees, though often the most overlooked by homeowners. Again and again, you'll see trees that will quickly spread to 50, 60, or 70 feet wide, planted in spaces only 20 or 30 feet deep, or varieties that will grow to 100 feet tall or that are planted right next to a single-story home, dwarfing the structure. This unhappy and expensive fate can be easily avoided by simply being realistic about how much space is

■ A large spreading ash forms the centerpiece of this backyard. A similar one fills the same role at the Victory Garden.

available in your yard and by believing the information written on the plant label. If the plant description says "reaches a spread of 20' in ten years, 40' at maturity," believe it! That day will surely come, and faster than you think!

Shape and intended use are equally important considerations, because trees come in a wide variety of basic shapes: upright and columnar, weeping and pendulous, multi-stemmed, conical, spreading and upright, etc.—all of which are associated with different and very distinct applications. A large conical tree might, for example, effectively screen you from the road but would probably be a bad choice for providing shade in a small yard, as its wide lower branches would take up too much room. A multi-stemmed tree might be ideal as a focal point off a small terrace, but a weeping tree in the same spot would only serve to annoyingly dangle branches on your head. You get the general idea: doing your research and knowing the eventual shape and size of the tree (which often differs from that of the immature specimen you bought at the nursery), as well as having a clear idea of how you intend to use it, are essential to the selection process.

Last, don't ignore a plant's growing requirements. Again, it pays to honestly evaluate your site and then choose material that will thrive in whatever conditions are present in your yard. Despite your best intentions, a shade-loving tree will never survive the full blast of the southern sun, nor will a moisture-loving tree do well in an arid garden.

Once you've accurately assessed these four criteria, it becomes reasonably easy to select a tree species that fulfills all of these requirements. Although this may sound somewhat simplistic given the number of possible plants available for any given purpose, you will be amazed at how many options won't work once you apply these strict criteria. For example, if you decide that a large flowering tree (say, over 50 feet tall) with spreading deciduous branches would be ideal for shading the back of your home and screening that tall building to the rear, you'll find that there's a limited number of species for your area that will grow to that particular height, flower, and also be deciduous.

Using Shrubs in the Landscape

SHRUBS ARE COMMONLY USED IN FOUR PRINCIPAL WAYS: as individual specimens, as part of foundation plantings (as we discussed in Chapter Three); as part of a hedge (as we discussed in Chapter One); and finally as part of a larger mixed planting or border. These plantings are employed either for privacy screening or simply for decorative effect, and can essentially be thought of as flower borders made of shrubs.

In fact, laying out a shrubbery border is achieved in much the same way as you would lay out a perennial planting (for more details on that, see Chapter Six). You begin by carefully choosing the site: to be effective, shrubbery borders need to be an integral part of the landscape, and should begin and end in a logical place, much like a hedge. This is fairly easy to do when the border parallels the edges of the property, as the shrubbery border will generally begin at the edge of some structure, like the house or garage, and continue to another logical point, such as the street or a neighboring house. The matter becomes a little more complicated when the landscape provides no ready-made terminus. In such cases, a good designer will often create one, locating a large tree or some structure such as a shed or gazebo to function as a logical ending point.

After determining the general scope of the border, the next step is to choose the specific plantings. We've listed some of our favorite suggestions in our Best Bets section, but in essence, you're free to pick and choose whatever material pleases you as long as it works well in your specific location and climate. The goal is to create a mixed planting that gives whatever privacy or screening you may require, while still pro-

■ This "perennial border" is actually comprised mostly of shrubs. Properly planned, shrub borders can be as floriferous as those comprised entirely of perennials, and will save you much labor in comparison to the traditional herbaceous border.

■ **In this mixed border, shrubs and perennials of varying textures and colors are creatively combined. A granite water feature provides a focal point.**

viding interest (flowers, form, bark, or berries) throughout the year. As you may suspect, this isn't always the easiest of design tasks, and creating a shrubbery border is definitely something you want to work out first on paper, keeping in mind the following guidelines:

- ***Plan your border for the future, not the present***. As you locate your selection on the plan, take careful note of the plants' eventual sizes and space accordingly. Although those tiny shrubs fresh from the nursery might look a little silly when first placed far from their neighbors, rest assured that if you properly prepare the soil and you water and feed them, your shrubs will quickly grow together to form a solid mass. On the other hand, plants placed too closely together will not only add to your initial cost, but will also quickly crowd each other out, ruining the effect and mandating expensive removals.

- ***If privacy is your main concern, be sure to include what designers call an "evergreen spine"—a line of evergreens—down the back (or if your planting is seen from two sides, the center) of the planting***. This will ensure that the necessary screening remains during the winter months when deciduous shrubs lose their leaves.

- ***Think in three dimensions***. Landscape planning becomes a difficult process only when you fail to work in three dimensions. Remember that plants can go under or above other plants, as long as light requirements permit. For example, small, shade-tolerant azaleas might surround the base of an upright conifer, or a dogwood might rise above a planting of winterberry. Three-dimensional plantings incorporating plants on multiple levels provide an especially rich effect. Also, don't forget to scale your plantings accordingly, moving from the tallest at the rear to the lowest in the front.

- ***Think four seasons when you choose your plant material***. We all spend a large amount of time looking from the inside out in the off-seasons, and our gardens should be

■ **A well-designed privacy screen not only delineates the boundaries of this yard, but also provides the perfect place for an impromptu lunch.**

planned accordingly. Shrubs with interesting bark, berries, flowers, or form in the winter months should be high on your list of priorities.

● ***When planning, don't rely solely on books or TV.***
Although programs and guides like ours can form a helpful introduction to the subject, nothing beats actually getting out and seeing plants in the landscape before you buy them. Visit a nursery on a scouting mission, or take a trip to the local park or botanical garden and see your potential selections in an actual garden setting. Viewing mature specimens is a particularly effective way to envision the kinds of plantings you're contemplating for your backyard.

Best Bets for Backyard Trees and Shrubs

Of course, any list of favorite trees and shrubs is highly subjective. But here are a few that we have found over the years to have outstanding qualities in form, flower, or foliage.

Species	Zone	Height × Width at Maturity (in feet)	Comments
TREES			
Abies lasiocarpa 'Glauca compacta'	4–9	10 × 6	Resembles a Colorado blue spruce, but softer in texture and with very restrained growth rate.
Acer griseum	4–8	35 × 35	Exfoliating bark and excellent fall color.
Acer palmatum 'Bloodgood'	6–9	20 × 20	Great leaf color; nice wide shape.
Betula nigra 'Heritage'	4–9	30 × 15	Exfoliating bark; borer resistant.
Carpinus caroliniana	5–9	40 × 40	Interesting bark with great fall color; native to Eastern North America; prefers moisture. Does not tolerate drought.
Cedrus atlantica 'Glauca'	6–9	80 × 30	Interesting growth habit; good blue color.
Chamaecyparis obtusa cultivars		variable	An excellent evergreen; there's a cultivar for every color, shape, size, or texture need.
Cornus kousa	5–8	25 × 15	One of the most ornamental deciduous trees; lasting blooms; not susceptible to disease.
Fagus sylvatica 'Cuprea'	5–8	100 × 50	Large and handsome, with copper-colored foliage and prominent flowers.
Liriodendron tulipifera	4–10	100 × 40	Very stately; with large flowers; the cultivar 'Fastigiatum' grows to half the normal width and is useful in small gardens.
Magnolia grandiflora	6–9	35 × 35	Evergreen with creamy, fragrant flowers in spring; numerous cultivars.
Malus spp.	4–9	variable	Multiple cultivars vary widely in size, flower color, berry shape, and retention; best chosen while in bloom at the nursery.
Picea glauca 'Rainbow's End'	2–8	10 × 10	A dwarf spruce with tips of gold summer growth light up like a Christmas tree.

Species	Zone	Height × Width at Maturity (in feet)	Comments
Prunus spp.	variable	variable	The cherry and plum genus varies widely; many excellent cultivars available for a variety of uses; choose while in bloom.
Stewartia pseudocamellia var. koreana	5–9	30 × 15	Lovely exfoliating bark; large flowers in summer.
Styrax japonica	5–9	25 × 15	Incredibly dense and fragrant late-spring bloom.
Viburnum sieboldii	4–8	30 × 30	More of a large shrub than a tree, with excellent white spring flowers; red fruit in fall.

■ *Cedrus atlantica* **'Glauca.'**

■ *Viburnum trilobum.*

Species	Zone	Height × Width at Maturity (in feet)	Comments
SHRUBS			
Berberis thunbergii 'Crimson Pygmy'	4–9	2 × 2	Compact, dense, strong bronze/purple color.
Corylopsis pauciflora	7–9	8 × 8	Nice leaf texture; great woodland/edge plant; yellow spring flower display.
Daphne x burkwoodii 'Carol Mackie'	5–9	2 × 2	Compact; gold picotee variegation; extremely fragrant spring flowers.
Enkianthus campanulatus	6–9	15 × 15	Very upright form; long-lasting red-pink flowers; scarlet fall color; 'Albiflorus' has white flowers.
Heptacodium miconioides	5–9	8 × 12	Late-summer fragrant white flowers; exfoliating bark.
Hibiscus syriacus 'Blue Bird'	5–9	12 × 8	Late-summer flowers; the best blue.
Hydrangea arborescens 'Annabelle'	3–10	6 × 6	Not too tall; huge white inflorescenses in summer.
Juniperus squamata 'Blue Star'	4–9	3 × 5	Dense spreading mound; sharp blue color.
Kolkwitzia amabilis 'Pink Cloud'	4–9	12 × 12	Its common name, Beautybush, says it all; deep pink flowers in early summer.
Spirea nipponica 'Snowmound'	3–10	6 × 4	Arching branches smothered with white flowers in spring; nicer than other similar types.
Viburnum spp.	variable	variable	Few viburnums aren't worthy of a place in the garden; some have extremely fragrant flowers; many have interesting fall berries and excellent autumn color.

Garden Basics:
Forcing Branches Indoors

OVER THE YEARS HERE AT THE VICTORY GARDEN, WE have slowly added new and interesting trees and shrubs to the backyard landscape, not only to beautify the garden, but also to provide ample branches for forcing indoors during the late winter and early spring. When brought into the warmth, branches of many of our most popular flowering trees and shrubs will burst into bloom just as they do outside, filling the house with the look and fragrance of spring at a tiny fraction of the cost you'd pay at the local florist.

Forcing branches couldn't be simpler. Depending on the species (see the chart page 123), carefully cut branches from your shrubs with sharp shears (being careful not to cut too many limbs and disfigure the plant), and bring them into your work space. (A location such as a basement or mud room where a bit of wetness isn't amiss is generally a good idea.) Next, decide on which containers you'll be using and prune your branches to fit, making sure to trim off any buds or small branches that will be below the water line when the container is filled. Don't forget to mash or make vertical cuts at the bottom of the cut branch. Then place your branches flat in a laundry sink, bathtub, or plastic bin and cover them with warm water. Leave the branches submerged overnight. (This process helps the branches emerge from dormancy.) The next day, remove the branches from their bath and place them upright in a bucket of water in a cool (60-degree) place with bright indirect light. Avoid warm locations with direct sunlight—remember, you're trying to replicate the cool, moist conditions of spring, when the branches would normally bloom, and overly hot, dry areas will only prevent the buds from developing naturally. Within one to three weeks, depending on the species, the flower buds will begin to emerge. When they do, arrange them in their display containers and place them around the house as desired.

■ **These pear branches form an inexpensive—yet spectacular—floral display.**

■ *Cercis canadensis.*

Best Bets For Forcing Branches

Botanical Name	Common Name	Flower Color	Best Time to Cut (Based on Zone 5)	Weeks Needed to Force	Comments
Abeliophyllum distichum	Korean *Abelialeaf*	White	Mid-January	1–3	Easy; similar to forsythia.
Aesculus hippocastanum	Horse chestnut	White to pink to shades of purple and red	Mid-March	2–3	Somewhat difficult.
Amelanchier spp.	Serviceberry	White	February	1–4	Easy fragrant blossoms.
Cercis canadensis	Redbud	Rosy to magenta pink	Early March	2–3	Worthwhile, but somewhat difficult to force.
Chaenomeles spp.	Japanese quince	Red-orange	Mid-February	4	Brilliant blossoms.
Cornus mas	Cornelian cherry	Yellow	January	2	Easy.
Cornus spp.	Dogwoods	White and pink	Mid-March	2–3	Easy.
Crataegus spp.	Hawthorns	White through red	Mid-March	4–5	Easy.
Cytisus scoparius	Scotch broom	Lavender	Late January	4–6	Somewhat difficult.
Deutzia spp.	Deutzias	White	Early March	3–4	Easy.
Forsythia spp.	Forsythias	Yellow	Mid-January	1–3	Extremely easy.
Fothergilla spp.	Fothergillas	White	March	2–3	Fragrant.
Hamamelis mollis	Witch hazel	Yellow	January	1	One of the shrubs to bloom in the spring.
Kolkwitzia amabilis	Beautybush	Pink	Mid-March	6	Easy.

Botanical Name	Common Name	Flower Color	Best Time to Cut (Based on Zone 5)	Weeks Needed to Force	Comments
Magnolia spp.	Magnolias	Creamy white to deep red	Early March	3–5	Larger-budded to varieties more difficult to force.
Malus spp.	Apple/Crab apple	White, pink to dark red	February to Mid-March	2–4	Double-flowering types force more slowly but last longer; very fragrant.
Philadelphus spp.	Mock orange	White	Mid-March	4–5	Extremely fragrant, though short-lived.
Prunus spp.	Cherry, Flowering almond, Plum	White and pink	Early February	2–4	Wonderfully fragrant.
Pyrus spp.	Pear	White	Late January	4–5	Excellent for forcing; fragrant flowers and interesting stems.
Rhododendron spp.	Rhododendron, Azalea	White through pink, lavender, lilac to red	Late February	4–6	Difficult; leaves even without flowers are quite decorative.
Salix discolor	Pussy willow	N/A	February	1–2	Can be dried once buds open; branches will root if left in water.
Spiraea spp.	Spirea	Generally white	March	4	Double-flowering types force more slowly but last longer.
Syringa spp.	Lilac	White through purple	Early April	4–5	Very difficult unless cut within several weeks of natural bloom time.

Table adapted from one issued April 1988 in furtherance of Cooperative Extension work, Acts of May 8 and June 30, 1914, in cooperation with the U.S. Department of Agriculture by the Cooperative Extension, University of Nebraska, Institute of Agriculture and Natural Resources. No visible copyright. http://www.ianr.unl.edu/pubs/Horticulture/g868.htm

Ask Michael:
Ponds and Wildlife

Dear Michael,
When I watch the show, I often catch a glimpse of a pond in the
distance. Michael, did you build it or is it natural, and what's the
story with all those ducks and geese I see?

Dug out by a farmer over a century ago, the pond is one of my favorite parts of the entire yard. It's approximately 100' × 60', six or seven feet deep, and is fed by a spring that emerges from the old house well and runs through the bog garden (see Victory Garden plan, page 44). Aside from the romantic allure of a pond to skate on and fish from (and we do both), the pure magic of the water itself is bewitching. From the reflections of the trees as they ripple in the summer breeze to the progression of ice as it slowly expands across the surface in the winter, the pond never fails to fascinate.

Incredible, too, is the diversity of wildlife that inhabits this place. Several species of wild ducks call the pond their home. The ducks and geese you've glimpsed on the show are likely our domestic flock. Those ducks and geese exist in an interesting interdependent relationship. The ducks (mostly an old heritage breed called Magpies) were originally brought in to help control the aquatic weeds and algae that are typical in small bodies of water in the high summer. It turned out that the ducks were not terribly adept when it came to self-preservation, and they proved to be easy targets for the occasional fox or coyote. At a loss for what to do, I consulted an old farmer friend, who advised getting several geese to guard the flock. Ever watchful and alert, the geese can generally "outfox" the marauders, giving a loud early warning that wakes the ducks from their self-contented reverie and allows them to flee to safety in the middle of the pond.

Beyond the dynamics of ducks and geese, there are many other forms of wildlife to be found in or near the pond. Frogs, snakes, and turtles croak and slither and bask on logs. Muskrats nest in the banks. A large blue heron periodically drops in to fish (inevitably scaring the bejesus out of our horse, Claudius, as it swoops down for a landing with its four-foot wingspan). Countless varieties of birds, including swallows, orioles, finches, cardinals, and mockingbirds, nest and play along the pond's banks.

Of course a pond such as this one isn't a common feature in a suburban or urban backyard, but even a small water feature can dramatically increase the presence of wildlife. A small pond that is prevented from freezing in the winter will attract birds year round. And if you add to your landscape plan native plants with berries that provide food to birds, and wildflowers that provide nectar to insects or are larval plants for butterflies, you'll find your backyard becomes filled with motion, life, and visual interest well beyond that of the plants alone.

DIGGING DEEPER: THE GARDEN CONSERVANCY

A PRACTICAL AND PLEASURABLE WAY TO GET IDEAS FOR your property is to visit other gardens, and one of the best ways to do that is through the Garden Conservancy, America's only national nonprofit organization dedicated to the preservation of the nation's gardens. Through its Open Days Program, the Conservancy invites the public to visit America's best and rarely seen private gardens. Its hope is to strengthen public commitment to garden preservation while encouraging the appreciation of gardens, in all their regional diversity, as living works of art.

In 1995, the Garden Conservancy published the first edition of its *Open Days Directory*, listing 110 private gardens in New York and Connecticut. Since then the *Directory* has evolved into a listing of hundreds of private gardens nationwide, with plans to continue its expansion. The Open Days Program is modeled after similar programs abroad, including England's popular "Yellow Book" and Australia's Open Garden Scheme. As of this year, nearly 400 private gardens in 22 states have opened their gates for the public's enjoyment. *The Open Days Directory* is available directly from the Garden Conservancy (see link below), as well as from book retailers throughout the country and on the Internet.

For more details on the Garden Conservancy's nationwide Open Days Program, visit them online at www.gardenconservancy.org.

■ Hobbs's Mission-style house was built on a steep hillside overlooking a dazzling vista of the Vancouver skyline. Much of the planting in the terrace area depends on containers.

Inspired Gardens

The Backyard of Thomas Hobbs, Vancouver, British Columbia

THE BACKYARD OF EXPERT PLANTSMAN AND GARDENER Thomas Hobbs's Mediterranean-style villa is a bold statement of two important gardening philosophies: the belief that a garden should serve as a private retreat created from a vision uniquely your own; and that the garden should also be viewed as a personal laboratory, a place in which to have fun and experiment with gardening.

When Hobbs first took on the challenge of his backyard, it was a virtual blank slate. Embracing the opportunity this presented, Hobbs was determined not to follow the traditional path of many Northwestern gardens that are largely dominated by rhododendrons and assorted broad-leaf evergreens. Instead he opted to transform the backyard completely, making it into a Mediterranean oasis. It proved to be an inspired concept.

The basic framework of Hobbs's garden is ingenious yet simple, effectively creating the illusion of depth and space in a modest-size yard. He achieved this by wrapping a series of

127

■ **The side garden off the dining room.**

small garden rooms around the house, and by always keeping something in reserve: low walls softened with flowering clematis and other climbing vines guides the visitor through the landscape toward the rear; arched doorways open to reveal dramatic views; and, finally, wandering walks lead to the principal feature of the backyard—a sweeping terrace of tinted cast-concrete pavers overlooking the Vancouver skyline.

This terrace also serves as the site of one of Hobbs's most highly prized garden treasures: an "antistress" machine in the form of a 20' × 5' foot slate-and-tile fountain that converts into a Jacuzzi at the flick of a button. This water feature is one of Hobbs's favorite indulgences and reflects his ultimate objective: to create a relaxed, well-designed outdoor living area that would bring a bit of the Riviera to Vancouver.

Once the hardscape was in place, Hobbs went on to fill the garden with a bounty of plants, trees, and shrubs. Selecting both flower and foliage to complement the rich salmon color of his home, he worked with a broad palette of species that included everything from the apricot-colored blooms of *Verbascum* 'Helen Johnson' and the richly colored purple bells of

Cerinthe major 'Purpurascens' to the unusual khaki color of his beloved 'Thornbird' bearded irises. Hobbs also mixed in some exceptional plants for contrast and accent, such as the wonderful lime-green *Euphorbia characias wulfenii* and the golden-leaved fuchsia 'Genii.' Ever experimenting, Hobbs continually pushes the northern boundaries of his Zone 8 garden, using tropical species previously thought not hardy enough for this area, such as the vibrant *Canna* 'Phaison' and the *Trachycarpus fortunei* windmill palm.

In order to create excitement in the landscape, Hobbs also makes a point of mingling the ordinary with the extraordinary throughout the garden. A six-foot-tall swiss chard with its multicolored stems and tactile foliage was used, for example, to delightfully accent the highly manicured entryway into his home—a perfect indication of his willingness to try something new. In Hobbs's view, hesitation has no place in the garden. "If something doesn't work, you can always dig it up, rip it out, and start all over again," says Hobbs. "Your backyard should be a personal expression of your life and taste. Take your space, make it your own, and do it in style."

■ A good lawn is like a good rug. It doesn't dominate the room but rather complements the other elements of the design, linking disparate features together.

Chapter 5
The Great American Lawn

Nothing is more pleasant
to the eye than green grass
kept finely shorn.

FRANCIS BACON
Of Gardens, 1625

■ **Here, the smooth green tract of grass acts as an effective foil for the varied and variegated shade planting behind.**

The Green, Green Grass of Home

A TRIP THROUGH ANY AMERICAN TOWN WILL QUICKLY reveal one sure fact: Americans are mighty attached to their lawns. Mile after mile of turf rolls out from foundations all across the country, carpeting the ground like one vast green blanket. But is this love affair a good thing? From an aesthetic point of view, probably not: while the right lawn in the right place acts as the perfect complement to other elements of the garden, too much lawn and too few plantings make for an extremely boring landscape.

The environmental impact of all this grass is also a concern: per square foot, there is no other type of planting that consumes as many natural resources in order to look good. From the petroleum products used to mow it, to the metals needed to rake it, to the chemicals that fertilize it, grass is a greedy ground cover. The amount of water grass requires is also a worry in many parched parts of the country. In the water-short Southwest for instance, installation of new lawns is forbidden in many cities, and municipalities caught between watering lawns and watering humans have begun to pay people to remove existing turf in their backyards.

The answer to these concerns, both aesthetic and environmental, lies not in eliminating grass entirely, but rather in moderation and proper planning. This can be achieved in several ways. First and foremost, to maximize the benefits of lawn in your landscape, decide just how much lawn you really need, and then tailor the design of the lawn itself for easy care and maintenance. Second, choose the correct type of grass for your part of the country. All turf is not created equal, and selecting the wrong type of grass for your area will at best mean a lot of extra expense and work, and at worst result in the total failure of the lawn. Third, you need to learn how to maintain grass properly. Although most of us think we know how to do it (after all, how difficult could it be to push a mower, right?), study after study has shown that most people violate the basic tenets of proper mowing, fertilizing, and watering, all to the detriment of both lawn and environment. In the pages that follow, we'll show you how to do everything you can to have a great lawn while saving energy, effort, and money.

DIGGING DEEPER: A LITTLE LAWN HISTORY

GIVEN THE UBIQUITOUS NATURE OF THE LAWN IN OUR landscapes, you might be inclined to think that large tracts of grass have always been part of the American gardening scene. In fact, the rise of the American lawn dates back only a century or so. Although fine lawns had always been much admired, until the early 1800s expanses of grass were extremely rare in American gardens, principally because of the cost of maintaining them. Before the advent of mechanized mowers, the only way to cut grass was with a hand scythe (a tremendously expensive and laborious process) or by allowing animals to graze on the grass (which resulted in a rather randomly cropped surface, as well as the inevitable animal offering . . .). Thus lawns were pretty much limited to the homes of the very rich, and even there they were used only sparingly and where absolutely necessary, such as in the courts designed for such upper-class games as boules (an early form of lawn bowling) and later, croquet.

This was all changed by two English gentlemen by the names of Edwin Budding and James Ferrabee, who in 1830 were clever enough to realize that machines used to cut the nap on wool cloth could, if slightly modified, be used to cut grass. In one stroke of the proverbial blade, the entire gardening world was turned upside down. What was formerly the exclusive province of the wealthy could now be had by anyone from maid to minister, and the popularity of lawns soared. Add to this development the rise of pressurized town water systems ideal for irrigation and the advent of chemical fertilizers (themselves an inadvertent product of munitions research in World War I), and by 1920, all the necessary elements required for bringing the American lawn to prominence—mowers, water, and fertilizers—were in place. The rest, as they say, is lawn history.

How Much Is Enough?

IF YOU'RE THINKING ABOUT LAYING OUT A NEW LAWN, or contemplating changes to an old one, the first question you need to ask is how much lawn you really need. The answer depends on your intentions for the lawn. Is the grass merely an adjunct to your garden, like a fine Oriental rug designed to set off your other horticultural possessions? Or do you intend your lawn to be a major entertainment or play area? If that's the case, what kind of activities do you have in mind? Unless you plan on using your backyard to play football or croquet, you'd be surprised just how little lawn area you actually require. Judging from studies done by municipalities where water use is critical, most people actually prefer a lawn area that's somewhere between 600 and 800 square feet. That's a relatively small area compared to the empty fields now found in many yards—in fact, it's just slightly bigger than the average patio or terrace.

Another way to assess your true grass needs is by determin-

■ **The attractive planting near the house is overwhelmed here by a great green sea of lawn. When there's too much grass in the landscape, the overall effect becomes dull and uninviting.**

ing all the areas of your yard where a lawn shouldn't even be considered: tiny island sections of the landscape without easy access (dragging that mower over the petunias is a pain); long, narrow strips (extremely tough to mow); steep or hilly areas (not only difficult but also dangerous to cut); and extremely shady areas where grass simply won't thrive. (Although you will often see seed and sod mix labeled "for shade," the fact of the matter is that most grass types, even those that will tolerate a bit of shade, much prefer sunny conditions and require infinitely more work and care in shady areas.) By delineating bad growing areas on your landscape plan and eliminating them from consideration, you'll be surprised how easy it is to reduce the amount of lawn in your yard.

Assessing What You Have

IF YOU'RE FACED WITH A PATCHY OR PROBLEMATIC lawn, you have two choices: try to renovate the existing surface, or put down an entirely new lawn. There's no hard and fast rule as to when your lawn is past all hope or resurrection, but in my experience, if weeds outnumber grass in your lawn area, or if at least 30 percent of the turf is dead from insect damage or disease, or if the surface is extremely lumpy or

■ **A de-thatching rake like this one works well for occasional use on small, limited areas. For larger jobs, it's best to rent a mechanical de-thatcher from your local home center.**

poorly graded, then it's probably best to cut your losses, rip out the old, and install the new.

If, however, your problem is spotty coverage in some areas or a minor weed problem, then a method called overseeding is probably for you. Overseeding works like this: In the spring or early fall, de-thatch the existing grass, remove any areas of weeds, fill in any depressions with good topsoil, fertilize, and apply a premium-quality grass seed over the entire lawn surface, including the old grass areas. (The de-thatching process removes just enough old grass to allow the seeds room to sprout through the existing lawn.) As the new grass emerges, it will knit together the various sections of old grass into a new, unified lawn surface.

Starting a New Lawn

ONE OF THE ARGUMENTS IN FAVOR OF STARTING AFRESH with a problematic lawn is that it offers the opportunity to enhance the soil beneath it. Given our repeated warnings throughout this book about the necessity of having the best possible soil for good growth, you probably won't be too surprised to learn that the key to a rich, green lawn lies in the soil beneath it. But what you may not realize is that all that effort spent in enhancing the soil will not only improve the quality of your grass, but will save you money. Grass growing in a rich, well-prepared bed will require less water, less fertilizer, and fewer (if any) chemicals than lawns grown in poor soils. What's more, in a well-maintained lawn, deep-rooted grass will be able to survive periods of drought and stress naturally, at the same time crowding out competing weeds. While thoroughly preparing the soil means more work up front, the long-term benefits are well worth it.

Before you can start your new lawn, however, you'll need a completely clean slate, and unless you are planting in an area that's never been covered by grass, you'll have to remove whatever remains of the existing failed lawn. Getting rid of old grass can be done in a number of ways, each with concomitant benefits and drawbacks:

- Treat the existing lawn with an herbicide to kill grass and weeds, then till under or remove the dead grass with a de-thatcher or power rake (effective, but involves the use of chemicals, which can taint the soil).

- Strip the existing grass with a sod cutter (extremely effective, but requires renting the machine).
- Use black plastic or mulch to smother the existing grass, then rototill (works well, but only practical for small spaces).
- Hire a professional with a grading machine to strip the old sod off for you (expensive, but quick and effective).

One method we definitely don't recommend is the common practice of simply rototilling the old lawn without first removing or killing the old grass. Although a significant portion of the old grass (along with any existing weeds) is indeed killed through the tilling process, a large part isn't, and it remains just below the surface ready to reroot. Tilling also produces thousands of little grass clumps—all of which will need to be arduously removed before you can establish a grade and level the new lawn bed.

After you've gotten rid of all surface rocks, debris, and old grass, the next step is to thoroughly prepare the soil bed. To do this properly, you'll need an accurate idea of your soil's current condition, especially in terms of available organic matter and pH level, which entails a soil test. While you can always add fertilizer and other nutrients after the grass is down, this is your last chance to improve the *structure* of the soil itself, and any and all work done now will pay off with big returns in the future. If your soil is extremely sandy or clayey, you should spread and till in several inches of organic matter (such as compost or rotted manure) over the entire lawn bed, cultivating the soil to the depth of six or seven inches. It's also important to adjust the pH. Grass prefers a rich soil with a pH just around 7. If necessary, add lime or acidifying agents now, as well as a starter fertilizer, according to the manufacturer's directions—new lawns are heavy feeders, and will require these nutrients in order to get off to a good start.

Leveling the Field

EARLIER IN THIS BOOK, WE TALKED ABOUT HOW important it is for you to establish proper grading and good

■ **There are times to call in the professionals—especially when you have a large property. Here, the heavy grading is being done by machine, with fine-tuning by hand.**

BUYING SOIL

If your house is brand new, you may be facing a major challenge: establishing a new lawn with little or no soil. Although it's illegal in many states, many contractors still manage to get away with skimming off the natural topsoil (or completely compacting it with heavy machinery), leaving new homeowners with nothing but an inch or two of rocky subsoil. By all means, resist the temptation of trying to amend this rocky mix by planting a quick coating of grass: the final result is inevitably a disaster that will rapidly require a complete makeover. Instead, hire a contractor to bring in sufficient topsoil to cover your lawn area to the depth of six inches. Make sure, however, that you purchase high-quality screened loam from a reputable dealer, preferably in a soil/compost mix. Also, keep in mind that whenever you import large quantities of soil, you can expect a certain amount of natural compaction, so you'll need to spread the soil and let it settle over a period of a month or so (preferably during a time when there's some rain) before doing any final grading.

{ thatch } *Thatch* is the term used to describe the dead remains of individual grass blades that build up in a lawn. While a certain amount of thatch is normal, large concentrations of it can prevent water and nutrients from penetrating the soil, essentially smothering the grass. Excessive thatch buildup can be removed either by raking or with a specialized de-thatching machine.

Open and check sod rolls before you bring them home. Rolls should be green, cool, and smell like freshly cut grass. If you smell a faint odor of composting grass clippings, shop elsewhere.

drainage when designing a landscape—unless, of course, you want to have water flowing back into your basement every time it rains. Lawn areas are no exception to this rule: not only is proper grading important for drainage, but a bumpy, lumpy soil surface will translate very quickly into a bumpy, lumpy lawn. In fact, counterintuitively, turf doesn't hide but actually magnifies any imperfections in the soil base below. Thus, you really want to make sure that your lawn surface is as well graded as it can be.

If you have a small area to level, this shouldn't pose any major problems as long as you have the proper tools for the job: a grading rake (a four- or six-foot-long rake designed to make leveling easy), an assortment of regular garden rakes, and some tool, such as a water level, that can determine the rise and fall of the land. In general, you should plan for a slope of $1/4$ inch for every foot, or 2 feet for every 100 feet. Simply determine the pitch required, and rake to suit. Grading is fairly arduous work and requires patience, but it's absolutely essential. Once you have your levels established, let the area sit for a week or two, making sure the soil is watered several times (either manually or by rainfall) to hasten the settling process. When that's done, correct any problematic areas and you're ready to plant.

If you are planning on a fairly large lawn, say more than 1,000 square feet, then you should probably consider enlisting the services of a professional landscaper. Not only is accurate

grading next to impossible to do manually over large areas, but to my mind at any rate, the time and effort required is much better spent working on the previous phase of soil preparation.

Seed versus Sod

ONCE YOUR LAWN SURFACE IS PREPARED, YOU'RE READY to start planting either with seed or sod.

Both have advantages and disadvantages. Sod, on one hand, provides a rich, green lawn that immediately covers the ground surface and smothers any emergent weeds. This instant gratification, of course, comes at a price: sod is exponentially more expensive than seeding, especially where large areas are concerned. Sod has another drawback: it does not offer the wide variety of choices that you find with seed, so if you are looking for a particular variety of grass, it may not be available. Sodded lawns can't be feathered, either. (Feathering is the process of subtly blending different types of grass seed to accommodate the various growing areas in a typical home landscape, gradually moving from sun to shade grasses under a large tree canopy, for example.) Thus you should choose sod only if the area in which you're planting grass has uniform growing conditions from one end to the other.

Seeding, on the other hand, is much less expensive, but has its own set of drawbacks—the principal one being that a substantial crop of weed seeds can become established in the time that grass seed takes to start growing (usually one to two months). In cold climates, weeds aren't such an issue if you plant in the fall (most weed seeds are annuals and don't start sprouting until the spring), but in warmer areas of the country a gardener doesn't have this luxury. Hand weeding or selective herbicide applications may be necessary.

In terms of maintenance, both sod and seed require about the same amount of work to get established, and will need the same amount of water afterward. Speaking of which, don't even think about leaving your new lawn in hot weather for more than a day or two during its first few months unless you have an automatic watering system.

Choosing
the Right Grass

THE KEY TO A SUCCESSFUL LAWN IS CHOOSING THE right type of grass for both your site and your climate. In general, grasses are divided into two categories: warm- and cool-season grasses. Cool-season grasses work particularly well in areas north of Zone 7. These grasses tend to be finer in texture than their warm-weather counterparts and are sufficiently hardy to last through cold northern winters. Warm-season grasses, as their name implies, prefer hotter climates and will go dormant when the temperatures drop below 50 degrees F. Tall fescue, while generally considered a cool-season grass, actually is better thought of as a transitional material between the warm- and cool-season zones.

Warm-climate gardeners take note: unlike cool-season grasses, which are generally found mixed in lawns, warm-season varieties tend not to do well together and generally should not be used in combination.

Selecting Grass Seed

ALTHOUGH IT SOUNDS SIMPLISTIC, THE FIRST ESSENTIAL to planting a new lawn from seed is purchasing premium-quality seed. There are three main types of grass seed: straights, blends, and mixtures. Straights, as the name implies, consist of a single type of grass and are a fairly common form of warm-season grasses. Mixtures are a combination of several different varieties of a single species, such as a bluegrass. Blends are made from two or more types of grass, such as bluegrass and fescue.

For most gardeners, blended mixtures offer the best chance for success because they are the most adaptable to the variable conditions found across the average home landscape. In a bluegrass/fescue blend, for instance, the resulting lawn will appear uniform to the eye, but in reality, through natural selection, the bluegrass will dominate the sunnier parts of the yard while the fescues will thrive in shadier areas. In other words, using seed mixtures is the grass equivalent of hedging your bets. Another good thing about blends is that they are often formulated for specific conditions. Companies now provide special blends for sun, shade, and high-traffic areas, which removes a lot of the guesswork from trying to determine the proper species of grass for your space.

When buying grass seed, always buy the best you can afford. While less expensive seeds may appear to be a bargain, often they contain more inert matter (read: dirt) and weed seeds than premium mixtures. Many cheap blends also often contain a high percentage of annual rye grass. While a small amount of this quick-growing grass allows the lawn to green rapidly and provides excellent cover for the slower-growing perennial species, too much annual rye grass in a seed blend will result in a largely annual lawn—a very pretty sight the first summer, but a major disappointment the following spring when you discover that substantial portions of the grass didn't reappear!

Cool- and Warm-Season Grasses

COOL-SEASON GRASSES

Grass Type	Description/ Comments	Planting Method and Water Requirements	Varieties
Bentgrasses (*Agrostis* spp.)	Shallow-rooted low-growing grass. Does well in the northeastern and northwestern regions of the country. Creeping bent varieties primarily used on golf courses and putting greens. Prone to thatch without aggressive management. Velvet bentgrass exceptionally fine-textured and tolerates lower soil, fertility, and pH conditions.	By seed; some varieties by sod or plugs; plant in sun or partial shade. Requires weekly watering (at least one inch per week).	Creeping bentgrass cultivars include 'Providence,' 'L-93,' 'Penncross,' and 'Seaside.' Colonial bentgrass varieties: 'Astoria' and 'Exeter.' Velvet bentgrass cultivars include 'SR 7200' and 'Greenwich.'
Tall- and fine-leaved fescues: Chewing (*Festuca rubra communtata*), Creeping (*Festuca rubra*), Tall (*Festuca arundinacea*), Hard (*Festuca longifolia*).	Fine-leaved fescues tolerate more shade, are quite vigorous. Don't tolerate traffic well. Newer, improved Tall fescues resemble Kentucky bluegrass but are lighter in color. Usually found as part of good grass mixes. Low-temperature tolerance not as strong as Kentucky bluegrass.	Tall fescue is available but doesn't form strong sods. Usually found in combination with Kentucky bluegrass sod mixes. Has normal watering requirements, but more tolerant of dry conditions where soil is deep.	Chewing fescue; Creeping red fescue; Sheep's fescue; Tall fescue; Hard fescue.
Kentucky bluegrass (*Poa pratensis*)	One of the most popular grasses in America. Fertile dark blue-green lawn, great for all-around use. Highly durable, thrives in full sun, will take a beating if given regular mowing.	Grown from seed or sod. Requires full sun, regular watering, and higher rates of nutrients.	'Adelphi,' 'Aquilla,' 'Baron,' 'Birka,' 'Bonnie,' 'Blue,' 'Majestic,' 'Midnight,' 'Parade,' 'Pennstar,' 'Touchdown,' 'Victa,' 'Windsor,' and many other varieties. 'Glade' and 'Nuggest' may do better in moderate shade.
Perennial ryegrass (*Lolium perenne*)	Quick to establish. Often included in mixes to provide cover for slower-growing species.	Seed or sod (in sod combination with Kentucky bluegrass); tolerates some shade.	'Yorktown 11,' 'Diplomat,' 'Citation,' 'Omega,' 'Derby,' 'Birdie Pennfine,' 'Manhattan.'

WARM-SEASON GRASSES

Grass Type	Description/ Comments	Planting Method and Water Requirements	Varieties
Bahia grass (*Paspalum notate*)	Low-maintenance grass that's not as fine as some other warm-season grasses. Does particularly well in hot, dry climates. Stays green and flourishes in poor soil.	Seed or sod; full sun or partial shade.	Easier-to-maintain varieties include 'Argentine,' 'Pensacola,' and 'Paraguay.'
Bermuda grass (*Cynodon dactylon*)	Attractive, high-quality, finely textured lawn. Can tolerate heat and is extremely durable in high-traffic areas.	Full sun; drought tolerant.	Common Bermuda grass good for poor soils; Hybrid Bermuda better for lawns.
Buffalo grass (*Buchloe dactyloides*)	One of the better heat-resistant, drought-tolerant grasses. Has a fine curly texture and gray-green blades. Grass is low maintenance, drought tolerant, does equally well in dry, clay, or sandy soil. Reasonably disease and pest resistant.	Plant in full sun using sod or two-inch plugs; water every two weeks, especially in arid climates.	Newer varieties include 'Texoca' and 'Prairie.'
St. Augustine (*Stenotaphrum secundatum*)	Deep-rooted grass well suited to shade. Fast growing and takes well to almost any kind of soil. Does best when soil is well drained and fertilized.	Can be planted using plugs in full sun or shade.	More disease-resistant varieties include 'Seville' and 'Floritam.'
Zoysia grasses (*Zoysia* spp.)	Slow-growing, high-quality grass that works well as a warm-climate lawn. Relatively trouble-free, has more climate latitude than some of the other warm-season grasses. Doesn't do well in northern climates.	Plant using two-inch plugs; prefers full sun, but also tolerates partial shade.	*Zoysia japonica* and *Zoysia tenuifolia*. Newer varieties that grow more quickly: 'De Anza' and 'Victoria.'

This chart was developed in consultation with David Mellor, author of *The Lawn Bible* and *Picture Perfect*; and W. Michael Sullivan, professor of agronomy at the University of Rhode Island.

Step by Step: Planting a New Lawn from Seed

ONCE YOU'VE CHOSEN YOUR SEED AND PREPARED YOUR soil well, it's time to get planting. You'll need to assemble the following:

- Grass seed
- A good-quality spreader
- Starter fertilizer
- Organic matter for mulch, which can be peat moss, hay, aged sawdust, fine compost, or whatever else you might have on hand
- A water-filled roller (these once-common tools are rather rare in households these days; most hardware stores sell them and tool supply stores rent them)
- Ample water and watering equipment

1 Place half the required seed in the spreader, and adjust the settings as recommended by the manufacturer. (Resist the temptation to sow more seed than required. Although the quantity may look insufficient to you, adding more than the recommended amount simply wastes seed and money. All those extra blades will merely crowd each other out and eventually die, actually slowing down the process of establishing a healthy lawn.) Begin walking in a straight line and cover the soil bed. To ensure even coverage, once you've completed the first pass, add the rest of the seed to the spreader and walk the area again, but this time perpendicular to the first pass. Load the spreader with starter fertilizer and spread according to the manufacturer's directions.

2 Place the covering material over the seed. A light covering of less than a quarter of an inch of organic material will help keep the seed moist during the critical germination period, as well as hide the seed from birds and other seed-eating critters. If you have access to a peat moss spreader (available at many rental centers), peat moss is a good way to go. Peat spreads easily and holds water well, making it the perfect light mulch for grass seed.

3 Roll the surface with a half-filled water roller. Light rolling presses the seed into the soil and speeds germination.

4 Water. Sufficient moisture is critical to good germination. In fact, allowing the seed bed to dry out any time after the grass sprouts and before the new seedlings have developed a sufficient root system will mean death for your new lawn. Immediately after seeding, water the soil bed thoroughly so that moisture penetrates at least four to six inches. After that, water enough to keep the top inch or so moist at all times. In hot weather, it may be necessary to water several times a day; if you're not going to be around, make sure to purchase a misting sprinkler and a programmable timer, or set your automatic irrigation system for several light waterings a day. After germination, slowly ease up on the watering until you reach the normal rate for lawns—the equivalent of one to two inches of water per week from either man or Mother Nature.

Don't walk on the bed for at least a month after germination. Keep kids and pets off the new grass by cordoning off the area to foot traffic until the grass has had a chance to get established.

1 Adequate fertilizer is essential to any lawn, whether started from sod or seed. Here, Kip spreads starter fertilizer by hand. Larger areas should be done with a mechanical spreader.

2 It's important not to create dips or depressions in the ground as you lay the sod; they will translate to the final lawn. Use a plank to avoid making hollows.

3 This specialty blade, called a linoleum knife, makes cutting turf pieces particularly easy.

Laying Sod

IF EITHER SCHEDULE OR IMPATIENCE PREVENTS YOU from growing a lawn from seed, laying sod may be just the kind of instantaneous solution you need.

The first step is to prepare your site. This means removing any old grass and any debris, preparing the soil as you would for a seedbed (see page 135), and leveling the site properly.

The next step is to determine how much sod you will need. Sod is sold in rolls of various sizes, one of the most common being 2' × 6'. Once you know the size of the rolls, it's simply a question of dividing the total square footage of your existing lawn by the square footage of a roll of sod to get the number of rolls you'll need. If your area is fairly square and you're able to measure it accurately, you should generally order 10 percent

more sod than the math indicates, as you'll need to allow for a certain amount of wastage and special cutting. If your lawn area is very irregular, ordering 15 to 20 percent more sod to encompass these extra irregularities is generally a good idea.

While sod can be planted at any time of the year (except the dead of winter when the ground is totally frozen), the ideal time is when the grass is actively growing, which means spring or fall for cool-season grasses and late spring for warm ones.

You can generally pick up generic sod at most local garden centers, but if you're going to be using more than just a few rolls, consider placing a special order for delivery right to your home. Not only is sod extremely heavy, but the rolls shed dirt and aren't particularly pleasant to transport in a passenger ve-

4 After a long day's work laying sod, you may be tempted to skip the compaction process—don't! Unless the sod roots make good contact with the soil, the sod won't take hold. Larger areas can be completed with a water-filled roller.

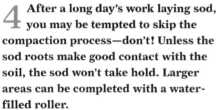

5 Water well after sod placement, and make sure the sod doesn't dry out in its first few weeks, or else you'll be starting the process over from scratch.

hicle. Placing a special order also will allow you to customize the type of grass you want; sod, like seed, is available in a variety of mixes, and selecting the best mix for your area is essential to getting a good lawn.

Unlike grass seed, sod is an extremely perishable commodity. Anyone who has mown the lawn, saved the clippings for compost, and left them in the sun for a few hours knows how quickly grass starts to heat up and decay, and sod is no exception. Left for too long in rolls, sod will quickly cook and destroy itself. That means it's imperative not only that you prepare to lay your sod the moment it arrives, but also that you carefully check the condition of the sod before purchase or accepting delivery. Here are some important factors to look for:

- Good sod should feel cool to the touch, not hot, and be moist, not sopping wet. Hot sod is already partially decomposed, and extremely wet sod is very heavy and hard to handle. If at all possible, order your sod for delivery in the early morning; this generally means that it will be cut and shipped the night before, assuring the freshest possible turf for your new lawn.

- Avoid any sod that seems yellowed or has blades of uneven length; this may indicate that it has been rolled up for too long. You should also try to avoid buying sod that has already been rolled out; although rolled-out sod can survive for quite a long time on the ground or even on concrete, the quality of the turf decreases slightly each day.

- Make sure the rolls of sod are consistently thick, with at least a half-inch of root mass below the blade. This will insure that the grass will hold together when laid down and quickly bond with the soil beneath to form a solid lawn.

Once the bed is prepared, the actual process of laying down sod is a reasonably simple one. You will need the following materials:

- A knife for cutting (An old serrated kitchen knife will do just fine, though once used for sodding, the blade will be permanently too dull for kitchen work, so choose carefully. Retractable utility knives also work well.)
- Two wooden planks: one large enough to walk on, the other a foot or so long to use when pounding the sod edges together
- A rubber mallet
- A water-filled roller
- A wheelbarrow to transport the sod
- A hose and nozzle for watering
- A rake for small level adjustments

The best time to lay sod is in the early morning, before the heat of the sun has a chance to dry out the rolls. Lightly water the soil in the planting area—not enough to make it soggy—and remember to spread starter fertilizer over the soil bed. (This is something that should be done during the soil preparation phase, but in the rush to get the new grass rolled out, it's easy to forget.)

Begin laying out your sod against a straight edge, such as the side of the house or the edge of a walk. If there are no straight edges in your design, take a piece of string and two stakes, run a straight line down the center of your sod bed, and lay the sod pieces to either side of that, being careful to walk on your plank so as not to rut the soil area. Unroll one piece of sod after another, making sure that the edges of the rolls come in direct contact with each other or another hard surface, such as the side of the walkway. The edges of the rolls are the first to dry out if they're exposed to air, and when they desiccate, unsightly gaps form. To avoid this, take your small plank, place it over the seam, and pound the joint with the mallet to make sure that the edges bond together as tightly as possible. As you proceed, you'll also want to stagger the rolls so that each roll ends in a slightly different place than the one next to it, to avoid creating an intersection of four seams that will dry out even faster.

Generally the variable lengths of the sod rolls will mean that each roll will end in a slightly different place; if they don't, cut

random rolls shorter so that they form a running bond pattern, just as in laying bricks. When you reach the new lawn's perimeter, simply cut the sod to fit using a knife, and then proceed on to the next row. Always remember to use your plank rather than stepping directly on the sod (any small dips or depressions that inadvertently form can always be removed by lifting the sod and using a rake). Also, if you have an irrigation system installed, don't forget to cut around each of the sprinkler heads, or you'll have quite a mess on your hands the first time you try to water.

When you've finished laying the sod, roll the lawn with the water-filled roller to take out any small bumps and surface imperfections; then water immediately and thoroughly. Then give your lawn a daily watering to ensure that the sod doesn't dry out before the rolls have had a chance to bond with the soil below. This generally takes upward of about a week. At this point, slowly move to a more regular watering schedule, always keeping a vigilant weather eye open for extremely dry and hot conditions that can severely damage a newly sodded lawn.

And one final tip: While the newly laid sod will look just like a well-established lawn, it's important to resist the tempta-

PREVENTING THE UNPREVENTABLE

If something unforeseen happens and your planting is delayed, you can store rolled sod for up to three days in the shade as long as the weather remains cool—below 60 degrees or so Fahrenheit—and you lightly water the rolls to prevent desiccation. In warm weather, 24 hours is the maximum sod can remain rolled up without starting to decompose. If you are completely stuck, you will have to unroll the sod, place it in the shade, and keep it well watered until you're ready, rolling it back up to transport the sod to its final site when it's time to plant. Obviously this causes a lot of extra work, as well as degradation to the sod, so this procedure should be used only in emergencies.

tion to walk on it—it really needs three to four weeks before it can handle any kind of serious foot traffic.

Know When to Hold 'em, Know When to Roll 'em

MANY OVERZEALOUS GARDENERS INTUITIVELY FEEL more is better, but in the case of fertilizer, more can lead to deleterious results. At best, an overfertilized lawn is more prone to disease; at worst, it's dead from burnout. All that unused fertilizer doesn't just sit there, either: each heavy rain carries it off into streams and lakes, with fatal results for aquatic life. This doesn't mean, however, that you shouldn't fertilize your grass; lawns are heavy feeders, and without a regular feeding they will lack the vigor required for thick growth, which is the best protection your lawn has against weeds.

When to fertilize depends entirely on whether you have warm- or cold-season grass. In general, you fertilize warm-season grasses every six to eight weeks during the active growing season from late spring to early fall, avoiding feeding in the very early spring, which only encourages annual weeds, and very late in the fall, which can damage the lawn. Cool-season grasses should be fertilized only once in the late spring and again in the early fall, skipping the summer season entirely, when most grasses go semidormant. (The only exception to this is for areas that remain temperate throughout the summer, where cool-season grasses don't go dormant.) The fall feeding is particularly important for cool-season grasses: this autumnal burst of nutrients strengthens the lawn against winter damage, as well as providing the energy required for rapid greening in the spring.

Never fertilize your lawn when the grass is dormant (you are just wasting time and money), and try to choose a dry day several days in advance of any predicted heavy rain. Once you've applied the fertilizer (sticking strictly to the manufacturer's directions), slowly apply enough water to moisten the top four to six inches of soil, making sure to avoid any runoff. A misting sprinkler, or short bouts of your irrigation system at several-hour intervals, works well to water in fertilizer, allowing the nutrients to penetrate into the grass's root zone, where you want them.

Lawn Maintenance

HAVING SPENT SO MUCH TIME AND ENERGY PLANNING and planting your lawn (or having benefited from someone who did), you'll naturally want to take the best possible care of your grass. While whole tomes have been written on lawn care and maintenance, we've found over the years that many people wind up killing their grass with kindness in the form of too much or too little mowing, too much water, or too much fertilizer. Here, then, are some quick pointers to avoid the most commonly encountered mistakes.

Watering

The number-one error in caring for lawns is frequent shallow watering. While that quick spray with the hose may seem beneficial to you, frequent applications of small amounts of water causes grass roots to remain close to the surface instead of seeking water deeper down. In essence, your grass becomes addicted to constant small doses of water and loses its ability to withstand drought. The first time you leave on vacation or don't have a chance to water, the lawn goes dormant and turns brown. While this kind of dormancy is a natural reaction to drought and isn't fatal, parched grass isn't much fun to look at. To avoid browning off, water your lawn thoroughly once or twice a week, giving an inch of water each time.

To do this accurately you'll need to determine how much water your sprinklers apply during a given period, something that can be accomplished with a simple test. Position several old coffee cans or wide-mouth glass jars around your sprinkler, turn on the water, and measure how long it takes for an inch of water to accumulate in all the cans. (You want to use several cans because most sprinklers have a tendency to deposit water unevenly. Multiple cans allow you to average out the required time.) Once you have familiarized yourself with the parameters of your watering system, you'll be able to accurately deliver water when and where your lawn needs it.

Mowing

When I was a kid, my mom used to cut my hair. She had one of those little home barber kits, and quite frankly, she did a pretty good job for a while—that is, until the blades dulled. As the steel lost its edge, my haircuts became more and more erratic (not to mention painful, as the clipper pulled rather than cut my hair) until finally nothing short of duress could get me to submit to a haircut. Fearing baldness if she continued, I finally convinced my mom to retire the home clippers, and my hair has been happy ever since.

Believe it or not, your lawn shares this same trauma every time you mow with a dull blade. Think about it: each time you mow, you cut the "hair" of your lawn, and without a sharp blade, you're bound to leave rough, jagged cuts. Not only does this hacking cause unsightly browning of the lawn tips, but the jagged cuts are essentially wounds on the grass blades and can form entry points for a variety of lawn diseases. In addition, dull blades, according to some studies, can use up to 30 percent more energy—either yours in the case of manual mowers or fossil fuels in the case of powered models—than a properly sharpened mower. So if you want a healthy lawn, and want to save energy at the same time, get your mower blades sharpened several times a season. (Here at The Victory Garden we keep several identical blades on hand for just this reason, rotating them out as they become dull.) Blades can be sharpened for about $10 at most lawn and garden centers that sell mowers, or if you are handy, you can sharpen them yourself. (See Garden Basics, page 147.) Either way, a sharp blade makes mowing the lawn a much more pleasant and effective experience.

Cutting your grass to the correct height is another often overlooked tenet of proper mowing. Cut your grass too short and at worst, you scalp and kill it; at best, you'll rob the grass of most of its ability to generate energy from the sun. The less blade surface available for photosynthesis, the weaker the plant becomes and the more care will be needed from you. If, on the other hand, you regularly allow your grass to grow too long and then cut it back severely, you end up putting tremendous strain on the roots, which in turn weakens the entire structure of the lawn. (Also, grass left to grow too tall has a tendency to develop excess thatch, or dead grass, which will then have to be manually removed.)

The key here is knowing the proper height for your particular variety of grass, and adjusting your mowing schedule so that you never remove more than a quarter to a third of the grass's total blade length at any one mowing. That means mowing more often during periods of active growth, such as the spring and fall, and less often during the high summer (or winter for warm-season grasses), when the lawn goes partially dormant. Here's a table that shows the correct mowing heights:

Grass Type	Ideal Mowing Heights in Inches
Bahia	2–3
Bent	0.25–1
Bermuda, common	0.75–1.50
Bermuda, hybrid	0.5–1
Blue gramma	2–3
Buffalo	2–3
Centipede	1–2
Fescue, fine	1.5–2.5
Fescue, tall	2–3
Kentucky bluegrass	1.75–2.5
Ryegrass, annual	1.5–2
Ryegrass, perennial	1.5–2
St. Augustine	1.5–2.5
Zoysia	1–2

This chart was developed in consultation with W. Michael Sullivan, professor of agronomy at the University of Rhode Island.

■ A rain gauge like the one shown here is an essential tool in water conservation—this is the only way to accurately assess how much water your sprinkler or irrigation system dispenses over a set period of time.

SHARPENING YOUR MOWER BLADE

Sharpening mower blades isn't a difficult process. To remove the blade, first make sure that the mower is off and the ignition key removed. (In mowers without an electric start, disconnect the spark plug to prevent accidental ignition.) Find the appropriate wrench (don't use pliers, or you'll damage the nut) and remove the blade, being careful to note which side of the blade is up. Secure the blade in a vise, and then slowly draw a metal file across the beveled edge of the blade. You'll want to sharpen the blade with several smooth passes of the file, making sure not to cut into the metal enough to alter the existing blade angle. After sharpening both sides with an equal number of strokes, check for balance by carefully placing your finger in the mounting hole. Remount the blade right side up.

If all this sounds too complicated, you can always do what we do: buy several blades and rotate them, sending the dull blade out for professional sharpening while another is in use.

Common Lawn Problems

Try as we might, it's nearly impossible to keep a lawn totally disease and trouble free. But when armed with the right diagnosis, there is a solution for virtually any situation that may arise.

Name	Description	Damage Description	Remedy
PESTS			
APHIDS	Aphids are small (⅙ of an inch) sucking insects with long legs and an oval body.	Like chinch bugs, they suck the juice right out of the blades of grass, causing them to turn yellow, then orange, and finally brown.	Insecticidal soap can be effective. Ladybugs and lacewings can also keep them naturally under control. Generally these are not a problem in home lawns.
ARMYWORMS	Yellow or gray ground color tinged with pink. The back of the larva is greenish black with a narrow, sometimes broken, stripe.	If left uncontrolled, they can destroy an entire lawn in a few days. Most likely to do damage at night (a good time to spot/catch them) or on cool, cloudy spring days.	Many different insecticides are effective in ridding lawns of both armyworms and cutworms. *Bacillus thuringiensis* is a good biological form of control.
BILLBUGS	Adult billbugs and larvae love lawns. Adult insects are one inch in length and brown/black in color. They are distinctive with their long snoutlike nose. Larvae looks like a small piece of moist white rice.	The easiest way to detect their presence is that the dead grass will pull away easily from the crown and roots. They can also leave telltale signs that look like sawdust. In the South, they are particularly drawn to Bermuda and zoysia grasses; in the North, they like bluegrass.	Use resistant varieties of turfgrasses in reseeding impacted areas. Kentucky bluegrass cultivars with high resistance to billbugs include 'America,' 'Adelphia,' 'Eagelton,' 'Eclipse,' 'Fylking,' 'Kenblue,' 'Midnight,' 'Unique,' 'Wabash,' and 'Washington.' The cultivars 'Broadway,' 'Cheri,' 'Columbia,' and 'Sydsport' all appear susceptible to billbugs. Endophytes are a beneficial fungal organism that lives in association with the plant.

Name	Description	Damage Description	Remedy
CHINCH BUGS	Chinch bugs are tiny (⅙ of an inch long), and black with red legs.	Grass blades have brownish spots with a yellow halo around them. Blades of grass eventually turn brown, similar in appearance to a drought-stressed lawn.	Respond well to traditional insecticides; insecticidal soaps are also effective. It's also best to take a preventive course of action by planting endophytic lawn varieties that are resistant to chinch bugs.
CUTWORMS	Cutworms are similar to armyworms, though a bit longer (1.75 inches), and curl themselves up in a tight circle when disturbed. Creamy brown in color; often spotted or with stripes.	They feed on grass blades with the same telltale markings as that of armyworms. They feed on green tissues and may consume the crown, which results in death of the plant.	Same as armyworms. Entomopathogenic nematodes are emerging as a good control mechanism.
WHITE GRUBS	White grubs grow up to one inch in length. They form the shape of a letter C, and are distinctive for their creamy white color. Grubs are actually the larvae of beetles, and the type depends on which region of the country you live in. They feed on grass roots.	Irregular-shaped brown patches, which expand quickly and can easily be pulled up out of the lawn. Grubs aren't partial to any particular variety of lawn. They do their greatest damage in late summer to early fall.	Grubs are best treated while still young. The best way of detecting their presence is by digging up a large patch of grass and examining the root system. If more than eight grubs are present in a square foot, there's a problem that needs treatment. Traditional insecticides are effective, as are entomopathogenic nematodes.

Name	Description	Remedy
DISEASES		
DOLLAR SPOT	Small straw-colored round spots one to three inches in diameter (the size of a silver dollar), especially problematic in the more humid parts of the country. Spots can blend together and darken with age. Little by little they can kill more sizeable areas of grass. Blades of grass, when infected, can have tan or purple streaks.	A problem common to Kentucky bluegrass or Creeping bentgrass, there are mixtures of grasses that are less susceptible. Try watering well, but less frequently, keeping the lawn well aerated, mown at the recommended height, and well thatched. Small increases in nitrogen fertilizer decrease severity.
FAIRY RING	Three- to twelve-foot partial or full circular rings of lush green grass, which then discolors or dies. Fairy rings can present themselves at any time. After grass has discolored or died, mushrooms or puffballs will be seen close to rings.	Fairy rings are often found in moist lawns that have had wood debris or naturally decaying organic matter. It helps to aerate the lawn and reduce the presence of any thatch.
LEAF SPOT OR MELTING OUT	Resembles long circular brown or blackish spots with dark edges appearing on the blades of grass. While leaf spot starts out as elongated spots, the entire blade of grass ultimately turns brown and the lawn itself starts to "melt out." Leaf spot is caused by the fungus *Dreschlera siccans* and *D. poae*, which arises as a result of overfertilizing, overwatering, and improper maintenance. Kentucky bluegrass is particularly susceptible.	Keep lawn slightly longer (no shorter than 1½ inches) and reduce the application of nitrogen fertilizer in spring and summer.
PYTHIUM BLIGHT (GREASE SPOT)	A fungus that causes leaves to look wet and slimy; it can cause a streaked pattern across the entire lawn. Grass turns a reddish brown and will eventually die. The dead areas often have a purple-gray-white fungus on them.	Reduce supplemental irrigation, especially under conditions of high humidity. Water deep and infrequently. Aerate appropriately and remediate poorly drained areas.

Name	Description	Remedy
RUST	If a lawn has rust, it will take on a yellowish orange hue. The damage usually occurs during warmer weather with long periods of moisture. Kentucky bluegrass and ryegrass are often susceptible.	The best treatment involves an ounce of prevention. Rust is more likely to occur in unkempt lawns. Therefore, keep the lawn well mowed and fertilized.
SNOW MOLD	As the name implies, snow mold is common in colder climates. White fungal growth appears, and blades of grass clump together. *Microdochium* species (pink) and *Typhula* species (gray) fungi are the cause of the disease. Snow molds are often found in shady areas. Patches of grass turn yellow and eventually die.	Improve water penetration by aerating troubled spots. It also helps to get sun onto shady areas. Keep grass mown at all times, and cut lower before snowfall in problem areas. Avoid using high-nitrogen fertilizers in fall in problem areas. Reduce snow accumulation features such as fences and windbreaks where possible.
SUMMER PATCH (FREQUENTLY INCORRECTLY CALLED FUSARIUM BLIGHT)	Disease starts out as circular patches of dead grass and then expands to areas as large as two feet across. Patches change from bluish purple to straw color (with the center of the circles remaining green) and then the areas eventually die. Frequent in areas with hot, dry weather where grass becomes drought stressed.	Grasses with shallow roots like Kentucky bluegrass are particularly vulnerable, so one solution is to change to a less susceptible grass, such as perennial ryegrass or Bermuda grass. Summer patch is best avoided by using less nitrogen, keeping the grass well aerated and a bit on the dry side so the water can penetrate properly. Keep grass at recommended mowing height.

This chart was developed in consultation with David Mellor, author of *The Lawn Bible* and *Picture Perfect*; and W. Michael Sullivan, professor of agronomy at the University of Rhode Island.

ALTERNATIVES TO LAWNS

■ **Above: Herbs make great ground covers too: here, santolina and lavender are set off by dwarf red *Berberis*.**

■ **Left: In mild areas of the country, ground covers like baby's breath and ajuga are ideal.**

■ **Right, clockwise: Dry areas of the country tend to favor low creeping succulents, complemented with gravel of various hues.**

■ **In many parts of the country, simply allowing grass to grow uncut will result in a natural meadow. Overseeding with a meadow mix will hasten the process. Remember, though: even meadows need to be cut once or twice a year.**

■ **Growing birches surrounded by unmowed fescue make a lovely alternative to the traditional lawn.**

■ The grass steps
at The Mount.

Inspired Gardens

Edith Wharton's The Mount

While remembered mostly for her novels, the Pulitzer Prize–winning author Edith Wharton left behind a considerable horticultural legacy as well. Not only did Wharton write two very influential books on architecture and design, *The Decoration of Houses* (1897) and *Italian Villas and Their Gardens* (1904), but she also surrounded her home, The Mount, with some of the most beautiful formal gardens in the United States, including an extremely creative example of how to use grass in the landscape.

Located in the Berkshire Mountains of far western Massachusetts, the Georgian-style mansion was built by Wharton and her husband in 1901. Its accompanying landscape—inspired by the gardens of Renaissance Italy—was the product of more than twelve years of meticulous work and planning. Wharton herself played a major role in the design of the gardens. In fact, she used the house and gardens as a laboratory for experimenting with the design philosophy she had advocated in her books, treating both house and garden as a single architectural entity united by the principles of "proportion, harmony, simplicity and suitability."

One of the key elements linking this ensemble together is an ingenious series of steps that link the north end of the terrace and rock garden with the more formal flower garden and

155

■ **The main house, with the grass steps in the foreground.**

lime walk below. Measuring over 80 feet long by 12 feet wide and descending a height of about 20 feet, these steps were constructed from grass instead of the standard stone and masonry, and were intended to be living architectural constructs that tied the house to the garden below. Inspired by Wharton's numerous trips to European gardens, The Mount's turf steps are one of only a few examples found in the United States.

How these unique steps were originally constructed remains a bit of a mystery. When the gardens recently underwent a $2.5 million renovation, a great deal of detective work went into trying to answer that question. The project manager and his team worked from historic photographs and unearthed archaeological remains, but the most they could surmise is that the steps were originally constructed out of wood, which, sadly, disintegrated over time.

As a product of their extensive research, the steps have now been returned to all their former glory, but with the help of some modern technology. In place of the previous wooden structure, a porous "pavement" system was installed that utilizes a series of plastic grids tied together with masonry wire to provide a solid support base. Once these supports were in place, a mixture of 60 percent sharp sand and 40 percent compacted topsoil was added to cover the structure, with sod laid on top and secured with six-inch-long spikes.

Given all this elaborate construction, one can perhaps understand why lawn stairs never really caught on with the gardening public: in addition to the building expense, a careful balancing act is required with a push mower, extensive hand trimming and weeding, and continual irrigation to prevent the risers and treads from drying out. Still, the effect is truly magnificent, and part of the surrounding landscape magic that transports today's visitors back to the gilded age of Edith Wharton's The Mount.

■ An heirloom narcissus
peeks out among the foliage
at the Victory Garden.

Chapter 6
Flower Power

When one turned over to sleep at night the scent was what some people would call "overpowering." So much the better, as far as I am concerned. To be "overpowered" by the fragrance of flowers is a most delectable form of defeat.

BEVERLEY NICHOLS
Merry Hall, 1951

ALTHOUGH MOST PEOPLE DON'T REALIZE IT, GARDENING follows fashion just like clothes do. And while garden trends may not move as quickly as hemlines march up and down, they are just as inevitable. Nowhere is this more evident than in the flower's ever-changing role in the American landscape. Sometimes viewed as the second-rate cousin to vegetables, while at other times perceived as the belle of the ball, annuals, perennials, and biennials have risen and fallen out of popularity many times over the last two hundred years, reappearing on each occasion in a slightly new iteration.

All this back and forth has historically meant (and continues to mean) a lot of uncertainty about how to best use flowers in the American landscape. In the Colonial era, for instance, flowers were relegated almost exclusively to the vegetable garden, and the few species available were grown not for their beautiful blossoms, but rather because they possessed some medicinal, herbal, or culinary quality. Whatever flowers appeared were simply a welcome byproduct. Then, in the early 1840s, with the huge technological advances in transportation and horticulture science, unknown annuals from far-off places like South America and East Asia (zinnias, petunias, and impatiens, to name just a few) began to arrive on American and

■ **Asiatic lilies are just one of the many imports brought to our gardens in the last two centuries.**

{annual, perennial, biennial} Annuals are plants that go from seed to flower and back to seed again in a single season. Perennials are plants that live for multiple years, their lifespan being measured in anything from months to decades, depending on the species. That much is pretty straightforward, but the so-called "tender perennials" begin to cloud the terminology a bit. Tender perennials are plants that in their native, tropical climates would normally be perennial, but in colder areas are grown as annuals. (In most cases, these tender perennials can be wintered over if a warm greenhouse is available.) Biennials are plants that produce only foliage during their first year and then flower, produce seed, and die in the second year, foxgloves being a prime example that's familiar to many. Clever gardeners can essentially "perennialize" biennials that self-sow by planting seeds two years in succession, so that one seeding generation will perpetually follow another.

■ Biennials, like the pale golden foxgloves shown here, are the "missing man" in modern American gardens.

■ While the palette of the shade perennial border is certainly less varied than that of the sunny border, in many ways it is more pleasing. The coordination between sympathetic colors—blue, blue-green, green, chartreuse, and white—is extremely soothing.

European shores. These novel flowers soon began supplanting traditional perennial and biennial flowering plants, and sparked a fashion for beds made entirely of flowers. These new plantings consisted almost exclusively of brightly colored annuals and were often positioned right in the center of another period novelty, the lawn.

This predominance of annual beds lasted until the late 1880s, when nostalgia for "simpler times" and "grandmother's gardens" began to grow. (The quotes here and elsewhere come from period guides.) Suddenly, "old-fashioned" was back in popular-

ity. Elaborate beds and borders dedicated entirely to perennials and biennials were all the rage, and annuals were not only out, but were now considered "crass" and "vulgar." Perennials continued their uninterrupted reign straight through World War II. But once the conflict was over, the lack of inexpensive manpower quickly made labor-intensive perennial borders an impossible luxury. The result? Largely flowerless landscapes, filled with bushes and grass, and a few easy-care annuals like marigolds planted in pots, which were touted as quick, colorful substitutes for expensive and high-maintenance perennial flowers. It was not until the 1970s that there was an inevitable counterreaction to these "monotonous lawn-filled landscapes" dotted with "over-hybridized" and "over-bred" annuals. Perennial borders were reintroduced, albeit this time without their biennial cousins, which seemed to mysteriously disappear from the American gardening consciousness.

The current state of affairs—according to the garden fashionistas—is that perennials are in but "only holding," preferably used as part of larger, mixed plantings that combine trees, shrubs, and flowers. Annuals, on the other hand, are rising quickly from their recent reversals, though this time not with the intention of supplanting perennials but rather complementing them, especially when used in containers. Biennials remain complete no-shows.

What this all boils down to is that even if you don't rigidly follow fashion, flowers have returned to the modern landscape and to have a successful garden today, it pays to hone your flower-growing skills. (Not to mention the fact that they are just plain pretty.) Before you get started, however, you need to decide how you envision using flowers in your yard: as an individual decorative element in the landscape, such as a bed or border; as part of a larger grouping, like a foundation or perimeter planting; or for more specific purposes, such as for cutting indoors. Depending on your plan, you'll find that each one of these aspects of flower growing requires a different approach in regards to design. Let's start with the most traditional method of growing flowers—the dedicated bed or border of perennials.

{a nonperennial perennial border?}

Although called perennial borders, most such borders aren't entirely perennial in that they contain a limited number of annuals, biennials, and woody shrubs. The British term herbaceous border, meaning a bed of nonshrubby plants, is probably a more accurate description, though rarely used in this country.

The Perennial Border

IT'S THE MOST ROMANTIC PICTURE IN ALL OF GARDENing, one that you see again and again on TV, in books, and in magazines: a long bed of colorful flowers set against an azure sky, bordered by a wide swath of emerald grass stretching gently across a pristine landscape toward a large and comfortable house. To some extent, this mythological landscape is what every gardener dreams of, and judging from the number of inquiries I've received over the years, not just dreams of, but actually attempts. Unfortunately, as many of you have reported, these efforts have often yielded extremely mediocre results, leaving many wondering exactly what went wrong.

In large part, these failures can be placed directly on the doorstep—or perhaps in this case, a better metaphor would be on the garden bench—of the media (and yes, I include myself

(continued on page 168)

■ **The Victory Garden perennial border "resting" between its two main bloom periods, the first in July and the second in September.**

■ A color wheel of shades (inner ring), pure hues (middle), and tints (outer).

MONOCHROMATIC SCHEMES

Monochromatic schemes use flowers of a single color, including its shades and tints, set off with masses of foliage. While undoubtedly dramatic, monochromatic schemes can also have a monolithic effect, making the garden appear to be a single mass. Probably the most popular of the monochromatic schemes outdoors are all-white gardens; while they are somewhat bland by day, their true beauty is appreciated at night, when the luminous white flowers, many highly fragrant, glow in the pale moonlight.

Design Basics:
THE COLOR WHEEL

Color theory works pretty much the same way outside as it does inside: warm bright colors—reds, yellows, and oranges—create an active, energetic atmosphere, while cool colors—blues, greens, and violets—set a calm, peaceful tone. Colors also affect how we perceive space: warm colors shrink distance, while cool colors elongate—something to keep in mind especially when designing small garden spaces.

To see how colors relate to each other, take a look at the artist's color wheel. The colors in the center of the wheel are called pure hues; they are the true base tones of the primary and secondary colors. Add white to these colors and you get what are called tints or pastels; add black and you get shades. Colors that are adjacent on the wheel are called analogous; those directly opposite are called, somewhat confusingly, complementary, as they don't so much complement as oppose. All color schemes, both indoors and out, are formed by making various combinations of analogous and complementary colors.

In essence, there are four basic types of color schemes: monochromatic, polychromatic, complementary, and analogous.

POLYCHROMATIC SCHEMES

Polychromatic, of course, means all colors, and that's exactly what a polychromatic scheme contains. Polychromatic schemes are the hardest for the beginner to pull off successfully, because to be effective, they need to carefully separate clashing colors with soft neutrals like gray, blue, or white, while individual colors must be sufficiently massed to avoid a dotted effect. The perennial border at the Victory Garden is technically polychromatic, though the scheme Kip designed uses blocks of related colors, gradually transitioning from pale, softer colors at the near end to brighter, warmer colors on the far end.

COMPLEMENTARY SCHEMES

Complementary schemes use opposing color combinations such as red and green, yellow and violet, or orange and blue. Properly pulled off, they can be very dramatic. A variation of this idea, and my favorite, uses three analogous colors and a dash of the complement in the middle color—for example, blue-violet, violet, and red violet, with violet's complement, yellow; or blue-violet, blue, and blue green, with a hint of orange.

ANALOGOUS SCHEMES

Analogous schemes are probably the easiest of all to work with, as they use colors in close relation to each other. A pastel scheme in mauve, pink, and blue is a good example; or a variegated garden of green, pale green, and pale yellow. Analogous schemes produce calm, harmonizing effects with wide appeal.

■ **The plan of the border here at the Victory Garden.**

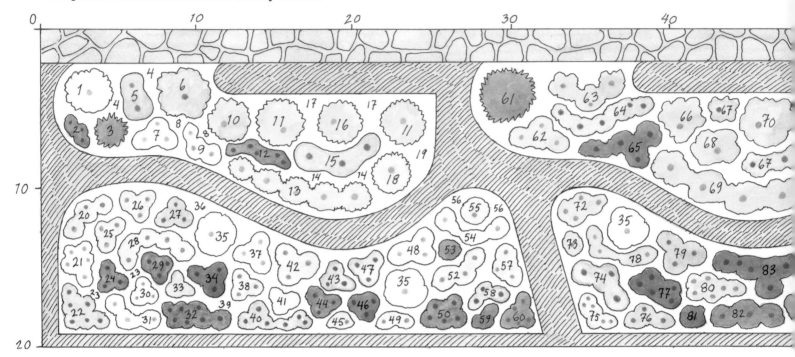

1. *Eupatorium* 'Joe White'
2. *Euphorbia dulcis* 'Chameleon'
3. *Miscanthus sinensis* 'Morning Light'
4. *Lilium* 'Casa Blanca'
5. *Aster laevis* 'Bluebird'
6. *Hydrangea macrophylla* 'Penny Mac'
7. *Anemone x hybrida* 'Honorine Jobert'
8. *Lilium* 'Gold Band'
9. *Baptisia pendula*
10. *Rosa* 'Teasing Georgia'
11. *Rosa* 'Graham Thomas'
12. *Nepeta sibirica*
13. *Rosa* 'Flower Carpet Yellow'
14. *Lilium* 'Jubileo'
15. *Perovskia atriplicifolia* 'Filigran'
16. *Rosa* 'Golden Showers'
17. *Lilium* 'Shocking'
18. *Rosa* 'Grand Prize'
19. *Lilium* 'Nippon Lady'
20. *Anemone tomentosa* 'Robustissima'
21. *Phlox maculata* 'Miss Lingard'
22. *Stokesia laevis* 'Bluestone'
23. *Lilium* 'Muscadet'

24. *Lobelia siphilitica*
25. *Phlox paniculata* 'Eva Cullum'
26. *Phlox paniculata* 'Nicky'
27. *Phlox paniculata* 'Blue Paradise'
28. *Digitalis x mertonensis*
29. *Penstemon strictus*
30. *Tradescantia* 'Navajo Princess'
31. *Geranium x cantabrigiense* 'Biokovo'
32. *Campanula carpatica* 'Blue Clips'
33. *Adenophora liliifolia*
34. *Campanula* 'Kent Belle'
35. *Artemisia x* 'Powis Castle'
36. *Lilium* 'Supremo'
37. *Phlox paniculata* 'David'
38. *Echinacea purpurea* 'Magnus'
39. *Callirhoe involucrate*
40. *Stokesia laevis* 'Klaus Jelitto'
41. *Echinacea purpurea* 'White Swan'
42. *Malva alcea* 'Fastigiata'
43. *Salvia x sylvestris* 'Blue Queen'
44. *Salvia x sylvestris* 'East Friesland'
45. *Campanula* 'Hot Lips'
46. *Salvia x sylvestris* 'May Night'

47. *Salvia x sylvestris* 'Blue Hill'
48. *Leucanthemum* 'Becky'
49. *Allium senescens* 'Glaucum'
50. *Campanula poscharskyana* 'Blue Gown'
51. *Lilium* 'Marlene'
52. *Sedum x* 'Autumn Joy'
53. *Aster novae-angliae* 'Alma Potschke'v
54. *Gypsophila paniculata* 'Bristol Fairy'
55. *Rosa* 'Our Lady of Guadalupe'
56. *Lilium* 'Lollypop'
57. *Chrysanthemum x morifolium* 'Venus'
58. *Campanula* 'Birch Hybrid'
59. *Veronica* 'Mann's Variety'
60. *Delosperma* 'Starburst'
61. *Miscanthus sinensis* 'Cosmopolitan'
62. *Oenothera fruticosa* 'Summer Solstice'
63. *Malva* 'Park Allee'
64. *Campanula lactiflora*
65. *Caryopteris* 'First Choice'
66. *Rosa* 'Habitat for Humanity'
67. *Perovskia x superba*
68. *Rosa* 'Outrageous'
69. *Rosa* 'Ladies in Waiting'

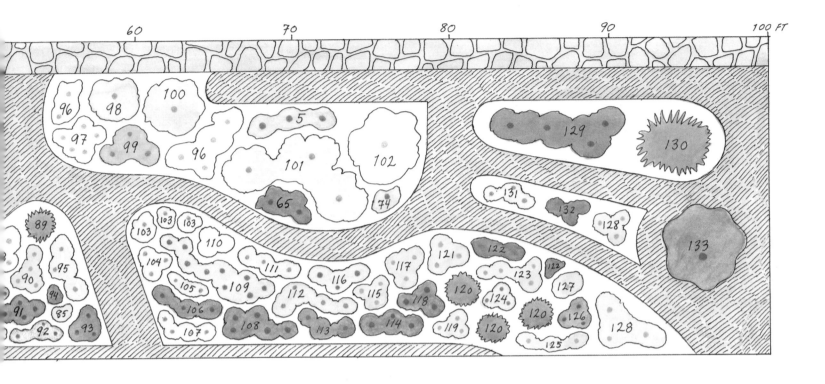

70. *Rosa* 'Crown Princess Margarita'
71. *Rosa* 'William Morris'
72. *Dendranthema* 'Sheffield'
73. *Hemerocallis* 'Apricot Sparkles'
74. *Aster oblongifolius* 'October Skies'
75. *Sedum pulchellum*
76. *Allium tanguticum* 'Summer Beauty'
77. *Salvia x sylvestris* 'Viola Klose'
78. *Coreopsis verticillata* 'Moonbeam'
79. *Phlox paniculata* 'Katherine'
80. *Verbascum x hybridum* 'Jackie'
81. *Tradescantia* 'Sweet Kate'
82. *Origanum laevigatum* 'Herrenhansen'
83. *Salvia forskaohlei*
84. *Aster novae-angliae* 'Purple Dome'
85. *Solidago sphacelata* 'Golden Fleece'
86. *Achillea* 'Terra Cotta'
87. *Adenophora bulleyana*
88. *Leucanthemum* 'Highland White Dreams'
89. *Miscanthus sinensis* 'Adagio'
90. *Coreopsis* 'Golden Gain'
91. *Veronica* 'Sunny Border Blue'

92. *Geranium* 'Hocus Pocus'
93. *Tradescantia virginiana* 'Concord Grape'
94. *Hemerocallis* 'Blueberry Sundae'
95. *Sedum* 'Matrona'
96. *Boltonia asteroides* 'Snowbank'
97. *Lilium* 'Snow Queen'
98. *Filipendula rubra* 'Venusta'
99. *Aster lateriflorus* 'Coombe Fishacre'
100. *Rosa rubrifolia* 'Glauca'
101. *Rosa* 'Ballerina'
102. *Heptacodium miconioides*
103. *Aster lateriflorus* 'Prince'
104. *Aster* 'Wood's Pink'
105. *Papaver orientale* 'Princess Victoria Louise'
106. *Sedum* 'Purple Emperor'
107. *Achillea millefolium* 'Oertel's Rose'
108. *Veronica austriaca ssp teucrium* 'Royal Blue'
109. *Aster x frikartii* 'Wonder of Staffa'
110. *Leucanthemum* 'Sunnyside Up'
111. *Achillea* 'Montrose Rose'

112. *Malva* 'Marina'
113. *Gaura* 'Crimson Butterflies'
114. *Nepeta* 'Walker's Low'
115. *Achillea x* 'Moonshine'
116. *Perovskia* 'Little Spire'
117. *Baptisia* 'Screamin' Yellow'
118. *Echinops bannaticus* 'Blue Globe'
119. *Coreopsis lanceolata* 'Sternthaler'
120. *Pennisetum alopecuroides* 'Hameln'
121. *Thermopsis caroliniana*
122. *Crocosmia x crocosmiiflora* 'Lucifer'
123. *Rudbeckia* 'Goldsturm'
124. *Agastache* 'Honey Bee Blue'
125. *Gaillardia x grandiflora* 'Golden Goblin'
126. *Gaillardia x grandiflora* 'Burgundy'
127. *Achillea x* 'Coronation Gold'
128. *Solidago rugosa* 'Fireworks'
129. *Lysimachia ciliata* 'Purpurea'
130. *Arundo donax*
131. *Sedum* 'Autumn Fire'
132. *Helenium* 'Mardi Gras'
133. *Hibiscus syriacus* 'Blue Bird'

in this group). To avoid discouraging the beginning gardener, we in the media have a tendency to underestimate and downplay the difficulties involved in designing and maintaining large flowering borders, much to the detriment of the amateur gardener. So let me now set the record straight right from the start: while the beginning gardener certainly *can* design and build a spectacular flower border; there are a set of essential site criteria necessary to achieve the flower-filled successes seen in all those glossies, qualities your yard either possesses or doesn't. Simply put, you either have the right conditions or you don't, and if you don't, gardening in large borders is not for you. This doesn't mean you can't have flowers in your landscape, but you'll need to incorporate them into your garden in different ways, as we'll discuss later on.

Sine Qua Non

THE FIRST AND MOST IMPORTANT REQUIREMENT FOR A successful perennial border is space—and a lot of it. Unlike many forms of gardening that can be expanded or contracted to fit into any given area, perennial borders can't be condensed successfully, especially when it comes to depth. To achieve the multilayered, interwoven effect of color you see in pictures, borders depend upon a very complicated tiered system of form, foliage, and flower planted in three height ranges: tall plants at the rear, a middle range down the center, and low plants toward the front. This triple-decker method requires very deep beds: at least 10 feet and preferably more—20 feet is not unheard of. Length is an important factor too, though slightly less crucial, the principle being that the longer the border, the greater the visual effect you'll achieve. A good point of departure would be a minimum length of 50 feet.

It goes without saying that a flower bed that's at least 50' × 10' is very time-intensive to create, not to mention a lot of work to maintain, so it's no wonder that the fashion for these borders arose in the late 1800s, when labor was extremely inexpensive. That's not to say that an amateur today can't build and maintain his or her own border, but it's not something to be undertaken lightly unless you intend to spend five to ten hours per week (and more in the spring) working in the garden.

Like hedges, perennial borders do best when growing conditions are uniform along their length, and this is often something difficult to achieve, especially in terms of sun and shade. Ideally borders should face due south, so that if and when plants reach for the light, they do so toward the viewer. Here at the Victory Garden, where we laid out and planted a 105' × 18' border several seasons ago, the bed actually runs from due north to due south. This was definitely a second-best solution, especially in the late fall when the sun is low in the sky; and some of the late-blooming species, like drunken sailors, careen southward toward the light and require staking, but this couldn't be helped.

During the early spring and early fall we also have to contend with the problem of shade generated from the large ash tree near the bog garden. This huge ash darkens the entire southern end of the border and forces us to use more shade-tolerant plants nearest the tree. Although that's not a problem in and of itself, by and large shade perennials have far less spectacular blooms in far less dramatic hues than their sun-loving cousins, requiring some fairly sophisticated machinations to make the shadier end of the border hold its own with the sunnier end. In short, if you have the choice, face your borders south in full sun to achieve the optimum results.

Even if you've only read a chapter or two of this book so far, you're probably more than aware of the need for good soil preparation in all aspects of gardening. Perennials borders are no exception, and in most cases, you'll need to do quite a bit of enhancement in terms of increasing humus content and fertility before you begin planting. Most flowering species are heavy feeders and thus require *very* rich soil. When we started our border here at the Garden, we worked in the equivalent of several truckloads of manure, as well as vast quantities of peat moss and nonsoluble fertilizer. Additionally, in the spring we top-dress with fertilizer, and whenever we have the opportunity to add or remove a plant, additional compost is added to the hole at that time.

Choosing Plant Material for Perennial Borders

AFTER ACCURATELY ASSESSING THE CONDITIONS IN your yard, and the costs and work involved in creating large borders, you are ready to proceed to the design stage. The question immediately then becomes, just how *do* you fill up all that space with flowering plants?

Well, there is no single right answer, because perennial borders, much like paintings, are individual artistic expressions—except in this case, you're working in concert with Mother Nature. There are, however, some guidelines, both horticultural and artistic, that can help you in the process.

The first rule of thumb is to pay close attention to color, both in terms of flower and foliage, as it's the key factor that knits all of those different specimens into a unified creation. Thus before you buy a single plant you should decide on a color scheme, and then rigidly stick to it, just as you would when

PERENNIALS FOR PARTIAL SHADE

■ *Campanula takesimana* 'Elizabeth.'

Anemone 'Honorine Jobert': Exquisite white flowers that grow on tall (3'–4') plants in late summer.

Campanula takesimana 'Elizabeth': Countless large stippled pink tubular bells that bloom well into the summer.

Cimicifuga ramosa 'Brunette': In late summer this produces deliciously fragrant white spikes on tall (3'–4') plants with bold bronze-purple foliage.

PERENNIALS FOR FULL SUN

Allium tanguticum 'Summer Beauty': This member of the onion clan has extremely attractive strap-like foliage, and many lavender flowers in July and August.

Aster oblongifolius 'October Skies': In September, a myriad of sky-blue blooms appear on bushy plants.

Boltonia asteroides 'Snowbank': This plant has a late-season explosion of daisy-like (1") white flowers.

Callirhoe involucrata: The purple rose "wine cups" appear throughout most of the summer on trailing plants that create bold color combinations wherever they wander.

Geranium 'Rozanne': Half-dollar-sized blue flowers flourish all summer and then some on robust plants with remarkably attractive foliage.

Phlox paniculata 'Katherine': Lovely lavender/white trusses of flowers are produced for much of the summer over mildew-resistant foliage.

Sedum 'Matrona': These late-season flowers are just a bonus atop their marvelous purple/pink foliage.

■ *Geranium* 'Rozanne.'

decorating a room indoors. While it's true that the constantly changing conditions of the great outdoors—sun, sky, and cloud—allow for much greater freedom in selecting pleasing colors than you would ordinarily have indoors, there's still no easier way to go awry in the garden than by combining colors that clash. If you don't trust your own color sense, either find a qualified person to help you or work within one of the already established color groupings using an artist's color wheel (see the Design Basics).

The second main consideration when designing perennial plantings is the sequence of bloom; in other words, timing the flowering so that portions of the border are continually in blossom. This is harder than you might think. Perennials, in contrast to annuals, don't burn their proverbial candle at both ends, and therefore need to reserve sufficient energy to survive from one season to the next. As a result, most of them have a fairly short blooming period, generally about a month, but often less, depending on the particular species and weather. (Very hot weather in the early spring, for instance, can dramatically shorten flower duration.) Figuring out a continual succession of bloom can be quite a daunting task, even for the professional, and while the perennial purists may scoff, the reality is that many perennial borders (ours included) rely on some annuals to get them through the interregnum periods—those weeks between the major perennial bloom times when not much is in flower.

You should also keep in mind when choosing your plant material that not all the color in perennial borders comes from the flowers: foliage plays an important role as well, either by highlighting contrasting hues (dark red foliage against orange and yellow works well, for example) or by linking together otherwise disparate colors. Gray-leaved plants, for instance, are particularly effective in softening transitions between bright colors, especially when combined with white, blues, yellows, and pinks, while chartreuse leaves do a perfect job of tying together yellows, greens, and blues.

A final point to remember when choosing plants is their eventual size. Again, this is where the beginner can easily go astray. Understandably it's often very hard, when looking at a small plant in a tiny pot, to realize that this little mass of leaves and stems will grow into a plant four feet wide and five feet tall, just as the label says. But rest assured, it will, especially if you've done your job correctly in preparing the soil and choosing plants suitable for the growing conditions in your yard. Thus it's really important to make sure the plants you choose are properly placed in terms of height—tallest material in the rear, middle height in the center, and shortest plants up front—and spaced sufficiently to allow for lateral expansion. And unless you are a genius in keeping hundreds of variables in your head, this means you need to make a detailed perennial planting plan.

Once your color scheme's in place, the easiest way to get started is to draw up a list of plant material suitable to your site and compatible with your chosen color range, arranging these potential selections into three groups: tall, middle, and low. Next, using graph paper or a computer program, make a scale drawing of your site, and begin locating individual plants on your plan. Of course, this is much easier said than done, but in general you are trying to create bands of compatible colors using plants in much the same way an artist creates a watercolor with paints. In fact, several perennial designers I know start their border plans exactly in this manner, filling in spaces with large swatches of color that are pleasing to the eye, then afterward deciding on which plants will fit the bill.

While this may sound counterintuitive, planning the colors first and the plants second actually makes the plant selection process much easier. Done this way, you self-limit your choices and thus avoid another classic beginner's mistake: using too many different kinds of plants in too few numbers. To be at all effective, colors need to be seen in large swatches, and in general this often means using three, five, seven, or even nine individual plants of the same species to create a sufficiently prominent effect. If you take a look at the plan of the Victory Garden border, for instance, you'll notice that only rarely is a single specimen indicated. Most

■ Different strokes for different folks: while the yellow-brown of this rudbeckia and the purplish-red of this phlox aren't exactly my cup of tea, the combination is certainly dramatic.

plants are grouped in combinations of threes, fives, and sevens, and Kip and I agree that if we were ever to do this process again, we would use even fewer species of plants, and more of each type.

And of course, we will *indeed* get to do it again, because perennial borders are always a work in progress. Even professionals rarely get it right the first time, and we are constantly adjusting our combinations, removing plants that failed (or, more often, that we failed to properly plan for in terms of height or color), and adding new varieties that will enhance individual groupings.

Garden Basics:
Perennial Maintenance

COMMON GARDENING LORE HAS IT THAT PERENNIALS are easier to maintain than annuals, but that really isn't the case. Both share equal weeding, watering, and fertilizing requirements, and while it's true that annuals require the extra effort of replanting every year, perennial borders certainly aren't exempt from yearly maintenance. Perennial beds must be thoroughly cleared of dead foliage, either in the late fall or very early in the spring before the first spring bulbs emerge. When exactly you embark on this mission depends entirely on personal preference: some people like the look of the seed heads and stalks in the winter, especially when they catch the snow, and feel that the garden appears barren when swept clean of any plant material. Other people maintain that the garden looks messy with all that dead foliage hanging around, and argue that pests and disease problems are reduced by the prompt removal of spent foliage in the fall. This last belief is one we've found to be especially true with a few plants, such as iris (over winter, the dreaded iris borer larvae are found in their dead leaves), but less certain with the majority of perennials. There's also the issue of resetting perennials. Once every four to six years, the entire border must be dug out (generally in the early spring); overcrowded plants

■ **The last rite of fall: Kip cutting down the dead perennial stalks after the first freeze.**

must be divided; the soil must be replenished with ample quantities of manure and compost to insure optimal bloom; and the entire border must be replanted. All this adds up to a lot of work any way you look at it—very much worth it, but still a lot of work.

Ask Michael:
Best Time to Plant or Transplant Perennials?

Dear Michael,
I'm confused: should I divide and transplant my perennials in the
fall or in the spring? The books I read seem to offer contradictory
advice.

For years I've been reading about the benefits of fall perennial planting and transplanting, and I can certainly understand its appeal. Anytime you can shift a horticultural task from the already overloaded spring to the much more relaxed autumn, you're undoubtedly ahead of the game. However, fall planting, especially when you're dividing or transplanting material, is not always the best choice. We've found that here in our Zone 6 New England garden, for instance, fall planting can be extremely risky and result in huge losses if the cold weather sets in earlier than expected. In this scenario plants just don't have enough time to establish sufficient root growth before the ground freezes, and they winterkill. The risk diminishes the farther south you go, but for most of the central and northern part of the country east of the Rockies fall planting should be avoided, especially if transplanting. One of the few exceptions to this advice is peonies: peonies can only be dug and transplanted in the fall.

An Annual Affair

SO FAR WE'VE BEEN TALKING PRETTY MUCH EXCLUSIVELY about perennials, but annuals play a substantial role in the landscape as well. Freed from the worry of surviving to live another season, annuals pour their energies into a flowery blast of color from early summer right through to frost, which for those of you in warmer areas of the country can sometimes mean

right up to Christmas and beyond. This performance makes annuals invaluable anytime a lot of flower power is needed—in container gardens, for instance, or in cutting gardens, and/or interspersed among the perennials to boost the drama of the display. Without annuals, in fact, we'd be doomed to having entire areas of the garden fall out of flower for large sections of the year.

So why not just garden with annuals exclusively? Well, you can, and to some extent, here at the Victory Garden we do. Right behind Kip's office is a parterre garden devoted entirely to annuals. Every spring, Kip spends hours scouring the catalogues and selecting varieties to combine for the best possible display. Then he orders the seeds, grows his own plants, sets them out, and tends the garden over the course of the summer. Fortunately these days that means mostly just weeding and watering, though that wasn't always the case. Until fairly recently, many annual varieties required deadheading—the removal of the spent blossoms—in order to continue flowering. If allowed to set seed and fulfill their purpose, they stopped blooming entirely. This, of course, was a tedious and time-consuming task, and one of the main reasons large annual gardens remained relegated to the Victorian era with its endless supply of cheap labor. Nowadays, however, most annuals are truly ever-blooming and many require little if any deadheading, a result of selective breeding that makes them much more attractive to the time-pressed gardener.

The annual result of all this annual labor never fails to teach us (and thus, if we've done our job right, you) many valuable lessons about growing individual varieties, as well as providing an excellent introduction to the incredible number of new varieties continually arriving on the market.

The trouble with massive annual gardening is largely the issue of practicality, both in terms of time and money. Gardens planted completely with annuals are expensive, as the entire cast of characters needs to be replaced each season. There's also an issue of availability. Many of the best annuals grown today are available only as seed from specialty cata-

■ The annual garden behind Kip's office, surrounded by containers also planted with annuals. The white plants in the foreground are *Matricaria* 'White Wonder' and *Zinnia* 'Star White,' set off by the blue of *Ageratum* 'Blue Horizon.' In the area above, white *Erigeron* 'Profusion' and the pink geranium 'Black Velvet Rose' are combined with the tall *Salvia* 'Sea Breeze.'

logues, and will never appear at your local garden center. That means to have some of these beauties in your garden, you'll need to search through the catalogs for seed and grow your own (or convince a local specialty grower to raise them for you). While not difficult (see Weekend Project, pages 180–181), starting your own annuals does require a certain amount of time and commitment on your part, as well as sufficient space and facilities to get your seedlings prepared to face the great outdoors.

Using Flowers in the General Landscape

FOR THOSE OF YOU WITHOUT TIME OR INCLINATION TO create dedicated flower beds, there is one other option: incorporating flowers into the general landscape. And quite frankly, this is something we should all be doing in any case. For reasons I've never quite understood, there's a certain hesitancy among gardeners to include herbaceous flowers among other types of general plantings, especially foundation and perimeter beds. It's almost as if people feel that flowers don't have a sufficient pedigree to be included with woody plantings. Nothing could be further from the truth.

If, for instance, you've followed our advice for foundation plantings, using wide beds of materials in descending heights, perennials and/or annuals are ideal to front the border, providing a burst of much-needed color as well as the softening effect of delicate foliage. Remember, as we've discussed previously, the idea behind foundation plantings is not to line up a single row of shrubs against a wall, but rather to make the house appear as if it were set down by magic in the midst of a garden. Flowers are ideal for this.

Flowers in containers are another great way to get the benefit of bloom without the bed, and have the added advantage of portability and replaceability. For instance, here at the Victory Garden, each season we pot up a considerable number of flowering containers for use on the various terraces and porches around the house. The great thing about these containers is that if a plant isn't looking its best, or if the shifting season makes you long for a change, a quick makeover is as close as the nearest potting bench. Generally, we switch the containers three times during the course of the year: once in spring, then in early summer, and finally in early fall. This annual ritual is one of my favorite tasks in the garden, as removing the worn, tired flowers and replacing them with fresh blossoms offers immediate gardening gratification.

Finally, if you're a vegetable gardener, don't forget about in-

BEST BETS

Marigold 'Snowball.'

ANNUALS

Ageratum 'Blue Horizon': Fairly tall at 16"–18", its new blooms do a good job of masking spent flowers, obviating deadheading. Works well as a cut flower and stays in scale when combined with other bedding annuals.

Geranium 'Black Velvet Rose': The brilliant flowers are nicely offset by the very dark zonal leaves.

Gomphrena 'Woodcreek Rose': An everlasting, its flowers don't fade away, but persist as new ones are added.

Marigold 'Snowball': The best of the so-called whites, though actually more of a cream, an aspect that makes it even more valuable in the border.

Salvia coccinea 'Cherry Blossom': The bicolor flowers are lovely and prolific on this tallish (18"+) open-structured plant.

Salvia farinacea 'Sea Breeze': The blue-white bicolor spikes are a refreshing alternative to the old standard 'Victoria.'

Sweet alyssum 'Snow Crystals': Absolutely the best of the whites, its flowers are large for the species and are produced freely; the result is more of a plush quilt than a carpet.

Vinca 'Blue Pearl': The soft lavender-blue flowers are a pleasant break from the usual colors of the species.

Zinnia angustifolia 'Star White': Less susceptible than other species to foliage disease, it produces hundreds of flowers on a compact plant and outperforms the other standard 'Crystal White' in our garden.

cluding flowers in the vegetable patch. Not only are flowers a welcome sight in the vegetable garden, but placing a varied and bright profusion of blooms among the veggies solves the problem of finding sufficient space to grow cutting flowers for indoor use. After having worked so hard to create a harmonious display, many gardeners are loath to cut from the general border. But if you include some of your favorite flowers along with the vegetables, you in effect create a small cutting garden in between your vegetable rows, making it easy to harvest a few blooms each time you venture out to pick a few tomatoes or beans.

In terms of flower selection for cutting, choose whatever flowers you find most pleasing: annuals like dahlias, zinnias, celosia, or sunflowers; perennials such as iris and peonies; bulbs like lilies or tulips; or a combination of all three. When choosing plants, don't forget to include those with interesting foliage to use as fillers.

Many of the ornamental grasses, for instance, are ideal for this, as are plants with textured leaves such as ferns, or those with subtly colored blossoms such as lady's mantle.

■ **Simple and dramatic: sometimes less is more in container plantings, especially if the plant material has a strong sculptural form, like these agaves.**

CREATING A MASSED TULIP DISPLAY

Ever wonder how the Dutch create those spectacular tulip displays? Well, so did we, and we set out make our own here at the Victory Garden. As we discovered, the process is not particularly challenging, but it does involve some very careful planning, some very precise planting, and *a lot* of tulips—more than 1,500 in fact. Here's how to go about it:

■ Step one: After deciding on a color scheme, and carefully selecting tulips with similar bloom times and appropriate heights (tulips vary widely in each category, so you need to plan carefully), we laid out grid lines traced in the soil to make sure the bulbs were positioned precisely. It's important that the beds be well drained; waterlogged soil is lethal to tulips.

■ Step two: Here are the bulbs laid out before planting. Placing the bulbs on the soil first allows you to make sure each variety of bulb is placed in its proper location.

■ Step three: Carefully plant the bulbs one at a time, at least six inches deep—and dedicate several hours to the process!

■ And voilà! Instant color in the spring. One caveat though: most modern tulips are essentially annuals, so this kind of display is a one-time—though admittedly spectacular—affair. After blooming, the bulbs here were dug out, composted, and the space planted with summer annuals. (See the next page for what this looks like.)

Growing Annuals from Seed

■ **Kip filling the flats with soilless mix.**

ANNUALS ARE GENERALLY DIVIDED INTO THREE GROUPS: hardy, half-hardy, and tender. Hardy species can withstand several degrees of frost and thus may be planted outdoors well before the frost-free date. Half-hardy annuals will tolerate a light frost. Tender annuals should be started indoors or, where summers are long, may be seeded directly into prepared beds.

There's no great trick to sowing annuals directly into the garden; just follow the directions on the seed packet. Emerging seedlings will need to be monitored closely to make sure they do not dry out or become snacks for opportunistic insects. Some annuals, such as lavatera, actually perform better sown directly outdoors.

For annuals that *do* require the extra coddling of indoor planting, the first step is to get things organized: you'll need a long table or bench in an area like a greenhouse, basement, or garage where you won't mind spilling a bit of dirt on the floor. Access to water is also important (a hose is really best, but a watering can will do). You'll also need a few trays that are about two inches deep. I use special plastic seed starter trays called flats, which have clear plastic lids and are available at most garden shops or home centers. These trays come in two types: open, undivided units, and divided units that have a series of small compartments. The open trays will require you to transplant the plants into larger pots as they grow—using the compartmentalized trays will eliminate this unnecessary step and is a great timesaver.

Finally, you'll need soilless mix. This special potting mix is typically a combination of peat moss and vermiculite, and has the advantages of retaining moisture and being sterile. Young seedlings are particularly susceptible to a fungal disease called dampening off, which causes the little stems to rot away at the base. Using a sterile mixture helps avoid this problem. Don't use regular potting soil, or soil from the garden, as this will just lead to more problems later on.

Fill your containers with the soilless mix (see Step 1). Then water them thoroughly, and allow them to drain. (Watering first prevents the seeds from washing away after planting.) Sowing large seeds is easy. You make a small indentation in the soilless

Make a small indentation in each cell.

Select about three seeds for each cell (then cover to their thickness with mix).

Kip gently watering the seeds several days after planting. Although the spray looks heavy in this picture, it's actually quite fine, and Kip is holding the rose head deliberately far away from the flat to minimize any disturbance to the surface of the soil.

mix with your thumb (see Step 2). Then separate out three seeds from a handful (see Step 3) and place them into the indentation. Cover them with a layer of soilless mix. Although the exact depth varies from variety to variety, seeds should generally be buried to a depth twice their diameter. Burying them any deeper can prevent germination. Extremely small seeds can simply be scattered on the soil surface and pressed in gently with your hand or a wooden block, and then covered with a clear plastic lid or plastic wrap to seal in the moisture. Several days after planting, water the seed flats again. Use a fine spray and hold the hose head far from the flat to minimize any disturbance to the soil (Step 4).

Though some seeds need light for germination, the most critical factor is soil temperature. Most annual seeds need a fairly warm, constant soil temperature—about 70 degrees—in order to germinate successfully. This is nature's built-in safety mechanism to prevent seeds from sprouting before outside temperatures have risen sufficiently to support the plant. One of the best ways to achieve adequate warmth is to use one of the special heat mats found at any nursery or garden shop. These devices are like little electric blankets that sit under the

flats keeping the soil, and the seeds, at a constant, cozy temperature. Place the flats and pad in a sunny space (fluorescent lights hung three to four inches above the flats will do in a pinch), check the flats daily, and water gently when the soil begins to dry, which when covered with plastic may take several days to a week. Remove the lids from the flats after germination, and water again only when required.

Once your seeds have sprouted and are several inches high, they may need to be thinned out. As the nighttime lows warm into the 40s, it's time to move your plants closer to the garden, though they shouldn't be put directly outside. Seeds sunburn easily and need time to get adjusted to the higher light levels and temperature swings found outdoors. A good transition is to place them in a cold frame for several weeks, remembering to keep them well watered, and to make arrangements to raise and lower the frame top as temperatures move up and down outside. (Young annuals are completely intolerant of frost or high heat and will quickly freeze or burn if exposed to extreme temperatures.) Once all danger of frost is past, it will be time to transplant your charges into the garden.

Step by Step: Preparing a New Flower Bed

Soil sample

The very first step in starting a new garden—whether it be for flowers, shrubs, or vegetables—is to take a soil sample for testing from your proposed beds. This should be done several weeks before your planned excavation, as you'll want to allow yourself adequate time to acquire whatever soil amendments (see page 48) you may need well ahead of your digging date.

Remove sod

If your intended beds are currently covered with grass, the next step will be to remove the sod. Although you may be tempted to simply bury or till in the sod, don't; all of those little bits and pieces of grass near the surface will simply try to reroot and create an instant weed nightmare. Instead, remove the grass by taking a sharp spade and cutting out a 2' × 2' square. Then slide the blade horizontally under the

roots to separate the grass from the soil, and place the grass in a wheelbarrow. (Old sod makes excellent fodder for the compost pile.) If, however, the area is large, you may want to rent a sod remover that will cut and strip the soil away for you.

Once the bed has been cleared of all plant material, loosen the soil thoroughly using a spading fork (see illustration 1).

Add amendments

Once the soil has been thoroughly loosened, and you have your soil analysis in hand, add the necessary soil amendments directly to the top of the soil. These amendments will likely include peat moss as well as fertilizer, which should be evenly cast over the bed (see illustration 2).

3

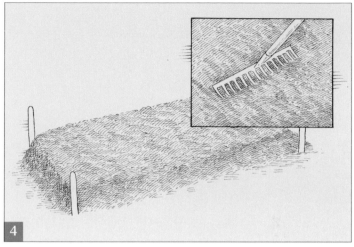

4

The amendments should then be dug in thoroughly. This may be done manually using the spading fork again (see illustration 3), or with the modern convenience of the rototiller. If you want to go the extra mile, nothing provides such depth or superb mixing as the age-old double-digging method. The only problem is that double digging is extremely labor intensive, requiring not only time, but a very strong back as well. To double dig a bed, divide the area into a series of two-foot rows and remove the earth in the first row, placing the soil in several carts or wheelbarrows. Amend the soil at the bottom of the trench you've dug. Next, take the soil from the second row and deposit it into the first, mixing in amendments as you go. Then amend the second trench and place the soil from the third into the second, and so on. To fill the last row, use the soil in the wheelbar-

rows. By the time you're done, you will not only have created a superbly prepared bed twice as deep as beds made using the spading fork or the rototiller alone, but will also have worked off quite a number of calories!

Level the bed

Whatever method you use, when done you should level off the finished bed using a rake (see illustration 4).

One final note: don't be too concerned if, when adding large quantities of organic matter for the first time, the final soil level of your new bed is several inches higher than the surrounding area. Organic matter decomposes quickly, and in most cases, given some time and a few soaking rains, the ground will soon lose some loft and settle closer to its starting point. If for some reason the difference in grade is still a problem, you can retain the bed with some type of edging. If the bed abuts a lawn, then you may simply "air-prune"—use an edging tool to cut a narrow, shallow trench where bed and sod meet.

183

Inspired
Gardens

The Boerner Botanical Gardens, Milwaukee, Wisconsin

IF YOU'RE INTERESTED IN DESIGNING WITH PERENNIALS, one of the best ways to get a feel for the subject is to visit local gardens and see how other gardeners take individual plants and weave them into the magical creation that is a perennial border. And if you're anywhere near Milwaukee, Wisconsin, you're in luck, because one the best examples of formal styled perennials borders in the United States is located there, at the Boerner Botanical Gardens.

First conceived in the late 1920s, the more than 600-acre garden and surrounding park came very close to never existing. Originally purchased by Milwaukee County in 1929, the land sat fallow through the early part of the Great Depression, a victim of the nationwide catastrophe. Fortunately, Milwaukee County's landscape architect, Alfred L. Boerner, saw past the dark days of the crisis and pushed the project through to completion as a mark of faith "not only for ourselves, but for our children and grandchildren." Harnessing the combined forces of the Federal Works Progress Administration (WPA) and the Civilian Conservation Corps (CCC), Boerner and hundreds of workers sculpted a magnificent set of gardens from

■ A stone seat and two topiaried euonymous (*Euonymus alata*) lend a Mediterranean flair to this Zone 5 garden.

what had been empty fields of corn stubble. Today's visitor will find a rose garden (now home to the American Rose Selection test trials); a bog garden and nature walk; a rock garden, created from an old gravel pit with 1,000 tons of weathered limestone; an herb garden; a massive annual garden; as well as numerous fountains, walks, and waterfalls, and a handcrafted stone garden house.

Perhaps most remarkable of all are the two formal perennial borders that flank the Garden House. Over 100 feet long and 10 feet wide, these beds now contain more than 1,260 different varieties of perennials, providing visitors with a sequence of bloom that begins with the earliest bulbs in the spring and ends in autumn with the last of the fall perennials. Not only are these borders an ideal place to see the artistry of good perennial design at work, but the adjacent trial gardens give the visitor an invaluable insight into how individual plants will perform in tricky Midwestern growing conditions.

Today, Boerner Botanical Gardens carries on the tradition of forward thinking initiated by Alfred Boerner with the recent addition of a massive new Visitors and Education Center (along with accompanying gardens), designed to promote excellence in Midwestern gardening. This new center, combined with the beds and borders of the Botanical Gardens, make the site a mecca for anyone desiring to use the magic of perennials in their own landscape.

■ There are few things more delightful than the first tomatoes of summer. Here, the variety 'Favorita' hangs, tantalizingly on the vine at the Victory Garden.

Chapter 7
The Edible Garden

To get the best results you must talk to your vegetables.

HRH PRINCE CHARLES

Quoted in *The Observer*, September 1986

Why Grow Your Own?

IN THIS DAY AND AGE, WITH A SUPERMARKET ON EVERY corner and fresh produce available in abundance year-round, you may be wondering why on earth you'd want to grow your own vegetables. Well, there are several very good reasons, but I suppose the primary one is flavor. If you have ever bitten into a tomato still warmed by the sun, or felt that delightful snap as you picked your own succulent asparagus, you'll understand that there is no possible way that anything from a store—or even a farm stand—will ever taste as good as produce that is brought directly from your garden to your table. Even within a few hours of picking, vegetables begin to lose their flavor.

■ **The Spanish onion, one of our favorite members of the extensive onion clan.**

190

Growing your own closes that gap and puts you first in line for an incredible culinary adventure.

The second reason is variety. Did you know, for instance, that there are hundreds of different kinds of tomatoes, each bred for a specific purpose—some for eating out of hand, some for sauce, some for storage, and even some for stuffing? The same is true for cucumbers, corn, lettuce, peas, and squash. Each has numerous tasty cultivars perfect for specific uses that you'll never see at the store. The sad fact of the matter is that most produce in the market today is bred not for specific use, or even for flavor, but for shelf life and appearance. That means if you're interested in some of these hard-to-find varieties, you'll have to grow them yourself.

Finally, there's the emotional reward of growing your own food. There is nothing quite so satisfying as going out to your garden at sunset and harvesting the well-grown cabbage or carrot or cucumber you've raised for yourself, and then seasoning your prize with aromatic snippets fresh from the herb patch.

In fact, there is only one reason I can think of *not* to grow your own produce—the moderate effort involved—but I can also assure you, once you have tasted the fruit of your own garden, you'll never be happy again with what's presented to you in the local market.

Selecting the Site

PERHAPS THE MOST CRITICAL FACTOR FOR SUCCESS IN the vegetable garden is choosing the right location. The garden *must* be situated in the sunniest part of the yard. (The old adage is to locate your vegetable garden in the same place you'd want a swimming pool to be.) Sun is key: what you get out of the vegetable garden is directly related to how much solar energy goes into it. With anything less than six full hours of direct sunlight, the results will be marginal at best. If you are forced to choose, morning light is preferable to afternoon light, because on torrid summer days plant metabolism begins to shut down, and so any light that's received later in the day simply goes to waste. The site of a vegetable garden must also be well drained, meaning that the cultivated beds should be free of standing water at all times, even after a heavy rain.

■ **The Victory Garden vegetable garden mid summer. The tents here are protecting the Swiss chard and cucumbers from the beet leaf miner and striped cucumber beetle, respectively. This simple method is almost 100 percent effective.**

Preparing the Soil

IF YOU ARE OPENING A BED IN NEW GROUND, YOU'LL want to remove the sod, if any, and take a soil test, which will determine how much extra preparation the soil will need. Vegetables are extremely heavy feeders (they have to be in order to produce a bountiful harvest) and in most cases, that means you'll need to add lots of organic matter. (See Chapter Two for more on this subject.)

Though the use of peat moss as a soil amendment has become somewhat controversial in recent years (there is active debate on the renewability of the peat bogs that provide the moss), here at the Victory Garden we still like to use peat when preparing new beds, spreading a couple of inches or more evenly throughout.

Unlike other organic materials like compost that are full of living organisms, peat moss is a biologically inactive organic material. Thus, it won't "evaporate" quite as quickly as other organic materials have a tendency to do, providing what in the short term gardeners of old used to call "tilth"—improved soil consistency and quality. We also try to add generous amounts of compost along with the peat during the initial soil preparation.

It's at this beginning point, and at this time alone, that you should use a rototiller in the vegetable garden. Obviously, using a machine at this initial stage results in a huge saving of time and effort, allowing you to quickly blend the amendments into the soil. But there are some distinct disadvantages to tillers as well, the principal one being the risk of overtilling of the soil. Too much rototiller use can destroy the soil's structure, turning it into a homogenized amalgam with the consistency of that smoothie you had for breakfast.

Which means that here at the Victory Garden at least, all tilling subsequent to the initial soil prep is done with a spading fork. Of course this is rather time-consuming, but it's more than worth it, as spading by hand cultivates the soil without destroying its structure. And once your soil is in tip-top shape, never tread on already prepared beds! Compaction defeats all the work you've just achieved by closing the air pockets in the soil necessary to convey water and nutrients to plant roots. Simply put, compacted soil means a poor harvest.

Organic versus Inorganic at the Victory Garden

ONE OF THE QUESTIONS PEOPLE ASKED US MOST frequently is whether or not we grow our vegetables organically on the show. The answer is to a great extent, yes, though not completely. Naturally, we don't have any particular desire for pesticide residues on the food we eat, nor do Kip and I relish handling toxic concentrates, but if we're faced with problems that can't be dealt with by other means, narrowly targeted chemical options, preferably from organically based compounds like pyrethrins, are something we do utilize on occasion.

When it comes to fertilizer, nothing is automatically ruled out either. For many years, ordinary 10-10-10 was the mainstay at the Victory Garden. When used with a practiced eye and a sparing hand, excess soluble nitrate buildup both in the soil and in runoff should not be a problem. The trick, of course, is to apply only the amount the plants can actually utilize. It takes some skill to get this right, but if the base soil has been adequately provided with rich organic matter, you shouldn't have to worry if you err on the lean side when adding supplemental granular plant food.

In years past, we also made use of a low-analysis fertilizer based on chicken manure. More recently we've gone over to a 5-5-5 formula self-described as "organic"—meaning that the ni-

trogen is in a chelated form, rather than in the form of soluble salts. In addition, we make extensive use of a completely non-soluble fertilizer containing substances such as bone meal and Milorganite. It's not a bad idea, when two or three fertilizers of different compositions are available, to use them in combination with each other.

Some heavy-feeding crops that stand a long time in the field—sweet corn in particular—may require a side dressing sometime during the growing season. Other crops such as lettuce, peppers, and carrots seem to do fine even without any additional fertilizer. The organic matter we've provided, plus residual nutrients from prior use of the beds for other crops, is all that's normally needed.

Design Basics: Laying Out a Vegetable Garden

VEGETABLE GARDENS ARE USUALLY LAID OUT IN straight parallel rows. To some extent, this is a carryover from times when the farmer had to guide his team back and forth across his fields. Though "horsepower" now appears in the vegetable garden only in the mechanical sense, linear layouts are still a good idea. Straight, ample rows make common garden chores like pushing a wheelbarrow or harvesting the crops much easier than narrow, twisting pathways.

Although exact design will vary according to your site requirements, in general your planting beds should be no more than four feet wide, allowing for easy reach into the middle of the beds from either side. It's also a good idea not to make your beds so long that it takes half the morning to walk from one side to the other; consider instead breaking up long stretches of beds with intersecting perpendicular paths.

Ideally, the paths between the beds should be about two feet wide. If you make them any wider you waste tillable ground you can ill afford to lose; any narrower and you may find it very difficult to work between the rows, especially by midsummer, when plants have a tendency to sprawl. At the Vic-

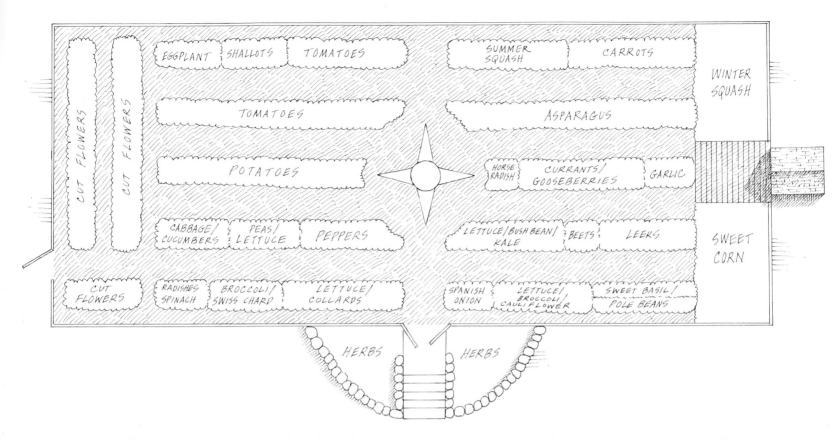

■ The layout of the Victory Garden vegetable beds, as they appear today. I designed the garden, with its central stone medallion, grass walks, white fencing, and decorative cedar tool shed, to be both useful and good-looking all year round.

tory Garden, our paths are made of grass. Gravel, mulch, or even hard paving are all other options, depending on how fancy you want your garden to appear.

There has been a lot of debate in gardening circles about whether or not vegetable beds should be raised. Here at the Garden, we find that at least a few inches of height is beneficial, both in terms of drainage and allowing the soil to warm up slightly faster in the spring. Contrary to what many people expect, a raised bed does not need to be enclosed by timbers or any other material. If the raised beds are as flat and level as possible with their sides sloping at a 45-degree angle, and if the soil is in good condition, gravity will hold the soil in place, and rain will pass right through without causing erosion.

Ready, Set, Seed

WITH SOME EXCEPTIONS, SUCH AS ASPARAGUS, horseradish, and rhubarb, which are perennials purchased ei-

ther bare-rooted or in pots, the vegetables grown in the vegetable garden are annuals or biennials started from seed.

Seeds can of course be purchased from a variety of sources, but one of the best ways to access the incredible possibilities out there is to shop through catalogs. These days there are literally hundreds of catalogs from which to choose, even some that specialize exclusively in single species such as tomatoes, peppers, or potatoes, offering hundreds of different varieties.

It's this plethora of choices, though, that often gets the beginning gardener into trouble: there are so many possible selections that the process can quickly become overwhelming. One good way to narrow your choices is to find catalogs with a local or regional bias, especially if it is clear that the seed company conducts vegetable trials and perhaps even develops new cultivars through their own breeding program. This way you get the benefit of years of experience without having to test out unfamiliar varieties in your own garden.

Another way to narrow down your catalog choices is to dis-

■ **This venerable seed box has helped organize the Victory Garden for more than 20 years.**

card those that give descriptions without substance. Glowing phrases like "delicious," "produces fantastic yields," and "superlative" lose their significance when constantly repeated. If you're finding too many of these kinds of descriptions, and very little else, then perhaps you should consider shopping elsewhere. On the other hand, those that possess statements about "resistance to diseases" or give indications of "innovative advances in breeding" are certainly worthy of your attention. The point of growing your own produce, after all, is usually less about subsistence than about bringing to the table food items of extraordinary quality or tantalizing novelty, and it pays to find catalogs that help you do just that.

Once you have your seeds in hand, the next step is to organize your selections by what needs to be planted and when, exactly as you would with flowers. If you are planning only a few crops, that's pretty easy. At the Victory Garden, however, we've learned from long experience that we need to pay close atten-

tion to the hundreds of different varieties we grow. Some have a planting window of only a week or two, which if missed means they're done for that season. So Kip has created a rather ingenious box that he uses year after year to organize his seeds.

Vegetable seed starting begins earlier than you might think. Because many common crops have extremely long growing seasons, seed starting begins in late winter and early spring, months before it would be safe to do so outside. Early starters include leeks, onions, tomatoes, peppers, eggplant, and even the first crops of lettuce, broccoli, and cabbage. While these don't absolutely have to be started indoors, they benefit immeasurably from getting a head start.

The techniques for starting most vegetables indoors are exactly the same as those used for starting ornamental annuals (see Annuals, page 180). The vegetable season commences in February with the sowing of leeks, and is followed shortly thereafter with our first crops of lettuce and broccoli in the greenhouse. For a complete list of what we sow, how, and when, see the master vegetable table on pages 201–206.

The real key to this seed starting process is our greenhouse. Unfortunately, without a cold frame, greenhouse, or some other venue such as an artificial light table for raising seedlings, you'll need to purchase already started plants at a local nursery. This means that you'll be limited to the varieties offered at the garden center, or to those crops such as carrots, radishes, spinach, and a few others that can be sown directly into the soil outdoors. If you have strong preferences in regard to cultivars you would like to raise in your garden, however, it is worth trying to persuade your local professional grower to carry them. Often their selections are based on little other than established habit or personal preference, and if you give them enough lead time, they will be more than happy to order whatever you'll need. There is one caveat, however: vegetables mass-produced in six-packs, especially the smaller-sized type that come eight to the flat, sometimes suffer through growing conditions that are less than ideal. Rugged, weedy plants like tomatoes usually recover from the stress of cramped roots rather easily, but others—broccoli and cauliflower, for instance—may be permanently affected, resulting in a poor crop or none at all. The moral of the story: if there is any way for you to contrive sufficient growing space, you should really try to grow your own.

■ **The Victory Garden cold frames. After the weather warms and the seedlings are set out in the garden, we remove and store the covers. This area then becomes the perfect place for growing heat-loving crops like melons.**

Step by Step: Building a Cold Frame

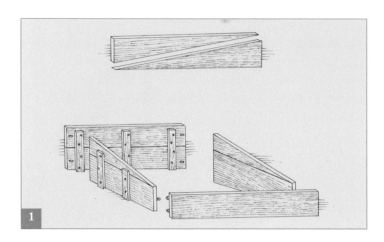

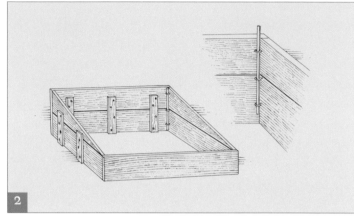

ADDING A COLD FRAME TO YOUR GARDEN CAN significantly lengthen your growing season. Instead of having to wait until it is warm enough to sow seeds outdoors, or the costlier alternative of purchasing plants that have already been started at nurseries, you can sow your seeds early in flats and set them out in a cold frame to grow. Essentially a mini solar-powered greenhouse, cold frames provide ideal protection for young seedlings in their transition to the outdoors.

Although many ready-made catalog versions are now available, including some very cleverly designed fabric types that can be folded away at the end of the season, they are often quite expensive. If you're the handy type, a quick and easy (and more durable) cold frame is just an hour or two away.

To build a cold frame, you'll need the following materials:

- 32 feet of pressure-treated one-by-one
- 8-foot pieces of pressure-treated two-by-eight (3)
- 1¼-inch galvanized box nails
- 10 galvanized eye screws
- 4-foot piece of ½-inch dowel (1)

- 8-foot pieces of pressure-treated two-by-four (2)
- 4 × 4-foot piece of 2 × 4-inch mesh galvanized dog wire (1)
- ¾-inch galvanized #14 staples
- 4 × 4-foot piece of 4-mil plastic sheeting (1)
- heavy-duty galvanized or brass loose-pin hinges (2)
- 4 × ⅜-inch carriage bolt (1)
- 8-foot piece of pressure-treated one-by-four (1)
- 3-inch galvanized corner brackets (4)
- 8-foot wooden battens, ¼ × 1½ inches (2)
- 1½-inch galvanized #8 screws (36)

1. Assemble the front, back, and side pieces

Cut a 48½-inch two-by-eight diagonally, as shown. The cut can be made with a table saw, or by using a circular saw with a cutting guide tacked in place. These diagonals will eventually become the slanting top pieces of the cold frame.

Next, cut the cold frame sides, front and back, from two-by-

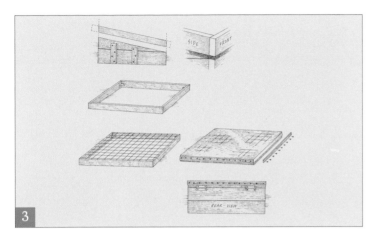

eight lumber. For the sides, cut two pieces 45 ½ inches long. For the front, cut one piece 48 ½ inches long. For the back, cut two pieces, 48 ½ inches long.

Now assemble the sides by nailing one-by-three cleats in place, as shown. Assemble the two back pieces the same way.

2. Add dowels for easy assembly and disassembly

Insert eye screws near the ends of the sides, front, and back. Connect the four sections together by threading half-inch wooden dowels through the aligned eye screws. These dowels can be removed to easily disassemble and transport the cold frame when not in use.

3. Frame the cold frame top

Cut two-by-four lumber for the cold frame top. The two side pieces should be 45 ½ inches long. The front and back pieces should be 48 ½ inches long. Note that the ends of the side pieces should be cut at an angle to align with the side pieces of the base.

Nail or screw the four top pieces together. Then cover the top of the frame with galvanized wire fencing (with four-inch holds) and staple the fencing to the two-by-fours with galvanized staples.

4. Complete the cold frame

Lay clear plastic (polyethylene sheeting) over the fencing, cut so that there is a three-inch overlap of plastic all around. Fix the plastic in place by nailing furring strips along the outside of the two-by-four frame. Attach the top to the cold frame box with loose-pin hinges.

The top of the finished cold frame can be held open with an adjustable vent stake secured to the front rail with a carriage bolt and wing nut.

■ The first of the cucumbers begins to emerge. You can just get a glimpse of the cages (tomato towers turned sideways) that keep the fruit off the ground.

Vertical Gardening

MANY CROPS IN THE GARDEN ARE BEST GROWN vertically for efficient use of space. The most famous of these is the indeterminate tomato, with varieties that produce fruit continuously on rampant vines. Allowing them to sprawl on the ground not only would be an inefficient use of garden space but also would tend to promote foliage diseases, making the fruit more vulnerable to rot, not to mention the snacking of interested fauna.

While some people prefer to stake their tomatoes, a process that requires constant pruning and tying, at the Victory Garden we like to use sturdy, long-lasting cages made of concrete-reinforced mesh. These cages are easy to create—all that's required is a roll of steel mesh and a pair of light-duty bolt cutters. Normally the heavy-gauge steel wire is welded to form a 6" × 6" grid. Cut from the roll a piece ten panes (five feet) wide plus the open-ended wires from an eleventh pane. When the piece is bent around on itself and the free end wires folded over the leading vertical wire, you have a cylinder five feet tall and just over 18 inches in diameter. Then cut away the horizontal wire on the bottom to create prongs for insertion into the soil. Because steel is subject to rust, to prolong the life of your tomato cages be sure to store them out of the ground during the winter, stacked horizontally in pyramids. Eventually, even with the best of care, the prongs on the bottom of the cage will rust and break off. When that happens, simply cut off the lowest remaining horizontal wire and continue to use the cage, which will now be a mere six inches shorter than before.

Old tomato cages, even after they have been trimmed a number of times, can still be put to good use. For one thing, short cages are perfect for determinate (nonvining) tomato plants, such as most paste tomatoes. Old cages also serve as perfect staging platforms for cucumbers. Because of constant depredations from the cucumber beetle, a common pest in the eastern part of the country, we can't raise cucumbers the old-fashioned way on trellises—there is simply no easy way to apply a row cover to such a large vertical structure. So Kip found a great compromise, laying old, worn-out cages on their sides. The vines scramble happily over the wires with the fruit suspended a foot or so aboveground, the cages providing enough room for the cucumbers to hang straight and unblemished, while still allowing the vines to be easily tented.

Other vegetables, however, simply have to be grown on a trellis—pole beans are a prime example. Although you occasionally see a traditional tripod, or "teepee" frame, used for this purpose, the vigorous bean vine can become congested at the top where the poles are joined, defeating the main purpose of any trellising system, which is to spread the vines over a broad surface so as to maximize their exposure to sunlight.

Instead we prefer to make trellises out of lengths of one-by-one wooden pieces cut to any desired width and height by screwing them together where the horizontal and vertical pieces intersect. A reasonable size for the apertures is eight to twelve inches square. Another possibility is wire fencing, with six-inch openings that allow easy access to both sides during harvest. We often use nylon netting sold for this use in 5' × 15' units. Two of these placed one above the other provide a 10-foot vertical run that is just right for pole beans. While every type of trellis mentioned here requires two sturdy end posts for support, the nylon mesh needs in addition a horizontal crosspiece at the top to keep it from sagging or even collapsing under the weight of mature plants laden with a heavy crop.

■ The simple bean trellis allows extra room for these ambitious climbers. Here at the Victory Garden, we are growing the pole bean 'Fortex' with sweet basil in front of it. When the bean season is over, the trellis is simply and easily taken down.

Planning to Get the Most from Your Garden

TO MAXIMIZE YOUR VEGETABLE GARDEN SPACE YOU'LL want to keep your plot fully planted, and that involves the practice of crop rotation, which means never planting any botanically related crops in the same bed two years in a row. Following this guideline not only reduces the chance of cross-infection from soil-borne diseases and insect pests, but also allows you to mine the same ground a bit more efficiently by rotating groups with different nutrient requirements.

Here at the Victory Garden crop rotation takes on an added twist, as most of our beds are used for two or more different crops in a single season. Not only does this mean that we have to pay very close attention to soil fertility, but lack of forethought can cause severe scheduling problems. Imagine: it's early July, time to plant a late crop of snap beans, and there is only one open bed in the whole garden—exactly where we planted the beans last year! Situations like this can usually be circumvented by some careful planning with pencil and paper, using a schematic drawing of the vegetable garden layout. We make multiple copies of the base drawing and every season pencil in which crops we intend to assign to particular beds for that year, cross-checking against what went where the year before. The only flaw to this system seems to be remembering in the spring where we stored the plan the previous fall!

STORING SEEDS

If you grow a wide range of vegetables in your garden, buying seeds can get rather expensive. Seeds that are planted out in broad swaths or long rows—such as spinach or carrots—are often quickly used up in a single season, but seeds of plants that require generous spacing—such as lettuce, cabbage, and tomatoes—often end the gardening year with considerable quantities remaining. These seeds can be preserved by storing them in a place where the temperature remains below 50 degrees (a refrigerator is ideal), using reasonably airtight containers such as zip lock bags or in that rapidly disappearing commodity, empty 35-millimeter film canisters. (Just don't forget to label your seeds—they all quickly start to look alike!) Viability, the seed's ability to sprout, varies by species and decreases with time in storage. Tomato and lettuce seed, for instance, will easily keep several years. Brassicas, cucurbits, legumes, and many others should last two years without much reduction in germination. The only exceptions: carrots, parsnips, or any member of the onion family lose their viability too quickly for long-term storage and should be replenished annually from fresh stock.

■ **Red cabbage about to begin forming a head.**

The Victory Garden Vegetables

For over thirty years we have been testing new vegetable varieties appearing in catalogs against the old favorites. This list is the winnowed summary of our experience—our best and brightest. Of course, there is no substitute for your own experience in your own garden. For the most part, specific cultivars are named; sometimes we indicate a type or class of vegetable. With few exceptions, the plants cited here are purchased as seed. Detailed descriptions may be followed by the names of other cultivars deserving honorable mention (HM).

Name	Recommended Varieties	When Sown/ How Grown	Insect/Pest Problems	Insect/Pest Remedies	Comments/ Recommendations
BEETS	Though they are not pretty, for a winter keeper nothing beats the sweetness of 'Long Season.'	Sown directly in the garden three months before first frost.	Beet leaf miner	Lightweight row cover until onset of cool weather	Beets like extra lime; they should not be harvested until they've had a month or more of cool weather.
BROCCOLI	In spring, 'Goliath' and 'Paragon'; for warm-season harvest, 'Windsor'; for fall harvest, 'Arcadia' and 'Eureka.'	Spring crops sown in greenhouse two months before last frost; fall crops sown outdoors in flats three months before first frost.	1. Club root 2. Cabbage butterfly	1. Solarization 2. Bacillus thuringiensis	Grows in rich, well-limed soil.
POLE BEANS	No other pole snap bean we've tried can compare to 'Fortex'; the bigger they get, the better the flavor.	Sown directly in the garden when soil warms up, a week or two after last frost.	Mexican bean beetle	Rotenone/pyrethrin	Requires a sturdy trellis at least eight feet tall.
BUSH SNAP BEANS	'Nickel' is a superb French filet bean, prolific and stringless, which holds its petite size well. HM: 'Derby,' 'Jade.'	Sown directly into garden when the soil warms up.	Same as for pole beans	Same as for pole beans	Successive crops may be sown up until 10 weeks before first frost.
CABBAGE	For long-term storage we've had great success with 'Huron'; fast-growing small-headed types such as 'Dynamo' and 'Savoy Express' are best for fresh eating. HM: 'Gonzales,' 'Arrowhead II.'	Storage types may be sown outdoors in flats 16 weeks before first frost; small-headed types may be sown with the first broccoli and successively thereafter until 10 weeks before the first frost.	Same as for broccoli	Same as for broccoli	Well-limed soil.

Name	Recommended Varieties	When Sown/ How Grown	Insect/Pest Problems	Insect/Pest Remedies	Comments/ Recommendations
CARROTS	Baby carrots such as 'Baby Sweet' are not regular carrots picked young, but those that sweeten up precociously. Most of the carrots we grow are Nantes types: 'Nelson' is sweeter than others during hot weather; 'Bolero' has consistently been outstanding harvested in fall or stored. HM: 'Touchon Deluxe,' 'Scarlet Nantes,' 'Rumba.'	Early sweetening varieties may be planted several weeks before the last frost, directly into the garden. Regular varieties are planted later, three months or so before the first frost.	Small mammals, such as voles	Cats, traps, or poison bait; otherwise a physical barrier, such as hardware cloth dug into the soil along the perimeter of the bed	Cool weather enhances sweetness. The soil must be loose and/or sandy to produce long, well-formed roots.
CAULIFLOWER	'Violet Queen' is no ordinary cauliflower; the heads are purple before cooking and we feel that it tastes much better than the white kind.	Sown in flats along with the fall broccoli, about three months before the first frost.	Same as for broccoli	Same as for broccoli	Purple-headed cauliflower requires no blanching or tying and is delicately textured, needing less cooking time than white cauliflower or broccoli.
CHINESE CABBAGE	We grow it for fall only and think highly of 'China Pride' and 'Lettucy Type.'	Sown in flats outdoors six weeks to two months before first frost.	Same as for broccoli	Same as for broccoli	Spring-sown Chinese cabbage tends to bolt without producing good heads at the onset of warm weather.
COLLARDS	We admire 'Champion' for its compact habit. HM: 'Flash,' 'Hevicrop.'	Sown outdoors in flats two months before the first frost.	Same as for broccoli	Same as for broccoli	A month or more of cool weather improves the flavor. It is cold-hardy to at least 25 degrees F.
CUCUMBERS	The only types we are partial to these days are bitterfree parthenocarpic varieties: 'Aria,' 'Diva,' 'Sweet Success.'	Sown directly into the garden after the last frost up until 10 weeks before the first frost.	Striped cucumber beetle	Use row cover until the onset of female flowers.	We like to grow them on old tomato cages placed horizontally so that much of the fruit is held off the ground.

Name	Recommended Varieties	When Sown/ How Grown	Insect/Pest Problems	Insect/Pest Remedies	Comments/ Recommendations
EGGPLANT	The most reliably prolific Asian-style variety we have grown is 'Orient Express'; good standard types are 'Black Bell' and 'Classic.'	Sown in flats in the greenhouse two months before the last frost.	Verticillium wilt	Solarization	If the unusual shape and skin color turn your head, most catalogs offer many interesting variations on the more familiar theme.
KALE	'Blue Ridge' and 'Winterbor' are both excellent for harvest from the middle of autumn on.	Sown in flats outdoors about two months before the first frost.	Same as for broccoli	Same as for broccoli	As with collards, cold weather is a benefit.
LEEKS	'Rikor' is a very long early type for fall harvest; 'Arkansas' is a stouter winter-hardy type.	Sown in the green-house, in plug trays, three months before the last frost; moved to the garden two months later.	Occasional onion maggot	Row cover during May	Transplant into six-inch-deep trenches, backfilling as the plants grow taller to blanch the shank.
LETTUCE	'Ermosa,' 'Nancy,' 'Sangria,' 'Buttercrunch' (butterhead); 'St. Blaise,' 'Apollo,' 'Medallion' (Romaine)	Sown in flats—in the greenhouse starting about two months before the last frost, and outdoors when the weather warms up—every two weeks.	Slugs	Various baited molluscicides; beer traps	Proper spacing (about 12 inches) ensures good head development.
ONIONS	Nowadays we grow only large, mild onions such as 'Mars,' 'Super Star,' 'Candy,' and 'Ailsa Craig Exhibition'; 'Copra,' however, is an excellent seed-grown variety for long-term storage, and 'Stuttgarter' the best storage onion from sets.	Sown in plug trays about February 15; set out in mid-April as young plants.	Onion maggot	Row cover	The primary purpose of the row cover is to push the seedlings to produce the most robust plants possible before lengthening days trigger bulb formation. The better you do in the early stages, the larger the onions when harvested in August.
ORIENTAL VEGETABLES	The different kinds of greens available are easy to grow and too numerous to mention; another vegetable, the huge white Chinese Lo Bok radish 'Everest,' is one of our favorites.	Best sown for cool-weather harvest, directly in the garden.	Pests will vary according to the plant species. We have found such problems to be minimal.		Many of the greens can be grown in trays in the green-house for additions to winter salads or stir-fries.

Name	Recommended Varieties	When Sown/ How Grown	Insect/Pest Problems	Insect/Pest Remedies	Comments/ Recommendations
PEAS	'Eclipse' is a new shelling type that holds its sweetness longer than traditional varieties. HM: 'Maestro,' 'Lincoln,' 'Improved Laxton's Progress,' 'Alderman.'	Sow peas, two seeds per cell, into peat strips. The seeds will germinate in about a week inside a moderately warm greenhouse, in 10 to 12 days inside a cold frame; plant the peat strips entire, in shallow trenches as soon as the soil can be worked.	None in our area		The importance of an early start has to do with the pea plant's intolerance to hot weather conditions. Unseasonably warm weather can occur in May or June, compromising crops from later, direct sowings.
PEPPERS	One of the highlights of the summer garden is when our sweet peppers ripen to red or yellow. Varieties abound, and good examples are 'Red Knight,' 'Red Dawn,' 'Yellow Bell II,' and 'Labrador'; 'Laparie' is an excellent Italian ramshorn type. The roster would not be complete without a few hot peppers, notably jalapeños, anchos, or Anaheims, with perhaps a cayenne thrown in for drying.	Sown in flats, in the greenhouse, about two months before frost-free; transplanted outdoors a week or so after all danger of frost has passed.	Most modern peppers have disease resistance bred into them.		Go easy on the fertilizer— it's fruit, not foliage, you're after. And be sure to let the peppers ripen to their full color, when they are at their sweetest.
POTATOES	We've stopped growing 'Yukon Gold,' because they can be had at almost any supermarket. The scores of cultivars available (many of them heirlooms) create a problem for the ambitious gardener. Some must-trys: 'Red Gold,' 'Anoka,' 'Augsburg Gold,' 'German Butterball,' 'Desiree,' and 'Russian Banana.'	Start your seed potato in eight-inch-deep trenches a few weeks before your frost-free date; hill the plants as they grow.	1. Colorado potato beetle 2. Potato leaf hopper	1. Bacillus Thuringiensis var. san diego 2. Rotenone/ pyrethrin	Have your seed potatoes shipped to you several weeks before it's time to plant them out. Set them someplace indoors where they will receive plenty of sunlight and begin to show green sprouts. This will speed their growth once they are planted in the garden.

Name	Recommended Varieties	When Sown/ How Grown	Insect/Pest Problems	Insect/Pest Remedies	Comments/ Recommendations
PUMPKINS	Our friend and heirloom expert Amy Goldman sends us an amazing selection of seeds every year. Varieties we've grown include 'Rouge Vif d'Etampes.'	Sown directly into the garden a week after frost-free date.	Squash vine borer	Use row cover until female flowers appear. Try to get the vines to root along the stem. Apply rotenone to the base of the plant if in doubt.	Try growing some that produce hull-less seeds.
SHALLOTS	'Dutch Yellow' produces good yields of large bulbs that are relatively easy to peel.	Planted shallowly several weeks before frost-free date.	None		Save your best bulbs for planting next year.
SNAP PEAS	Our new favorite is 'Sugar Sprint,' but several other varieties are excellent.	Same culture as with other peas, but starting in peat strips is even more important due to their poor cold-soil vigor.	None		Dried branches, "pea brush," provide valuable support.
SPINACH	'Tyee,' 'Olympia,' and 'Melody.'	Sown directly into the garden as soon as the soil can be worked in the spring and then again six weeks or so before first frost.	Beet leaf miner	Row cover when the fly is active	Spinach is very cold-hardy, and late plantings can be harvested into the winter.
SUMMER SQUASH	Picked young, there is hardly a bad one; we especially like 'Zephyr,' 'Butter Scallop,' and the Middle Eastern cousa types, 'Ghada' and 'Clarita'; for zucchini, our choices are 'Raven' and the amazingly delicious 'Costata Romanesco.'	Sown directly a week after frost-free date. Successive sowings may be made until 10 weeks or so before the first frost.	Same as pumpkin	Since summer squash is a much shorter vine, getting them to root along the stem is much less likely—a second crop is the best way to ensure a continuous supply.	Pick them small and avoid zucchini glut!

Name	Recommended Varieties	When Sown/ How Grown	Insect/Pest Problems	Insect/Pest Remedies	Comments/ Recommendations
SWEET CORN	We do not have specific advice about which of the hundreds of varieties you should grow, just that "sugar enhanced" (se or se+) types are sweeter with longer shelf life than normal types, and compared to the "super sweets" have better early seed vigor and do not require isolation.	Planting time varies according to type and depending when you would like to harvest.	Corn earworm and European corn borer	Bacillus thuringiensis subspecies kurstaki	Plant a sufficient number of rows to allow for wind pollination.
SWISS CHARD	The smaller stature of 'Silverado' makes it perfect for growing under row cover.	Sown indoors in flats a month or more before frost-free date, or outdoors in mid-May,	Same as beets	Same as beets	Nine plants spaced 15 inches apart should be plenty for a small army.
TOMATOES	It would be nearly impossible to give a full account of praiseworthy tomatoes we have grown. 'Brandywine' is essential, and its modern counterpart, 'Brandy Boy,' shows great promise, but we like 'Rose' even better. Our favorite cherry tomato is 'Favorita.' HM: 'Yellow Brandywine,' 'Evergreen,' 'Garden Peach.'	Sown indoors two months before frost-free date.	Most modern varieties have disease resistance bred into them.	For leaf blights, sadly, there is no cure, though keeping the foliage as dry as possible is a reasonable preventive measure, as is fungicidal soap containing copper.	The easiest way to grow tomatoes is in cylindrical cages made from concrete-reinforced mesh.
WINTER SQUASH	For ease of culture and best eating quality we prize butternut squash, especially 'Butternut Supreme.' HM: 'Cornell's Bush Delicata,' 'Sweet Dumpling,' 'ChaCha,' 'Sunshine.'	Same as pumpkin.	Same as pumpkin	Same as pumpkin	Butternut squash is resistant to the borer, and according to many the best-flavored of them all.

Growing Culinary Herbs in the Vegetable Garden

GROWING HERBS, A HUMAN ACTIVITY PROBABLY AS ancient as gardening itself, is as popular today as it has ever been. Though culinary herbs are probably the first to come to mind, there are many other themes: medicinal herbs, herbs grown for intense fragrance, and herbs from literature and lore, to name but a few. Many herb gardens are strictly ornamental, from the very formal and intricate knot gardens to the most informally staged swaths and swatches of soothing blues, greens, and grays.

Here at the Victory Garden, our emphasis has always been on herbs for use at the table, and these we like to grow right alongside the vegetables, for several reasons. The first is that just like vegetables, many of the most common culinary herbs either are annuals or are treated like annuals, and that makes them easy to grow alongside the veggies that require similar culture. The second reason is an aesthetic one: the heavy harvesting of herbs for the table often isn't the prettiest of processes, especially in an ornamental garden. Thus, for those varieties we really like to cut in quantity, such as fresh basil for pesto, or parsley for gremollata, the vegetable garden setting—where we can snip, snip, snip to our hearts' content—is ideal.

Here's a table of the herbs we grow en masse in the vegetable garden, with some suggestions on culture; without exception these can also be grown individually in pots.

■ **Rows of dill, cilantro, and parsley grown in the vegetable bed.**

Name	Recommended Varieties	When Sown/ How Grown	Comments
SWEET BASIL	'Nufar YR,' 'Genovese,' and 'Siam Queen'	Sown in flats, in late spring.	No need to rush—sow late so that it comes in with the tomatoes, but before it goes into flowering mode.
CILANTRO	'Santo'	Successive sowings can be made anytime throughout the growing season directly into the garden.	There are two types of people: those who love it and those who hate it. Summer wouldn't be summer without cilantro!
DILL	'Bouquet'	Sown anytime from May through early July directly into the garden.	We grow it not so much for the seeds as for the fragrant foliage; also, you can't have dill pickles without it.
PARSLEY	'Krausa' (curly), plain-leaf Italian	Sown in the greenhouse early April.	In the fall, pot up a plant or two for the sunroom or kitchen window, and you'll have fresh parsley all season long.
SUMMER SAVORY		Sown indoors a few weeks before last frost or directly into the garden late spring.	The essential seasoning for snap beans

■ **Save those grass clippings—they make the perfect mulch for vegetables.**

Maintenance

ONCE YOUR CROPS ARE UP AND GROWING, GARDEN maintenance becomes a primary concern, and here you have no better ally than that unsung hero of the garden—mulch. Mulches serve the vegetable gardener in several ways. Besides the obvious tasks of inhibiting weed growth and aiding water conservation, mulch breaks the force of water falling from overhead and thus prevents erosion and crusting of the soil. Likewise, in a well-mulched bed mud doesn't get splashed all

over the plants, reducing both the need to wash crops in the kitchen and the incidence of certain foliage diseases. The cooler, moist area under the mulch is an environment where earthworms can thrive near the surface of the soil, which is where most plant roots are deployed.

Unlike other areas of the landscape, however, where you'd want the mulch application to last the entire season, vegetable garden mulches need to be impermanent. Most vegetables are annuals after all, or at least treated as such, and many of these occupy space in the garden for only part of a season. As the beds are continually being cultivated, a permanent mulch of, say, bark chips would be rather inconvenient, forcing the gardener to rake it off with each replanting.

Fresh grass clippings are the perfect mulch for many vegetables, especially small plants like lettuce, which are closely spaced and stay in the garden for a relatively short time. One caveat, though: Grass clippings should be used within a couple of hours of mowing. If you wait too long, they turn rank and slimy from the internal heat they start to generate as soon as they are put in a pile. The clippings should be spread liberally in the garden beds to cover all the bare soil around the plants— two or three inches is not too much, for in a day or two the grass will completely dry out, forming a thin, continuous tan mat that lasts well over a month. Crops that take longer to develop, such as broccoli, may need a second mulching after the first wears out. Any mulch residue can be turned into the soil after the crop is harvested. If grass clippings are not available, a thin layer of buckwheat hulls is an acceptable substitute.

For larger plants, especially those that grow throughout the summer, our mulch of choice is salt marsh hay. It's durable and can often be reused in the fall to insulate crops still standing in the field. When salt marsh hay is unavailable, any kind of straw will do. Straw contains some weed seed that may germinate, but typically this is only a minor nuisance.

In past years we have used black plastic film as mulch for crops such as tomatoes, squash, and melons, but nowadays we use it mainly for peppers and eggplant. Black plastic mulch has the added benefit of trapping heat. The downside of black plastic is that although it provides almost perfect weed control, it is rather tedious to install, and using tremendous quantities of plastic doesn't strike us as being terribly environmentally sensitive. For limited uses, however, black plastic works fine. After cutting the plastic to size, its edges are anchored to the soil with U-shaped pins or bricks, or else are tucked into a shallow trench dug along the bed's perimeter. Then X-shaped incisions are made with a knife where the young plants are to be inserted.

The watering requirements for the vegetable garden are similar to those for the rest of the landscape—an inch or two (more in very hot weather) of water per week during the active growing season. Unlike other plants, though, which don't mind getting their leaves wet, there are a number of plants in the vegetable garden such as beans, tomatoes, and potatoes that are susceptible to various foliage diseases promoted by wet conditions. Although we can't do anything about the rain falling from the heavens, we can alter the way we distribute water, and thus for the tomatoes in particular we use soaker hoses buried under the mulch rather than overhead watering.

Of Pests and Pestilence

AFTER SO MUCH TIME, EFFORT, AND EXPENSE HAVE BEEN invested in the vegetable or herb garden, it's only natural to take a dim view of sharing the harvest with uninvited interlopers. My grandfather always used to say, "Ten percent to the weather, 10 percent to pests, and 10 percent to God. The rest to us, and if anyone besides the deity steps over the line, whack 'em!" Though the specific disease and insect problems you may face in other parts of the country may differ from the ones we have to deal with in New England, most of the practices we describe here will cover a broad range of similar problems. (For specific crop pests and problems, see page 201.)

For those of you interested in gardening with the least amount of pesticides possible, spunbonded polypropylene fabric row cover is perhaps the most useful innovation available to the modern gardener. While light and water freely pass through the fabric, insects are stopped cold, practically eliminating the need for insecticides on crops that don't rely on pollination, such as Swiss chard, radishes, brassicas, and beets. (Those that require pollinators, such as cucumbers and squash, can be covered for part of the season until the plants are mature enough to flower.)

■ Above: Young peppers beneath a black plastic mulch: the plastic not only prevents weeds and conserves water, but also retains heat—perfect conditions for peppers.

■ Below: Watering tomatoes from below with a soaker hose like this one helps to prevent foilage diseases.

209

The material comes in two weights, a heavier one that has the added benefit of insulating your crops on cold nights and a lighter-weight type that prevents unnecessary heat buildup in the warmer months. Some gardeners simply drape the fabric over the plants, but we generally prefer to create tents. For crops of shorter stature, heavy-gauge wire can be bent into custom-sized tent supports. When taller plants need to be covered, eight-foot lengths of flexible PVC electrical conduit make excellent hoops for creating a Quonset-style enclosure, with bricks or stones used to hold the edges of the fabric down.

The most economical way to purchase row cover is by the roll, 100 feet or more at a time. This is enough to last most gardeners many years. (If you're careful not to tear or soil it, the fabric can be reused again and again.) Unfortunately, the rolls do not always come in convenient widths, so we generally buy one that's 30' × 100' and cut the widths we need from its length. Keep in mind that especially with taller plants, you'll need a considerable width to encompass the added height. At the Victory Garden, for example, to cover our four-foot-wide rows filled with two-foot-tall plants, we need a cover a little more than nine feet wide.

■ **A close-up of the row cover and hoops over the Swiss chard.**

GARDENING IN AUTUMN

All too often gardeners set out their tomato plants, lettuce, cucumbers, and zucchini in late spring and call it a season, meaning that by Labor Day, the vegetable garden is pretty much forgotten. This is truly unfortunate, because they then miss what should really be the crowning climax of the vegetable garden: the fall harvest. Here at the Victory Garden early plantings are only a dress rehearsal for the main event, the late-season garden that fills the larder, carrying us right through winter into the following spring, when the cycle begins all over again.

Here's just a partial list of the vegetable abundance the autumn garden provides:

- **Spinach** sown a month or so before first frost can be harvested until the garden becomes a solid block of ice.

- **Lettuce,** started *before* Labor Day and held under a double layer of row cover, will normally remain crisp and sweet for a final, culminating Thanksgiving Day salad. Placed in a cold frame, it will often last all the way to Christmas.

- **Crops like leeks, kale, collards, or Brussels sprouts** can be harvested into the winter if there is good snow cover, or if the plants are mulched deeply with hay and then perhaps covered with fabric to prevent windburn.

- **Uprooted cabbage plants** can be stored upside-down in a trench dug in a garden bed. When they are covered with a very deep layer of hay to prevent freezing, they will keep at least to St. Patrick's Day, and may be harvested anytime during the winter.

- **Carrots** can be left in the ground and dug all winter long—provided you can keep the ground from freezing. (In all but the coldest areas, a thick layer of hay often works well.)

- **If you do have a greenhouse,** or any other well-lit space that can be kept within tolerable temperature ranges, then you can grow fresh greens even in the dead of winter. Fill a nursery flat or any kind of shallow tray with potting mix and stir in a bit of your fertilizer of choice. Water it down thoroughly, make furrows with the edge of a wooden label, and sow your favorite mesclun blend. In just a few weeks, when the crowded seedlings are four or five inches tall, cut bunches of them with scissors and enjoy a mixed winter salad without paying a small fortune per pound. Be sure to sow a new crop every three weeks or so.

■ Here I am, greedily making off with the butterhead lettuce 'Sangria.' This picture was taken in October, with at least a month of harvest to come, showing just how extended the home-grown season can be, even in the north.

Mammalian Marauders

LARGE MAMMALS OFTEN PRESENT QUITE A PROBLEM for the vegetable grower. Sometimes the best defense is nothing more than a good fence. At the very least, it's nice to know that your dog won't be tramping all over your garden. But the situation can get a lot more serious than just an occasional stray pet. In many parts of the country, the most common trespassers are rabbits, woodchucks, and deer.

Rabbits are perhaps the easiest of the three to deal with: they are easily stopped with as little as a two-foot-high barrier of chicken wire or other fencing with small apertures. Be warned, though, that an ordinary picket fence will need to have some additional mesh fastened to the interior to prevent rabbit entry. Rabbits are master contortionists and have no problem slipping between narrow pickets!

Woodchucks are an entirely different story. Not only can they dig very well—which often requires that metal fencing be sunk a foot into the ground, or sunk six inches deep and bent at a right angle away from the patch—but they can also climb, and will stop at nothing when faced with the prospect of feasting on some fresh produce! Faced with a woodchuck invasion,

a floppy fence, one that is virtually impossible to climb, is often recommended. Unfortunately, this isn't the most aesthetically pleasing solution. We've discovered, however, that chicken wire or other wire fencing threaded through a double row of dense growing privet is not only invisible, but has proven to be an effective means of fencing off the depredations of this especially indefatigable beast.

Fortunately for us, deer have never been a problem in the garden—at least not yet. To prevent deer from devouring your garden, however, your only defense is a tall fence—eight feet high or more—or a hedge that's threaded with deer mesh. Other methods, such as coyote urine or noisemakers, have generally proven to be pretty much useless.

Quick Tips: Autumn Soil Enhancement for Better Spring Harvests

AUTUMN IS PROBABLY THE BEST TIME TO WORK ON THE soil in the vegetable garden. Once the majority of the beds have

USING SOLAR POWER

Solarization is a method of using sunlight to heat planting beds to a temperature at which pathogens borne in the soil are reduced to tolerable levels, or even obliterated. Solar heat is collected by covering the infected bed with a double layer of six-millimeter clear plastic sheeting. (Thinner plastic is more likely to break down under outdoor conditions, and will be difficult to reuse.) The two layers must be separated by a couple of inches or so to provide a space for trapping heated air. PVC pipes or lengths of common lumber work well to create this separation;

three pieces are used, one in the middle of the bed and one near each edge. It is important that the middle spacer be a bit higher than the ones at the edges, and that the plastic is kept taut by firmly anchoring its perimeter, so that the covering will shed water.

The soil must be moistened thoroughly before the bed is covered with plastic, because it is water that collects and conducts the heat that is generated. Here in our northern latitude we have attained soil temperatures in excess of 120 degrees F. Six hours at that heat level is sufficient to rid our soil of

clubroot and verticillium wilt; at slightly lower temperatures the time needed for effective control may be much longer—days or even weeks.

In southern latitudes, the potential for heat buildup is much greater due to higher ambient temperatures and the more favorable angle at which sunlight strikes the earth. As a possible alternative to toxic chemical remedies, solarization seems worth a try when dealing with nematodes and whatever else is attacking your plants through the soil.

been cleared of the remains of the summer planting, you're free to replace the nutrients and trace minerals that the season's vegetables have depleted.

One of the best ways to improve the quality of the vegetable garden soil is by sowing what's called a "cover crop" such as winter rye. Once grown, the rye is then turned over back into the soil, providing a completely organic fertilization method that adds both nutrients and organic matter. Here at the Victory Garden, the ideal time for planting winter rye in our Zone 6 garden is the latter half of October, just after the first few frosts but a full month or two before the ground freezes over. Winter rye flourishes in cold weather. (Gardeners north or south of this line will need to adjust their schedules accordingly to provide the allotted two months of cold but freeze-free growing time.)

Don't be lulled into planting too early or too late, though: premature planting will cause luxuriant growth that is very difficult to turn under come spring. Planting too late, on the other hand, will make for extremely sparse and insubstantial growth.

Before the rye seed is actually sown, an inch or two of compost should be worked into the soil. If you haven't made enough of your own, you can always buy it by the cubic yard from commercial sources. At the same time, add a touch of ground dolomitic limestone to restore the calcium and magnesium that's leached out or been taken up by plants in the course of the growing season. Lime also helps keep the soil pH at the ideal level of about 6.5.

In early spring, as soon as the ground thaws, the winter rye is turned under. It's best to do this by hand, not with a rototiller. The object is not to churn the rye and soil into something resembling a tossed salad, but to invert it—blades down, roots up. Rye grass takes at least two or three weeks to decompose after it has been turned under, and would delay your earliest crops by that amount of time if all your beds were filled with it. To allow for timely spring planting (of peas, for instance), as well as the chance to enjoy some late-autumn crops the previous fall, it's best to leave a small portion unsown with rye each year and then rotate that unsown section about the garden with each passing season.

DIGGING DEEPER: THE TROUBLE WITH HEIRLOOMS

IN RECENT YEARS ESPECIALLY, WITH MANY GARDENERS waxing nostalgic for simpler and less hectic times, growing heirloom vegetables has become a fun and interesting way to touch a part of our culinary past. In the days before taste and texture were sacrificed in favor of shelf life and perfect appearance, many fine vegetables were introduced—some bred especially for the home gardener—that would put some of their modern counterparts to shame. And by and large, the only way you can experience the taste sensation these antique cultivars provide is to grow your own.

Another good reason to grow heirlooms is to preserve genetic variations that might otherwise be lost to posterity. Genetic diversity is a good thing in itself, and has in the past provided mankind with the solution to many a difficult problem. In the early 1970s, for instance, the American corn crop was threatened with almost total destruction by a particular type of blight fatal to modern hybrids. Economic disaster was avoided only by going back to older varieties that were resistant to the disease and crossbreeding this trait into modern cultivars. Buying heirloom seeds helps to support growers who preserve these antique genetic lines and provides valuable horticultural "insurance" against future calamities.

This doesn't mean, however, that all heirlooms are universally good and that all modern hybrids are bad, a bias that has been gaining currency in some gardening circles. Many older varieties have been abandoned for good reasons, such as poor disease resistance or spotty performance. Sometimes, new varieties are truly improvements over the old, as anyone who has eaten stringless string beans or burpless cucumbers can attest. The point is this: if you want a spectacular harvest that's the envy of your friends, don't be too influenced by gardening fads. Instead, choose varieties from new and old based on your own personal taste, as well as proven performance in your area.

Best Bets:
Top Tools for Vegetable Gardening

Here are the top five tools no vegetable gardener can afford to be without:

Spading fork—Every task involving loosening the soil, from turning in amendments to inverting winter rye to removing the root systems of expired crops, requires this tool. But don't confuse it with a pitchfork, and always choose one with flat (not square) tines.

Rake—Not just any rake, but a flat-back steel garden rake. With this, and this alone, you can put the final finish on your beds prior to planting or seeding. Don't confuse it with a bow rake, the curved tines of which are only good for dragging debris into piles or spreading bark mulch.

Planting board—An extremely simple but useful tool, this consists of a 4' × 4" piece of "one-by" lumber with notches cut into it every six inches. We make ours out of western red cedar because it's weatherproof. In addition, the unnotched side is beveled to a point for making seed furrows.

String line—In its crudest form, a string line is just two sticks with nylon mason's twine connecting them. Wrap 100 feet of twine around the two spikes and it will keep your rows precisely straight.

Floral shears—Any fine-bladed instrument will do. For harvesting beans, peppers, summer squash, and almost anything else that does not require excessive force to sever, these narrow shears, compared to standard hand pruners, negotiate tangled vegetative growth with finesse.

■ **The Victory Garden's famous planting board, a versatile tool you can easily make at home.**

■ **Three other Best Bet tools: the spading fork, the floral shears, and the flat-backed steel garden rake.**

Ask Michael:
Top Tomatoes

Dear Michael,
I'm intrigued with all the different types of tomato seeds now
available, both new and old, and I'm wondering which are your
favorites, and which you would recommend growing.

Well, that's a tall order! As an absolute tomato fanatic, I grow several dozen varieties each year at the garden, and my favorites seem to change with each passing season, though I must admit a special partiality to members of the Brandywine group for large slicing tomatoes, and a yellow called Sungold is my all-time favorite cherry.

Which tomatoes you should grow depends on what you plan to use the tomatoes for: eating out of hand, sauces, or preserving. That decision will greatly influence your final selections, as specific varieties have been bred for each of these applications. If you would like to get your feet wet and discover just how wide the world of tomatoes really is, here are eight varieties recommended by heirloom expert Amy Goldman, who's been a guest on our show many times, and who's an absolute doyenne of interesting and intriguing varieties.

'Eva Purple Ball'
'Aunt Ruby's German Green'
'Kellogg's'
'Hillbilly'
'Red Peach' (and 'Yellow Peach,' a.k.a. 'Garden Peach Fuzzy')
'Radiator Charlie's Mortgage Lifter'
'Schimmeig Stoo'
'Big Rainbow'

If you're interested in tracking down some of Amy's recommendations, these, and many others, are available from the following sources:

Baker Creek Heirloom Seeds	www.rareseeds.com
Sand Hill Preservation Center	www.sandhillpreservation.com
Seed Savers Exchange	www.seedsavers.org
Tomato Growers Supply	www.tomatogrowers.com
Totally Tomatoes	www.totallytomato.com

■ **Visions of tomato bounty grown by heirloom expert and frequent Victory Garden guest Amy Goldman.**

■ The vegetable garden at Monticello.

Inspired Gardens

The Vegetable Garden of Thomas Jefferson

"I have often thought that if heaven had given me choice of my position and calling, it would have been on a rich spot of earth, well watered, and near a good market for the production of the garden."

Thomas Jefferson, from a letter written to Mrs. Clark's fourth-grade class

MONTICELLO, THE HOME OF THE THIRD PRESIDENT of the United States, Thomas Jefferson, has long attracted visitors with its incredible architecture and bucolic setting among the rolling Piedmont Hills of Virginia. But for anyone interested in growing vegetables, Monticello is also a place of pilgrimage: Jefferson's 1,000-foot vegetable garden has recently been restored to its original glory, along with some very valuable lessons for today's gardener.

The vegetable garden, which was terraced into the side of Monticello (the name means "little hill"), evolved over 40 years and hit its peak in 1812. Built and grown with the help of considerable slave labor, the vegetable garden not only provided an important source of food during Jefferson's lifetime, but also served as an experimental garden where he tested different varieties of vegetables as well as the latest horticultural techniques.

217

For Jefferson, part of the experimental process included growing virtually anything he could get his hands on. Of course this included the basics, such as lettuce, radishes, and tomatoes—though not necessarily quite as we view these crops today. For example, prior to his growing them for culinary purposes, tomatoes were thought to be poisonous, and therefore were strictly ornamental, and lettuce was eaten only if boiled. Jefferson also cast his net about the world to bring home to Monticello some unusual and highly prized imported delicacies. These included everything from red globes, a colorful and nutty-flavored Italian artichoke, to Egyptian onions, a perennial grown chiefly as a curiosity or for early salad onions.

Jefferson believed his garden laboratory should include a sampling of as many different varieties of individual vegetables as possible. Implementing the equivalent of today's "trial gardens," Jefferson grew, for example, 15 different varieties of English peas (his favorite of all vegetables) and a large number of kale, including Delaware, Scotch, Russian, and Buda, varieties still grown by the modern gardener.

Jefferson, the scientist, also believed in recording in intricate detail the behavior and habit of everything he grew. These observations, made from 1766 until 1824, just two years before his death, later were assembled and became part of *Thomas Jefferson's Garden Book*. Annotated by Edwin Morris Betts, the work (which can be purchased on Amazon.com) is a prize resource for historical gardeners. It not only captures Jefferson's love of nature and other interests, but provides a detailed accounting of his garden activities, including both the successes and failures.

Jefferson was very clever when it came to testing different ways of extending the gardening season. Primarily a vegetarian, he was driven by the desire to have lettuce, spinach, and endive that could be harvested well into the winter as well as very early in the spring. To that end, Jefferson's strategies were relatively simple: situate the beds for optimum growth throughout the year; and take into consideration sun, shade, wind direction, and any other environmental factor that affects a plant's ability to flourish and survive. While such thinking is common today, in Jefferson's day it was truly revolutionary.

The wise 21st-century gardener would do well to borrow a few pages from Jefferson's gardening book: don't be afraid to experiment; hunt for new and interesting plants; garden critically, and keep a record of your successes and failures. Follow this bit of presidential advice and your vegetable garden is sure to win votes of praise next year.

For more information on Monticello, visit www.monticello.org. If you visit, be sure to check out their garden center. Monticello is home to a historic seed-saving program, so you can actually buy and grow many of the same varieties of fruits and vegetables that Jefferson cultivated during his own time.

Texas Bird Pepper
Capsicum annuum, var. galbriscul

■Thomas Jefferson was fascinated by the wave of newly discovered plants that flooded into America during the first part of the 19th century, and was the first person in America to grow many of these new species. This Texas Bird Pepper was one of his favorites, first raised by Jefferson at Monticello in 1812.

■ Gooseberries, raspberries, strawberries, blueberries, and blackberries. While costly and bland at the store, they are delicious and inexpensive when you grow them at home.

Chapter 8
A Berry Extravaganza

Oh, the incredible profit by
digging of ground!

THOMAS FULLER
History of the Worthies of England, 1662

ONE OF MY EARLIEST GARDENING MEMORIES IS PICKING raspberries with my grandfather. My dad and I would get up early in the morning before the late summer heat got too intense (there was no shelter in that raspberry patch) and drive over to my grandfather's house. There, under Gramps's watchful eye, we would grab our small woven baskets (which he saved especially for this purpose) and head out to the plot behind the garage. Looking back at it now, I bet Gramps didn't have more than a 50-foot row of raspberries, but being only three feet tall myself, that row of towering giants seemed to stretch on forever.

This size differential was, of course, the very reason I had been brought along on this particular expedition: raspberries give up their fruits jealously, many of them down low beneath their leaves. This was a pain for grown-ups forced to search for berries from above, but for pint-size children able to look up *under* the leaves, the raspberries didn't have a chance. Berry after berry fell into my greedy grasp and down into the bucket (okay, if the truth be known, about every third berry fell into my basket, the rest just happened to fall directly into my mouth . . .). Almost before I knew it, the row was picked clean. Despite my berry depredations (as well as the suspected but never proven diminution of the overall total by both my father and grandfather) we always managed to harvest close to 10 or 12 pints of berries, which were eagerly received by the various households in our extended family.

Now that I think back on it, berries of every variety figured prominently in some of my most vivid childhood memories. There was the time at my Uncle Vern's farm, when I was tossed off a horse into his prize strawberry patch. This happened to the utter horror of my mother, who from a distance not only saw me fly from horse to ground, but watched aghast as I then unsteadily arose seemingly covered in washes of red blood. . . . Then there were the family trips through Wisconsin's famous cranberry bogs. I still remember all of us marveling at how such a tasty crop could grow in such an unlikely place. . . . Oh, and how could I ever forget the time when my father and I went out looking for blueberries only to be chased away by a huge black bear bent on a similar mission?

Almost every gardener nowadays grows tomatoes or a few vegetables. Many people have at least a fruit tree or two in their backyard. But berries seem to be the neglected stepchild of the modern gardening world. They have virtually disappeared from our backyards, despite the fact that berries are among the most expensive food crops around. Just look at raspberries—a half pint of these organically grown little red gems will often set you back three dollars or more. That's a lot of money for a plant that pretty much grows by itself once planted, and whose required maintenance is limited to once-a-year pruning and fertilizing. . . . Granted, not all berries are quite *that* easy to grow, but when compared to many vegetable crops they are a veritable cinch, and should be included in every home garden.

So, here's how to get started with some of our favorite berry crops: raspberries (and other brambles), strawberries, blueberries, gooseberries, and currants.

Raspberries

OF ALL THE BERRIES, PERHAPS THE EASIEST TO GROW, and (for many) the most rewarding, are raspberries. In fact, their common name, brambles, is almost synonymous with "spiked weed." (If you've ever walked in the woods and had your sides shredded by sharp wild bramble thorns, you'll immediately understand what I'm talking about.) The trick to growing raspberries is not so much in culture but in selecting the right variety for your part of the country. In order to do that, it helps to know a little bit about the history of the raspberry.

Most varieties on the market today are descended from a cross between the European red raspberry, noted for its long, cone-shaped fruits, and the American raspberry, which had smaller but tastier berries. Both of these berries shared a preference for cool and relatively moist parts of world, with the historical consequence that until recently the majority of their progeny preferred similar climes. This meant that within the United States, growing good raspberries was essentially limited to the Pacific Northwest, New England, and the Great Lakes region. In the last couple of decades however, there has been a spate of new varieties designed to thrive in the warmer parts of the country (not for the deepest of the Deep South, but pretty close to it). When selecting the right berry for your part

■ Freshly picked
blackberries, with
blueberries in the
background.

223

■ **This simple trellising method keeps both berries and canes off the ground, while giving easy access to the fruits.**

of the country keep this background in mind, as it will be crucial to the success of what you grow (see the table on page 228).

Once you've eliminated berries that don't do well in your part of the world, the next thing to decide is whether you want a variety that produces one large crop a year (generally in July) or one of the "everbearing" types that produces a small crop in June and early July, then takes a few weeks off, and finally starts producing fruit again in late August until early frost on new canes. Why, you might ask, would you ever choose a variety that bears fruit only once a year when you could have raspberries aplenty for months at a time? The difference lies in the taste: some people feel very strongly that the once-a-year berries taste much better than any other kind of raspberry. Others, however (including myself), prefer some of the everbearing types. Color, size, and eventual use—eating out of hand, in jams, or in baking—will also play a part in your decision.

One of the quickest ways to get educated about raspberry varieties is by going to the berry farm nearest you during the harvest season. I guarantee that you'll be amazed at how much difference there is from one type of fresh raspberry to the next—something you'd never appreciate from those berries in a box at the supermarket. A quick field trip to the berry farm will also serve to guide you toward the berry varieties that do best in your part of the world. We've solved the seasonality question at the Victory Garden by planting some of the single-crop varieties (which Kip prefers) and the everbearing types that I like. (See the Ask Michael section, pages 240–241, for more information on how we choose what to grow on the show.)

In terms of layout, raspberries are generally planted in rows for easy harvest. Rows can be of any length, but you'll need to allow at least eight feet between rows if you're planning multiple lanes. In terms of culture, raspberries aren't terribly demanding, except in one respect: they can't stand wet feet. Try to site your bed in full sun on a slight slope that drains well, preparing the soil as you would for vegetables, making sure to mix in sufficient fertilizer and considerable quantities of organic matter. Keep the pH at about 6.5, slightly on the alkaline side. As with every other kind of crop, the better the soil preparation, the better the harvest. If possible, you should establish your bed in autumn for planting the following spring.

It's also not a bad idea to think about a trellising system as you're constructing the bed; raspberries must have support if you want to get easy access to the harvest. For the method we use, see Step by Step, pages 226–227.

Although it may sound unneighborly, free raspberry plants are the one gift you should always decline from gardening friends. While generally untroubled by insect pests (though raspberry cane borer can be a problem in the West), raspberries *are* quite susceptible to a number of viral and bacterial problems, especially verticillium wilt, which can cause entire stands of canes to wither and die in a few short weeks. These diseases are principally spread by infected stock, and once the disease spreads, there's no cure except removal. Your best defense is prevention, making sure all planting stock in your yard comes only from clean, inspected nursery sources.

The most cost-effective way to get started with raspberries is to order young plants through the mail. (Live plants in pots are sometimes available at local nurseries, but are much more expensive.) These generally come as bare-root canes—essentially foot-long sticks with a few roots that to the uneducated eye look about as alive as, well, dead wood. Never fear, though, because once properly planted, a healthy stand of raspberries will be waiting right around the corner.

Raspberry canes are normally shipped in the early spring, just at the proper planting time. When the canes arrive in the

■ **After fruiting, canes are cut to the ground.**

mail, soak them for a few hours in warm water to rehydrate them. (If you have to delay planting for a day or two, don't leave the canes sitting in the water. Wrap them in wet burlap or wet newspapers, and place them in a cool place.) Once outside, be sure to keep your raspberry roots under cover, especially when you take them out to be planted. Also try to plant your canes on a cloudy day—the roots of the bramble family are extremely sensitive to sunlight, and can be quickly damaged if exposed to the sun's direct rays.

The easiest planting method is to dig a hole (or trench) large enough to accommodate the spread of the root mass, and set the canes in the ground an inch or two deeper than they were while growing in the nursery. (The soil mark is usually fairly visible on the canes to guide you.) Next, cover the canes with soil and tamp down firmly. While the spacing of raspberries varies by variety and species, and by how quickly you want the row to fill in, generally they should be planted between 15 and 30 inches apart.

The first season, your work will be limited to keeping the bed well watered and weeded. The lucky few may get a berry or two that season, but this is rare. The berry bonanza arrives during the second and subsequent seasons, when the canes you planted begin to flower and fruit. Raspberry canes are fairly unusual in the horticultural world in that while their root system is perennial, the canes themselves are biennial, meaning that in the first year raspberries produce canes (called the primocanes) that don't flower. The following season, the primocanes, now called florocanes, fruit and then die. Meanwhile, these are replaced by the new growth of primocanes that arise from underground. There are exceptions to this rule: the once-a-year summer fruiting species do in fact function this way.

The everbearing varieties, on the other hand, actually produce a crop of berries on their primocanes late the first summer, which produce a poor second crop the following summer, then die. Once the florocanes are done fruiting in the fall, they should be removed at that time, or immediately in the early spring to allow the new primocanes to develop. Spring is also the time to fertilize the bed with a well-balanced fertilizer such as 10-10-10. Properly tended in this way, your raspberry patch should last at least 10 years before the plants need replenishing.

Step by Step: Building a Raspberry Trellis

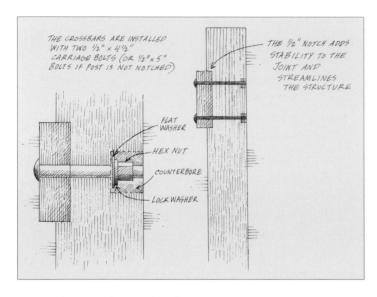

THE CROSSBARS ARE INSTALLED
WITH TWO ½" × 4½"
CARRIAGE BOLTS (OR ½"× 5"
BOLTS IF POST IS NOT NOTCHED)

THE ½" NOTCH ADDS
STABILITY TO THE
JOINT AND
STREAMLINES
THE STRUCTURE

FLAT
WASHER

HEX NUT

COUNTERBORE

LOCK WASHER

■ **Crossbar attachment detail.**

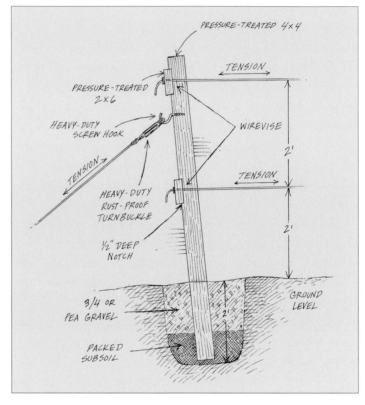

PRESSURE-TREATED 4×4

TENSION

PRESSURE-TREATED
2×6

HEAVY-DUTY
SCREW HOOK

WIREVISE

TENSION

2'

TENSION

HEAVY-DUTY
RUST-PROOF
TURNBUCKLE

2'

½" DEEP
NOTCH

3/4 OR
PEA GRAVEL

GROUND
LEVEL

2'

PACKED
SUBSOIL

■ **Finished trellis, side view.**

BUILDING YOUR OWN TRELLIS CAN APPEAR DAUNTING
AT first, but it's not really all that complicated, and if you're
interested in raising raspberries, a trellis is essential to pro-
moting optimum fruiting and greater ease in harvesting.

To build one complete trellis (with two stanchions), you'll
need the following materials:

■ 10-foot two-by-sixes (1)

■ 4.5- or 5-inch carriage bolts (8)

■ About two wheelbarrow loads of gravel (to fill holes)

■ 10.5-gauge trellis wire (four times the length you want your
trellis to be, plus 10 feet)

■ Wire vises (8)

■ 30-inch earth anchors (2)

■ Turnbuckles (2)

■ Hooks (2)

■ 8-foot four-by-fours (2)

■ 1-inch all-weather screws (to secure wire vises)

■ Flat washers (8)

■ Lock washers (8)

■ Nuts (8)

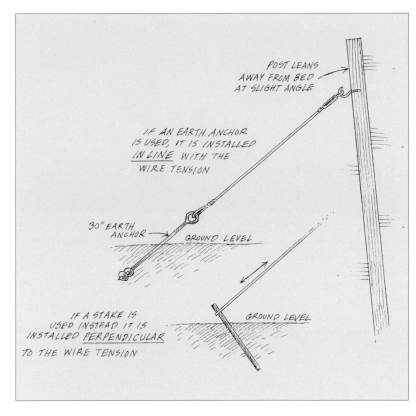

■ Post anchoring detail.

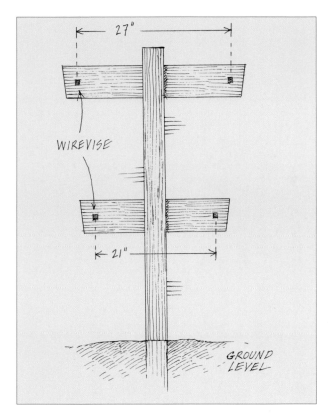

■ Finished trellis, front view.

1. Drill holes (about ½-inch) in crosspieces for the wire vises.

2. Attach 2 two-by-six crosspieces to the six-foot post with two carriage bolts at each joint.

3. Dig a two-foot hole for the post; pack sterile subsoil around the base and fill the remainder of the hole with three-quarters of the gravel.

4. String trellis wire through all four pairs of corresponding wire vises.

5. Install earth anchors and attach trellis wire to them and to the turnbuckle looped over the hook on each post.

6. Draw the wire until evenly taut.

■ Raspberry 'Latham.'

Best Bets: Selected Raspberries

Variety of Raspberry	Preferred Growing Region	Taste/Quality	Horticulture/ Comments
'ALLEN'	Northeast	Large black raspberries good for all uses: fresh, frozen, and in jams and jellies.	Very hardy; disease-resistant with ample fruit.
'BLACK HAWK'	Midwest	Very large black raspberries good for all uses: fresh, frozen, and in jams and jellies.	Very hardy plant that produces a lot of fruit; does well in hot, dry climates.
'BRANDYWINE'	Northeast	Very large, tart purple raspberries good for all uses: fresh, frozen, and in jams and jellies.	Hardy.
'BRISTOL'	South	Sweet, large black raspberries excellent for fruit jams and freezing.	Hardy plant, strong enough not to need support.
'DIRKSEN'	Pacific Northwest	Large, sweet berries good fresh, frozen, and in jams and pies.	Vigorous plants that produce big clusters of berries.
'DURHAM'	Midwest, Mid-Atlantic, upper Plains and Rockies	Medium to large berries that have excellent flavor; good for all uses: fresh, frozen, and in jams and jellies.	Hardy, long-yielding.
'JEWEL'	Southern Plains, mid Atlantic, Midwest	Very large black raspberries good for jams, jellies, and pies.	Extremely disease resistant; yields large crop of fruit.
'LATHAM'	Upper Plains and Rockies	Very large red raspberries with excellent quality fruit; very popular.	Disease resistant; grows vigorously and yields well.
'SODUS'	Midwest, South	Large purple raspberries great for eating fresh and for freezing.	Relatively easy to grow; disease resistant.
'TAYLOR'	Northeast	Considered by many to be the best-flavored red raspberry.	Vigorous and productive.

■ Strawberries
nestled in
the garden.

Strawberries

IN ORDER TO ENJOY GROWING YOUR OWN STRAWBERRIES,
you need to understand one critical fact: no matter what you
do, you aren't going to get those red behemoths you see in the
grocery store. Those "strawberries on steroids" are produced
by specialized growers who raise the plants as annuals in special plastic-coated beds that are literally injected with gas to
kill all pathogens and disease. (This method, by the way, has
come under attack recently, because one of the most commonly
used gases, methyl bromide, is incredibly toxic and breaks

down the ozone layer; it has been banned in many industrial-
ized countries.) Thus, unless you intend to duplicate these
methods, you can be assured that your berries will never look
like those bizarre giants in the supermarket. Which is actually
fine, because in return for a slightly smaller berry, your home-
grown strawberries will have a flavor that is unrivaled by anything you'll ever find in the store.

The first step in growing your own strawberries involves a
process similar to that for raspberries: deciding which varieties
you want to grow. Just as with raspberries, there are several different categories of strawberry. There are the traditional "June

Growing Strawberries in a Jar

IF YOU LIKE THE FRESH TASTE OF HOMEGROWN strawberries but don't have the garden space to devote to a large-scale strawberry bed, you're in luck, because one of the best and easiest ways to grow strawberries is in a strawberry jar.

Some of you may not be familiar with this peculiar-looking pot, though chances are you've seen them in nurseries and not known precisely what they were for. Generally made of terra cotta and standing about two feet tall, these cylindrical pots have multiple holes or cups in their sides in addition to the standard top opening. These side pockets are designed to take advantage of the strawberry's habit of sending out new plantlets or runners. As these runners emerge from the mother plant, they essentially form a drapery over the side of the pot, covering the jar with strawberries. Not only do strawberry pots look great, but growing the berries vertically removes them from direct contact with the soil, and in so doing

prevents many of the diseases common to growing berries in the ground. Strawberry pots have the added convenience of location. A jar or two placed next to the kitchen will provide fresh berries for your cereal all season long, provided that you've chosen the right varieties.

To begin your jar, you'll need a strawberry pot; some prefertilized soilless mix; some small strawberry plants (these can be either the same leafless young plants you use in the garden or already leafed-out plants in pots; in either case, you'll want to choose a self-pollinating, day-neutral variety for longest production); a marker; masking tape; a hacksaw or electric reciprocating saw and drill; and a short length of 1- or 1¼-inch PVC pipe that's no taller than your pot. This last item is crucial to the success of your jar, because the one distinct drawback of strawberry pots is that the plants on top receive the lion's share of water and nutrients, leaving their cousins in the lower pockets to fend for themselves. This piece of PVC pipe will take care of that problem by providing a drain to funnel water and fertilizer directly to plants on the lower levels.

To begin the assembly of your strawberry pot, hold your

piece of PVC upright alongside the pot and use a marker to indicate a point an inch or so below the rim of the jar. Next, cut your PVC pipe with the hacksaw or electric reciprocating saw using your mark as a guide, and then drill five or six holes about a quarter-inch wide on the lower third of the pipe. Place a piece of old shard over the bottom drainage hole of the strawberry pot (taking care not to block it completely) and then place the pipe directly on top of the shard. Take a piece of masking tape and cover the top end of the pipe to prevent soil or "the potting medium" from filling the tube while you work. Then fill the pot with soilless mix up to the first tier of planting holes and place a strawberry plant in each of the pockets, forcing them in from the outside. Continue upward. Next, place several plants in the top receptacle. If your plants aren't sufficiently large to hold back the soilless mix in the pockets, you may wish to cover the mix with a bit of sphagnum or florists' moss to prevent any erosion. After you're done, water well using the PVC drain (making sure to first remove the masking tape) and then place the jar in full sun, rotating it periodically. Water every few days as needed. As the plants begin to grow and flower, use a water-soluble fertilizer once a week, again making sure that some will flow down the PVC pipe.

bearers," which yield one crop a year that lasts for two or three weeks, in, as the name implies, June. (At least it's June here in Boston and in most northerly climes; for a locale-specific planting and harvesting schedule see page 233.) The second type of strawberry is called "day neutral," which means the berries bloom pretty much continually throughout the season. And just to make things even more complicated, there's a third type you'll sometimes still see, though these days they have pretty much been supplanted by the day-neutral varieties: everbearing. Contrary to common sense, everbearing strawberries don't bear fruit continually during the season as their name suggests, but instead bear once in June and again later in the summer. (Go figure!) In any event, which you choose will again depend on personal taste. In general, the June bearers produce a larger (and to my mind), sweeter berry than the day-neutral types, but the advantage of having berries throughout the season makes the day-neutral berries appealing as well.

The Strawberry Clan

THE STRAWBERRIES THAT YOU SEE ON YOUR TABLE today are the result of a tripartite, tricontinental collecting expedition that extended across two millennia. The Romans, with their love of delicacies, contributed the first part of the equation: they collected and grew the dainty wild European strawberry, *Fragaria vesca*. The first Europeans to North America found the second part of the puzzle: the Virginia strawberry, which was larger, sweeter, and juicier than its European cousin. The missing piece was discovered growing on the coasts of Chile and California: *Fragaria chiloensis*, the beach strawberry, whose fruits weren't particularly tasty but were large and showy. The beach strawberry and the Virginia berry were transported to gardens in both Europe and North America, where over time mixed cultivars of the three first appeared through natural pollination, and later on through direct hybridization. The first man-made "improved" berry was the 'Hovey,' produced in Massachusetts in 1838, and since its arrival, things in the strawberry patch haven't been the same.

Another deciding factor in choosing strawberries will hinge on whether or not a particular variety does well in your part of the country. Strawberries, like raspberries, have been bred to tolerate different climatic conditions. A third consideration is whether or not the variety does well in your garden. Unlike most plants that have a fairly predictable performance when given a set range of growing conditions, strawberries have a mysterious tendency to vary considerably from patch to patch and even within the same field. Subtle variations in soil acidity and drainage certainly play a part in this, but the exact reasons are sometimes hard to pinpoint. We've learned that finding the right berry for your garden is owed as much to chance as to anything else, and that it pays to order several different types and experiment.

There's one last factor to consider when choosing strawberries. Most varieties are self-pollinating, meaning that both the male and female parts of the flower are present and active in each blossom and therefore don't require any additional help to produce fruits. In some varieties, however (called self-sterile), only the female parts of the flower are active, which means you'll need to order another self-pollinating variety to provide sufficient pollen for the "self-sterile" plants.

In terms of strawberry culture, things are much more straightforward: strawberries like a rich, highly organic soil in full sun, and brook no substitute. (It probably bears saying again that work put into the soil now will be amply rewarded at fruiting time, and that the contrary also remains true: poor soils mean poor harvests.)

Strawberries are generally ordered from suppliers as bare-rooted plants. These tiny plantlets will be shipped at the appropriate time for your growing area, which in most cases will be early spring. Although there are several different techniques for planting strawberries—hill, mat, and space matted row—at the Victory Garden we prefer the matted row system for beginners. Not only does this method produce the most berries, but it's also easiest to maintain.

As the name implies, the matted row system utilizes the strawberries' natural tendency to produce small baby plants on runners that spread out from the mother plant over the course of the season. One mother plant, in addition to producing about a quart of berries a season, will produce an incredible amount of runners, so spacing for the matted row system should allow for an ample 18 to 24 inches between plants and three or four feet between rows. Although this may look huge in comparison to the tiny plants you're setting out, trust that if you've done your homework in preparing the soil, the berries will soon cover the distance.

It's important to note that when planting strawberries, correct depth is also a critical factor—too deep and the plant will rot, too shallow and it will raise itself up and out of the ground and eventually die. When planting your berries, make a hole that's large enough that you can fan out the roots, and deep enough that the midpoint of the crown of the plant (the place where the leaves emerge) is level with the soil's surface. When you're done planting, mulch the bed, and be sure to give your plants sufficient moisture. Strawberries are heavy drinkers and will need at least an inch of water a week. Mulching, by the way, is highly recommended for strawberry beds; not only does it cut down on weeds and conserve water, it also protects the fruit from direct contact with the ground, which can lead to rot.

The first year, your maintenance tasks will consist of keeping weeds out of the bed, watering, occasional fertilizing, and agonizingly, removing any small fruit that may appear. (Okay, you can let one or two plants mature, but that's all! Allowing a lot of fruit to ripen in the first year will seriously decrease the longevity of your strawberry bed.) With day-neutral types, however, you can harvest after a few weeks or so of deflowering. In the fall in northern climates, a covering of mulch is especially recommended: several inches of straw, hay, or leaves will protect the vulnerable crowns from winterkill.

The second season will bring your first harvest, and strawberries should continue in abundance for several years provided you keep the bed well weeded, watered, and fertilized. After that, however, you will notice a substantial decrease in the amount of fruit. Strawberry plants aren't particularly long-lived, and they need to be renewed every three to five years or so. Here at the Victory Garden, to avoid summers without berries, we simply plant what we call a migrating row: new plants are added to one end of the strawberry row each year, while old plants are removed from the other. Not only does this eliminate any gaps in the harvest, but you also get an opportunity each year to try out new varieties.

Planting Times for Strawberries

Planting time for strawberries varies considerably by region.

Region	Time
Deep South, Gulf Coast, and Florida	December
Mid-South	October or November
Central California	Midsummer
Southern California	Late summer
Pacific Northwest	April–May
Northeast, Central, Mid-Atlantic	May

This chart was developed in consultation with W. Michael Sullivan, professor of agronomy at the University of Rhode Island.

Given good maintenance practices such as meticulous weeding, mulching, and removal of dead leaves in the fall, strawberries are generally trouble free. Leaf rollers, weevils, and borers can sometimes be a problem, but they can be controlled through either chemical or organic means. Some varieties of strawberries are also susceptible to leaf spot, red stele (a type of root rot), and strawberry anthracnose, which are all fungal infections, but they too can be controlled with fungicides or by planting more resistant varieties.

Best Bets: Selected Strawberries

■ Strawberry 'Sure crop.'

Variety of Strawberry	Region Where Best Grown	Taste/Quality	Horticulture Comments
'ALLSTAR'	East to central Midwest	Very large, firm berries, great for eating fresh or freezing	Hardy midseason berries; do well through many pickings; resistant to red stele (a fungal root disease), with some resistance to verticillium wilt
'ANNAPOLIS'	Northern areas	Very large berries, good for eating or freezing	Early-season strawberries, disease resistant to red stele; winter hardy
'BISH'	Pacific Northwest	Great-quality fruit, excellent for eating fresh	Early- to mid-season fruit
'CHANDLER'	Southern areas, California	Medium to large fruit, terrific dessert strawberry	Early to mid-season variety; brilliant color; susceptible to red stele, but resistant to many viruses
'EARLIGLOW'	Mid Atlantic, Midwest, Northeast, West	Firm and sweet medium-size berries	Early variety with moderate to high yield; somewhat resistant to leaf spot, red stele, and verticillium wilt; full sun
'HOOD'	Pacific Northwest	Medium to large; firm, sweet berries	Early- to mid-season crop; susceptible to viruses; resistant to powdery mildew
'JEWEL'	Midwest, Northeast, and West	Large berries, great for eating fresh or freezing	Late mid-season berries; disease resistant
'POCAHONTAS'	Mid Atlantic, south-central U.S.	Medium to large sweet berries; great for all types of recipes; freezes well	Resistant to powdery mildew, but susceptible to red stele and leaf spot
'PUGET SUMMER'	Pacific Northwest	Great-quality fruit and flavor	New variety for very late season
'RED COAT'	Northeast and colder climates	Great flavor, good multi-purpose berries	Noted for winter hardiness; resistant to leaf scorch
'SPARKLE'	Northeast, Midwest, and Rockies	Round and firm, excellent for freezing	Mid-season berries; somewhat susceptible to leaf spot and verticillium wilt; resistant to red stele
'SURECROP'	Mid-Atlantic, especially coastal regions	Large, sweet berries; good for eating fresh or freezing	Mid-season variety; loves full sun and well-drained soil; very resistant to verticillium wilt; resistant to red stele
'TRIBUTE'	Northern U.S.	Large, slightly tart berries	Ever-bearing, day-neutral berry; tolerates leaf spot; resistant to red stele
'TRISTAR'	Northeast, Midwest, South	Excellent flavor	Day-neutral; resistant to verticillium

Blueberries

EVER SINCE WE STARTED GROWING OUR OWN blueberries at the Victory Garden a few years back, I've been totally spoiled. In fact, I no longer even consider eating store-bought berries. Even when they're available at a reasonable cost (which isn't too often), commercially picked berries are not allowed to ripen fully, which happens a couple of weeks after they turn blue. So the product you receive generally tastes more like blue mush, with a hint of blueberry, than the berries I know and love. Indeed, the pleasure of eating blueberries should be visceral: they're bursting with flavor, delicious almost to the point of delirium, and the only way you'll get to experience that is by growing your own.

Well, let me retract a bit: that's not entirely true. There's one other way to experience fantastic blueberries. If you're the outdoorsy type, you know that phenomenal berries also grow wild in many parts of the United States, where they've been valued by humans and animals for centuries. In fact, there are so many types of native blueberries (high bush, low bush, mountain, dryland, evergreen velvet, and others) that until 100 years ago there was very little effort made to hybridize new varieties, or for that matter, even to grow blueberries domestically. Now, however, there are a number of new cultivars on the market that combine the best qualities of several of the different blueberry types. They also provide the convenience of not having to search across hill and dale anytime you're hungry for the taste of blueberries, so it's more than worthwhile to include a few blueberry bushes in the home landscape.

Domestic blueberries are essentially divided into four main classes: low bush types; low-chill high-bush blueberries, which grow on bushes 5 to 15 feet high and thrive in zones 5 to 10; high-bush/low-bush cultivars, which are similar in appearance to the high-bush types but more cold-hardy, often to Zone 3; and rabbit-eye blueberries, which are much more tolerant of southern conditions in zones 6 to 9.

The aspect that most distinguishes blueberry culture from that of other berries is their need for acidity—a whopping 4.3 to 5.0 pH, depending on the precise variety. This kind of pH can be supplied only by isolating blueberries in their own bed and acidifying the soil with an agent such as sulfur or ammonium sulfate. (The former should be used in already fertile soils; the latter should be used where additional fertilization is required, as ammonium sulfate not only lowers the pH, but also adds nitrogen to the soil.) The acidifying agent should be dug into a bed positioned in full sun that has also seen the addition of ample organic matter. Once the blueberries are planted, an annual top dressing of sulfur or ammonium will generally be required in order to maintain the proper acidity. Mureate of potash is recommended to optimize fruit production. It's also advisable to mulch the bed well with bark (or pine needles if you have them, as they are slightly acidic, or even sawdust) and keep everything well watered.

The good news is that once planted, there's not much more to do with blueberries except harvest them. In subsequent years the bushes may need a bit of light pruning and removal of old or dead wood, but that's about it. In terms of pests and disease, birds will be your largest enemy—your winged friends prize blueberries even more than you do, sometimes forcing you to cover your bushes with netting just before the berries start to show. Like most berries, blueberries are susceptible to several insect pests, such as black-vine beetles and blueberry maggots, as well as several kinds of canker, fungal, and viral maladies. Fortunately, all are controllable through both organic and inorganic means.

■ **If you're lucky enough to have masses of blueberries, a blueberry rake like this one comes in quite handy.**

■ Blueberry 'Blueray.'

Best Bets: Selected Blueberries

Variety	Zones	Taste/Quality	Comments

LOW-BUSH BLUEBERRIES (*Vaccinium* spp.)

These short ground-cover plants (up to two feet tall) are native to cold climates. Planted mostly in the north, they grow wild in the Northeast and upper Midwest. Berries are pale blue to black in color with small seeds. Two cultivators worth trying are:

Variety	Zones	Taste/Quality	Comments
'BLOODSTONE'	5–7	Tart flavor, good for cooking	Prone to phytophthora root rot and anthracnose
'EARLY SWEET'	2–7	Tart flavor, small berries, good for cooking	Best low-bush variety; ripens early

LOW-CHILL (SOUTHERN) HIGH-BUSH BLUEBERRIES (*Vaccinium corymbosum*)

These tall multi-stemmed shrubs can grow up to 15 feet tall. They bear blue to black berries with small seeds and do well in moderate to hot climates. Many varieties do best interplanted with other cultivars for cross-pollination.

Variety	Zones	Taste/Quality	Comments
'BLUECROP'	4–8	Extremely large berries, good for all uses	Drought resistant; grows up to five feet tall
'BLUERAY'	4–8	Extremely large berries, excellent fresh, frozen, or for use in jams and pies	Handles extremely warm climates; grows upward of five feet tall; ready early to mid-season
'DUKE'	5–7	Medium-size berries, mild flavor	Ripens early, grows 4 to 6 feet tall; one of the most popular
'GEORGIA GEM'	7–9	Medium-size berries, excellent quality	Early-season variety

Variety	Zones	Taste/Quality	Comments
'JUBILEE'	5–9	Medium berries	Upright, compact bush bears well in heavy Southern soils.
'MISTY'	5–10	Medium-size berries, excellent quality	Extremely attractive bright blue-green foliage
'O'NEAL'	7–9	Medium-size, dark-blue berries; terrific quality	Does well in high heat; ripens early; great pollinator
'SHARPBLUE'	7–10	Medium-size berries, excellent quality	Foliage almost evergreen; blooms and fruit almost year-around
'SUNSHINE BLUE'	6–9	Medium-size berries with a unique tangy flavor	Dwarf variety, great for pots; does well in the South

HIGH-BUSH HYBRID BLUEBERRIES (*Vaccinium corymbosum*)

These woody shrubs grow three to five feet tall; most are well suited to northern climates. Berries are blue to black in color with small seeds.

Variety	Zones	Taste/Quality	Comments
'BONUS'	3–7	Promising newer introduction with large, excellent fruit	Ripens late
'FRIENDSHIP'	3–5	Sweet, small berries	Good for very cold climates
'NORTHBLUE'	3–7	Sweet berries, great for jelly and pies	Ripens mid-season; smaller yield than other high-bush varieties, though easy to pick
'NORTHCOUNTRY'	3–7	Sweet berries, good fresh or for use in jellies and pies	Ripens mid-season; excellent production
'NORTHLAND'	3–7	Small sweet berries, good fresh or for use in jellies and pies	Early ripening; requires cross-pollination
'NORTHSKY'	3–7	Small sweet berries with rich flavor	Ripens mid-season; dwarf type (to 18 inches), good for containers

RABBIT-EYE BLUEBERRIES (*Vaccinium ashei*)

Excellent for the South. Rabbit-eye blueberries can grow from 5 to 20 feet tall. Many require cross-pollination. Berries are blue to black in color with small seeds.

Variety	Zones	Taste/Quality	Comments
'ALICE BLUE'	6–9	Good fruit quality	Plant with 'Beckyblue' for cross-pollination
'BECKYBLUE'	6–9	Excellent fruit quality	Blooms early; requires another variety for good cross-pollination

Variety	Zones	Taste/Quality	Comments
'BLUEBELL'	6–10	Large berry with excellent flavor	Ripens mid-season
'BLUEBELLE'	6–9	Good flavor	Extended harvest season; excellent for home gardens
'BONITA'	6–9	Larger berries	High-yielding; plant with 'Climax' or other early bloomer
'BRIGHTWELL'	7–9	Great flavor	Late-blooming; disease-resistant
'CENTURION'	6–9	Good for making jams	Late bloom helps avoid frost damage
'CHOICE'	6–9	Good berry quality	Late-season; disease-resistant
'CLIMAX'	7–9	Good flavor	Early-season; needs cross-pollination
'DELITE'	6–10	Medium to large berries with sweet flavor	Late-season; grows up to eight feet tall; cold tender
'TIFBLUE'	7–9	Berries tart until fully ripe; excellent flavor	High-yielding and dependable

Gooseberries and Currants: The "Other" Berries

CHANCES ARE YOU'VE NEVER EVEN HEARD OF gooseberries, and currants may ring only a vague memory from sampling Christmas cakes and other pastries. If that's the case, you'll be surprised to learn that in America over a hundred years ago both of these berries were considered among the queens of the kitchen garden, and invaluable for making jams, jellies, tarts, and pies. A garden writer from 1833 describes the currant as "a most useful fruit, indeed indispensable to every garden. It possesses a remarkable combination of sweet and acid, that fits it for an almost endless variety of useful and agreeable preparations." Being particularly fond of currant jelly, I couldn't agree more!

The gooseberry was similarly lauded, and in fact, one of America's most famous 19th-century nurseries carried over 140 different varieties. Yet 50 years later, nary a currant nor a gooseberry was to be found in the American garden. What could possibly have happened to effect such a drastic change?

Unfortunately for the gooseberry and the currant, both members of the Ribes genus were caught up in the equivalent of a horticultural bum rap. During the late 1800s and early 1900s, when lumbering white pine was a huge business east of the Rockies, it was discovered that a disease deadly to white pines, the White Pine Blister Rust, spent part of its life cycle in members of the Ribes clan. If the Ribes plants were removed, the cycle was broken and the disease disappeared. Starting in 1918, in order to protect the timber industry, the growing of Ribes became illegal. Ultimately, however, it was discovered that it was wild members of the Ribes clan that generally acted as the rust host, not the cultivated members of the kitchen garden, but by then the damage had already been done: gooseberries and currants had been almost entirely eradicated from American gardens. It wasn't until 1966 that the poor currant and gooseberry were proven innocent of the crimes alleged against them and the federal ban was repealed.

That was terrific news for gardeners, because both currants and gooseberries are absolutely fantastic additions to the home berry roster. They also very much live up to their historical claims, and even better, are quite easy to grow. Gooseberries and currants are both small shrubs, and they require a culture quite similar to that of landscape ornamentals. A few bushes planted in full sun and fertile soil, given ample water (but please avoid overhead watering), will result in enough berries to make pies and jams for the entire household.

■ **Red currants, like the variety 'Jonkheer van Tets' shown here, are easy to grow and make a delicious jelly.**

DIGGING DEEPER: THE GENUS *RUBUS*, OR BERRIES BY EVERY OTHER NAME

THE *RUBUS* GENUS HAS PRODUCED A CONFUSINGLY large number of progeny, making berry nomenclature somewhat confusing. The wild European raspberry (*Rubus idaeus*) and the American red raspberry (*Rubus idaeus var. strigosus*), the parents of most of today's red-berried cultivars, have also produced a number of yellow- and white-fruited types, which are raised exactly like red raspberries. These, however, aren't to be confused with the native black raspberry (*Rubus occidentalis*) or the purple raspberries that are hybrids between the red and black types and have slightly different cultural requirements (primarily with regard to pruning). Nor should these be confused with loganberries, dewberries, or boysenberries, all of which are types of trailing blackberries, or distinct species or interspecific hybrids, and have cultural requirements different from those of red raspberries. A berry by any other name? Still delicious!

■ *Rubus ideaeus.*

THE VICTORY GARDEN COMPANION

Ask Michael:
The Missing Orchard

Dear Michael,
We often see you walking through your orchard on the way to other areas, but with the exception of one piece I remember you doing on pruning, you don't seem to talk much about your orchard on the show. How come? What do you grow there?

U h-oh. It seems we've been found out. The truth is that the orchard is something of a work in progress here at the Victory Garden. Fourteen years ago, long before I ever started doing the show, visions of having my own orchard danced in my head. So I ordered a number of year-old whips (essentially rooted sticks on semi-dwarf root stock) and planted the first trees: mostly heirloom apples like 'Roxbury Russet,' 'Summer Rambo,' 'Wealthy,' and 'Northern Spy,' as well as five or six others. I also planted some heirloom pears (Bosc and Anjou types) as well as several peaches, like the famous white 'Belle of Georgia,' which, having grown up in cold Wisconsin, were a complete novelty to me. Then I sat back and let the trees grow, expecting to get my first harvest after three or four years without much more effort. They were fruit trees, after all, and their purpose was to produce fruit. How much more difficult could it be?

Well . . . the trees matured and grew to be truly lovely, especially in the spring, when the pink, scented blossoms and the gentle hum of the bees make the orchard one of my all-time favorite places to be. The actual harvest, however, was another story. Although the peaches and pears did just fine, the apples were a disaster: warped, worm-infested lumps that appealed only to my horse Claudius (and sometimes not even to him!). In my youthful zeal it seems that I had not paid terribly much attention to the astounding number of pests and diseases that simply LOVE to infest apple trees, especially east of the Rockies, where apple maggot fly and plum curculio are a huge problem. (Folks in the West generally have a much easier time of it, and often can grow apples organically without a huge amount of additional effort.)

Nor, it seems, had I paid proper attention to pruning: somehow I had simply thought that you planted the trees, allowed them to grow, and then picked the apples. A visit from Ed Palmer, our pruning expert, clearly revealed that my practice resulted in nothing but sucker-infested, gnarled trees. In all fairness, I think my ignorance was influenced by memories of an ancient apple tree at my grandfather's that without much apparent care or attention produced what seemed to me to be loads of fruit each year. Unfortunately, Gramps is now long gone, and the secret of that particular tree has gone with him. What I do know for sure is that if I want any kind of decent harvest here at the Victory Garden, regular pruning and some kind of a pest prevention program are essential.

Thus, just last year, after we did a segment at the Tower Hill Botanical Garden in Boylston, Massachusetts, I decided to implement a maintenance program similar to the one they use, which tries to use the least toxic methods of pest control possible and combines organic and inorganic techniques. That means starting in the spring with a horticultural oil spray that suppresses mites, aphids, and scale, among other pests. Then, when the trees have about a quarter to half of their leaves, a fungicide/insecticide mix is applied to combat apple scab and the plum curculio. A second application is made seven to ten days later, or as soon as the trees are finished blooming. Finally in June they put out sticky red traps that mimic red apples to capture the apple maggot fly. Good cleanup in the fall is also essential to reduce the overwintering scab spores, and keeping the orchard floor well mown and free of falls (something never a problem with a horse or chickens around) reduces insect and rodent problems. These techniques, combined with good horticultural practices, seem to be enough to give the folks at Tower Hill a decent crop of apples. Let's hope the same can be said for the Victory Garden this coming year!

■ **Late fall is the perfect time to prune out the sucker growth in the orchard.**

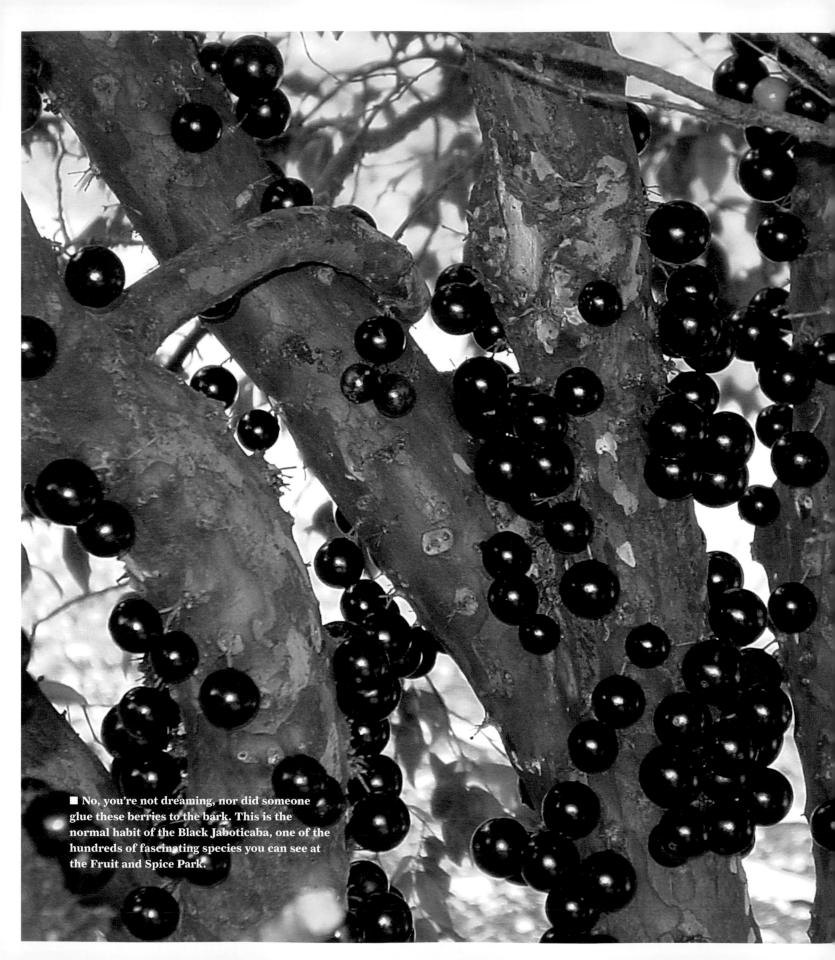

■ No, you're not dreaming, nor did someone glue these berries to the bark. This is the normal habit of the Black Jaboticaba, one of the hundreds of fascinating species you can see at the Fruit and Spice Park.

The Redland Fruit and Spice Park

IN A STATE KNOWN MORE FOR ITS THEME PARKS THAN its gardens, travelers to Florida will be delighted to find a real horticultural treasure awaiting them—the Redland Fruit and Spice Park. Located in Homestead, Florida, just outside Miami, this unique 30-acre tropical botanical garden contains a vast and highly unusual collection of fruits, vegetables, spices, nuts, and berries gathered from around the world.

The Fruit and Spice Park has more than 100 varieties of citrus, 65 varieties of bananas, 40 of grapes, and 60 of bamboo, to name just a few of its collections. The park is also home to some of the world's most unusual berries, each brought here with the specific intent of introducing new species to the American palate. "The time is ripe for this objective," says naturalist and park manager Chris Rollins. "Americans are developing a more diverse diet, and exotic fruits and vegetables are rapidly being mainstreamed both into our diets and onto our daily menus."

What's Rollins referring to? Well, here are a few berries you've probably never even heard of:

Pigeon grape (*Vitis aestivates*): A fruit that's native to south Florida, these berries grow on the vine. Dark purple in color, each individual berry is about 3/8 inch in size, and

243

■ **Barbados gooseberry.**

the berries grow in bunches. Harvested during late summer and fall, they are great eaten fresh or for making jelly. (Hardy to Zone 3)

Hill or Mysore raspberry (*Rubus niveus*): Native to India, the Philippines, and Indonesia, this berry is found on shrubs up to 20 decimeters long that are covered with fat, hooked prickles three to seven millimeters long. The berries are small and either dark red or black in color, with a memorably sweet and juicy flavor. They are great eaten fresh, for juice, or in making ice cream. The plants are known to be spread by fruit-eating birds and mammals and are in season from January through September. (Hardy to Zone 9)

Barbados gooseberries (*Pereskia aculeata*): This vine-grown fruit, similar in appearance to a gooseberry, comes from the West Indies. Ripe come spring, these berries are small and yellow in color, with a juicy pulp that is great eaten fresh or when preserved. This nonleafing vine is actually a member of the cactus family. (Hardy to Zones 9–11)

Otaheite gooseberry, a.k.a. Malay gooseberry (*Phyllanthus acidus*): Native to Madagascar, these berries are grown on shrubs and trees that can reach anywhere from 5 to 30 feet in height. High in vitamin C, they are pale green in color, medium in size, and have a distinctly sour taste. Traditionally grown for the April–June season, they are usually preserved or used in pies but are also used in beverages and sauces. When cooked with sugar, the pulp and juice will turn a characteristic bright red. (Hardy to Zones 10–11)

Jaboticaba (*Myrciaria cauliflora and M. jaboticaba*): This highly prized but slow-growing large shrub or small, dark-leafed, bushy tree can take eight or more years before it bears fruit. Native to the Minas Gerais region of Brazil, these berries produce small yellow-white flowers that appear in clusters of four directly on the main trunk of the tree from the ground up. In season year-round (at irregular intervals), these round, black, sweet berries are used fresh or frozen and for making wine. Similar in looks to purple grapes (one inch in size or slightly smaller) but with a thicker skin, they also have a fresh, grapelike flavor similar to muscadine. They are often eaten raw and can also be made into jams, jellies, and wines. (Hardy to Zones 10–11)

Guava berry: These attractive ornamental berries hail from the West Indies. Grown on small tropical American shrubby trees, the berries are small with yellow skin and have a sweet, aromatic pulp and one or two seeds. Harvested in the fall and winter, they are traditionally used fresh, in jellies, or as flavoring. They are also tasty in Guava berry pie, which in Florida is traditionally made by combining guavas and strawberries and the zest of a lemon. (Hardy to Zones 10–11)

If hearing about these berries stimulates your taste buds, you'll undoubtedly be glad to know that this highly unusual park is not only a feast for the eyes, but for the palate as well. Indeed, tasting is considered to be an important part of the Fruit and Spice Park experience, so if you want to do some sampling of your own or would like more information about the Redland Fruit and Spice Park, see the Resources section on page 283.

■ Urban gardens
don't need to be
large to be beautiful,
as this begon[ia]-
filled window box
attests.

Chapter 9
The Urban Garden

No man but feels more of a man in the world if he have but a bit of ground that he can call his own. However small it is on the surface, it is four thousand miles deep; and that is a very handsome property.

CHARLES DUDLEY WARNER

WE'LL PROBABLY NEVER KNOW EXACTLY WHEN THE FIRST determined gardener decided to tempt fate and create a garden in the city, but whoever that person was, his or her horticultural legacy stretches back at least 3,000 years. Urban gardens were known to have existed in ancient Egypt, and the delights and hazards of city gardening were well known to the Greeks and Romans as well. With the passage of time, however, urban gardening hasn't gotten any easier, and today gardeners face many of the same problems their predecessors faced thousands of years ago: cramped growing spaces, difficult light and soil conditions, and unpleasant sights and sounds. Still, the rewards of cultivating the urban oasis far outweigh the challenges, as there is probably no place on earth where the tranquillity of the garden is more keenly appreciated than in the middle of the bustling metropolis.

Nowhere to Hide

TAKE A QUICK LOOK AROUND ANY URBAN GARDEN space, whether it's a roof deck, balcony, or small backyard, and the one thing that becomes obvious very quickly is that in the

■ **Edible plants feature prominently in this small garden off the kitchen.**

city garden, there's no place to hide. Unlike the more spacious suburban yard, where you might leave a corner or two untended without serious ramifications, in town every square foot counts. Sometimes a postage stamp–sized space will have to do double, or even triple duty—serving as entertainment, relaxation, and gardening space all at once. Thus in order for an urban garden to function successfully, it needs to be well conceived right from the start, and that means not only paying attention to the rules of good design, but also taking careful consideration of a number of issues unique to city spaces.

Inside Out

BECAUSE IN TOWN, ARCHITECTURE AND LANDSCAPE ARE right on top of each other (sometimes literally so, in the case of roof decks!), there must be a direct working relationship between building and garden in terms of functionality, layout, and style. In other words, though we often talk about larger garden spaces as outdoor rooms, in the city, given the garden's small size and direct connection to the house, the garden truly becomes a working room in every sense of the word.

The first step to designing (or redesigning) an urban garden is to consider its relationship to the house. The eventual character and purpose of any outdoor area should be a natural extension of the adjacent indoor space to which it's attached. If access to the proposed garden is from the dining room, for example, the normal tendency is to extend the interior seating and entertaining areas of the dining room to the outdoors, creating a space from which family and guests can enjoy the landscape. If the planned garden space opens off a study, then perhaps a shady, private retreat is in order. If adjacent to the kitchen, then an herb and vegetable garden might be appropriate. On the other hand, if the garden is self-contained and can be reached only by indirect means (such as a roof deck or entrance off the street), then perhaps some type of multi-use space combining a number of different functions is what's required.

Not paying attention to this intimate relationship between house and garden or overriding these considerations with personal preferences generally results in an unsuccessful urban landscape; for instance, vegetable gardens accessed by

■ Crisp, clean, attractive:
the hallmarks of a successful
urban garden.

■ Paving can often be the urban gardener's best friend; notice how the long straight lines of the decking make this space seem much larger than it really is.

formal living rooms are an invitation for dirt and disaster indoors; nor do you want a grill and public entertainment area whose only means of entrance is through the master bedroom. These kinds of problems are best avoided by taking your cue from the house and molding your concept of the garden to fit the structure.

Whatever the eventual use of your urban oasis, it's extremely important that the garden's style and theme be uniform and consistent with that of your home; otherwise, you'll find yourself confronting a design disaster. A case in point: A while back I was called in to re-do a small urban garden that had been laid out only a few years earlier in a Japanese theme. The only problem was that the Japanese garden was in New England, attached to a Colonial house and the Colonial Revival living room that led out onto it. The result was a complete stylistic collision that dragged down both spaces, forcing a very costly and expensive re-do of the outdoor space. As my grandfather used to say, "Do it right—do it right the first time."

Other Issues

AFTER CONSIDERING THE GARDEN'S RELATIONSHIP TO the house, the next factor critical to successful urban design is a careful evaluation of the outdoor space itself. Once again, the general rules laid out earlier when planning your garden are made even more important by additional factors unique to city spaces.

Take urban sight lines, for instance. Small city spaces face a visual dilemma: often they are so tiny that the entire garden can be seen at a single glance—a factor that makes them seem even smaller than they really are. Very often too, their boundaries are defined—frequently for the worse—by their neighbors. This means you need to be extremely clever when considering sight lines in an urban garden and use every available trick of the trade to make the area appear as large as possible. In general, your strategy should be threefold: the first is to preserve, from at least one or two principal viewpoints, the longest sight lines possible through the space. This will give the illusion of the garden being much larger than it really is.

(Several visual sleights of hand, such as trompe l'oeil, can also help you here—see page 266.)

The second strategy is to imbue some sense of mystery and privacy by creating distinct areas of the garden that can't be seen all at once. The challenge here is to avoid chopping up an already small area into tiny, functionless chunks, although in very diminutive gardens, small subdivisions are often mandatory. If that's the case, changes in level, as well as using trellises, hedges, or screens, can achieve surprisingly effective results.

The third important concept is to maximize the sense of space by using borrowed vistas wherever possible. If, for example, you have a rooftop garden with magnificent urban views, then framing these views with upright evergreens or trellis features will not only enhance the look of your garden, but increase the perceived size of your space as well.

Sometimes, however, the problem in the city garden isn't about framing views, it's about blocking them. Ugly neighboring buildings, a litter-strewn vacant lot, or a busy street or highway all require some form of visual barrier between you and the outside world. Unlike the suburban garden, however, where dense, thick screen plantings can often be used to create a privacy shield, in the urban garden there is rarely sufficient space for such an option. In the city garden, tall, narrow hedges, fences, and trellises are pretty much the only solutions for creating this privacy barrier. Keep in mind that the strictures of good fence and hedge design discussed in Chapter One—such as beginning and ending at a logical point, and uniformity along the line—apply equally in town.

Muffling the excessive chatter of city life is also an essential consideration for the well-designed urban garden. Fortunately for the city dweller, the structural nature of urban garden spaces can sometimes come to the rescue. Large buildings and tall fences are excellent means of bouncing sound back to the street, and when covered with vines can further absorb unwanted noise. Thick planting will also help muffle the city's roar, and of course there is always the option of white noise: a gurgling water feature not only provides an excellent focal point for a small urban garden, it can successfully mask a whole host of city sounds.

■ **Small self-contained water features like this one are ideal for urban settings. They are easy to set up, are simple to maintain, and provide a constant source of pleasure in the garden with their cheerful sound, colorful fish, and decorative aquatic plants.**

The Urban Environment

OLD MOTHER NATURE ALSO TAKES ON A MORE INTENSE face in the city: it doesn't just *seem* hotter, shadier, windier, and drier in town, it really is! This has to do in great part with the proximity of large buildings and the microclimates they produce. Anyone who has ever taken a walk on a windy day between two skyscrapers knows what a gale they can create.

But the effects of buildings aren't limited to wind: large structures project a far denser shade with their shadows than that found in nature; and the sun's heat, when it does fall between the buildings, is intensified by reflection from steel and glass, and can become trapped in the surrounding stone and concrete. All this causes urban gardens to be far hotter and drier, and often shadier, than their country cousins. The urban gardener has to be more vigilant in accurately assessing the environment affecting his or her space than other gardeners, and adept at choosing plant material that will thrive in these erratic and sometimes stressful conditions.

Bad urban air is another problem, and one that doesn't just affect humans. Poor air quality can harm plants too, though by different means. Exhaust from autos, industry waste, and low ozone concentrations can damage sensitive leaves as well as deposit dirt and grime on the leaf surface, reducing the plant's ability to photosynthesize. While frequent washing can sometimes help, some varieties are far more susceptible to damage caused by air pollution than others, so once again the careful choice of hardy varieties is critical to urban garden success.

The Dirty Truth About Urban Soil

MAKING SURE THE SOIL IS IN THE BEST POSSIBLE CONDITION is important to any garden, but it's even more critical in the city, where you not only need to know the exact makeup of your soil, but the existence of any contamination. The most common contaminants in urban environments are heavy metals such as lead, mercury, and cadmium, which were deposited in the soil in the days when these were common additives in gasoline, paint, and other household products. Although these elements have largely been banned because of their toxicity, they are still present in most urban soils, especially around structures built before 1970. If you plan to do only ornamental gardening, soil contamination is less of a worry. If, however, you plan to plant and harvest fruit, vegetables, or herbs for human consumption, you'll need to have your soil tested before eating any of your crops. (Both private companies and the local agricultural extension offices do this sort of testing for a moderate fee.) If you discover your soil is unsafe for food crops, then you'll be faced with the choice of either having the topsoil removed and replaced or growing foodstuffs in raised beds with imported soil.

Another problem common to urban gardens is what a friend of mine facetiously likes to call "buried treasure"—

debris left from previous inhabitants that instead of being properly removed was simply buried. This is especially common in city backyards, where junk left over from the building's construction, such as bricks and chunks of concrete, are often buried and forgotten under a thin layer of soil. While this might have been tolerated if left undisturbed, any type of garden activity quickly brings all this material to light, much to the chagrin of the urban gardener. In fact, it's not uncommon to dig up old tires, tin cans, glass bottles, and a host of other garbage when starting a garden where none has existed before. If you're faced with this prospect, don't just ignore the problem and rebury the stuff. Good gardening requires debris-free ground, especially in city gardens, where the plants will rely even more heavily on water and nutrients from the soil to cushion them from adverse urban conditions. If you encounter any rocks, concrete, or other debris when working your soil, make sure to remove and properly dispose of them.

BEFORE YOU BEGIN: A CITY CHECKLIST

If you want a garden in the city, you need to plan ahead. This becomes obvious the second you proceed without thinking the process through: extra expenditures of effort, energy, and money are quickly the result. If you have any doubts about the validity of this premise, all you have to do is purchase a very large and expensive tree at a nursery, then haul it back in a car borrowed from a friend, convince three neighbors to help you get that unwieldy tree up the stairs, and arrive at the top only to discover that the plant doesn't fit through the roof hatch leading to the garden deck. Regrettable? Certainly. Avoidable? Absolutely.

Actually, access is probably one of the most critical elements to consider when first planning an urban garden. How you intend to get all of the materials you need into your garden space will be a huge factor in your plans, and may ultimately control what you can or can't accomplish. Before you start, measure all doorways, stairwells, elevators, and other points of entry to make sure plants and tools can easily fit through the space. If your only access is through the main part of the house, you may want to plan on laying tarps or other coverings over valuable floors and furniture during the principal part of the construction and planting process.

Also, if you don't have an off-street parking area adjacent to your garden, you're going to need to do some extra thinking about how you are going to get materials such as soil, compost, and plants into your planned landscape. If your garden is small and you don't need much in the way of extra materials, a friend stationed on the sidewalk to help you unload nursery purchases may be all that's required. If, however, you are planning a more extensive garden, you may need to reserve street space for deliveries. Most cities and towns will grant day-long no-parking permits that will free up the necessary road space. Many will also allow dumping of bulk deliveries such as soil directly onto the street as long as the material is moved into the garden within the time allowed by the permit, and provided the street is thoroughly cleaned up afterward. Make sure you file the proper paperwork before you start, or your landscaping efforts might run into a considerable amount of municipal resistance!

Best Bets: Trees for Urban Spaces

On the theory that trees in urban gardens have to look great in multiple seasons, here's a short list of trees that fit the bill:

CRAPE MYRTLE
(*LAGERSTROEMIA INDICA*)
A dramatic summer-flowering tree that can also be grown as a shrub, with large crapelike flowers that come in shades of purple, red, pink, or white. Keep an eye out for the newer hybrid cultivars such as 'Natchez,' which combine the flower size of *L. indica* with the disease resistance, hardiness, and interesting bark of sister species *L. faurei*. (Zones 7–11)

FLOWERING CRAB APPLE
(*MALUS* SPECIES)
For interesting form, gorgeous flower, and beautiful fruit, it's hard to beat flowering crab apples. Cultivars vary widely in disease resistance and flower color, as well as in fruit size, color, and winter retention, so it pays to do some investigation before buying. A favorite here at the Victory Garden is 'Donald Wyman,' which grows to 20 feet and retains striking bright red fruit all winter. (Zones 4/5–9)

JAPANESE MAPLE
(*ACER PALMATUM* SPECIES)
Hundreds of different varieties grow anywhere from 5 to 25 feet, depending on the species; many are admired for their spectacular weeping form, deeply serrated leaves that come in a variety of colors, and vibrant red, orange, and yellow fall colors. (Zones 5–9)

KOUSA DOGWOOD
(*CORNUS KOUSA*)
Prized for its white bracts in early summer, which are followed by pink or red fruits and crimson fall color, the Kousa dogwood is one of the showiest small ornamental trees. It grows to 20 feet. (Zones 4–8)

LILY MAGNOLIA
(*MAGNOLIA LILIIFLORA*)
This lovely small tree comes from China and is valued for its beautifully scented, lily-shaped purple flowers that bloom in the spring. It grows to 10 feet. Be on the lookout for 'Nigra,' with wine-purple flowers. (Zones 5–8)

SERVICEBERRY
(*AMELANCHIER* SPECIES)
This tree for all seasons has white blossoms in the early spring; purplish-black berries in the summer; brilliant orange fall color; and interesting multi-stemmed trunks with gray bark in the winter. (Zones 4–8)

WHITE FRINGE TREE
(*CHIONANTHUS VIRGINICUS*)
Native to the southeastern United States, the fringe tree sports fragrant white blossoms in early summer followed by blue-black half-inch fruit. (Zones 3–9)

■ *Chionanthus virginicus.*

Best Bets: Urban Perennials

Want to add a little spice to your urban garden? We've selected some of our best bets for easy-care urban perennials to help you create the maximum effect within a minimum amount of space. To that end we have chosen plants that grow slowly, thrive in city conditions, provide bloom throughout the season, and tolerate the partial shade common to most city gardens.

ASTILBE CHINENSIS 'PUMILA'
This tough dwarf variety has distinctive foliage and beautiful pink blooms. Quick spreading, it forms a dense mat, making it a terrific choice both for ground cover and as a cutting plant for arrangements. Astilbe likes moist soil and partial sun to partial shade. (Zones 4–8)

ASTRANTIA MAJOR 'BO-ANN'
This *astrantia* is a great late bloomer (summer to fall) that comes in a variety of shades from dusty pink to wine. Its compact habit works particularly well when combined with taller plants like foxglove. 'Bo-Ann' makes a great container plant, thriving best when planted in partial to full shade. (Zones 5–8)

BRUNNERA 'JACK FROST'
Want to add a little light to a shady area? 'Jack Frost' could be the perfect perennial for you, with its distinctive silver heart-shaped leaves and blue flowers. Its compact mounding habit makes it a good choice for the small urban garden, and the flowers will provide you with continuous color from late spring to summer. (Zones 4–8)

CAREX SIDEROSTRICTA 'VARIEGATA'
This carex has wide, almost *hosta*-like foliage with an upright habit. Its cream-bordered leaves will bring light into any partially shaded or shady area, and it works particularly well as an accent plant, especially as a foil for large-leaved *hosta*. (Zones 6–8)

HELLEBORUS 'PINK LADY'
Commonly known as the "Lenten Rose," helleborus brings lots of early bloom into the garden followed by strong foliage later in the season. The intense color of 'Pink Lady' is unusual for helleborus, making it a great choice when used as a tall ground cover. It is also a tough plant that will thrive in partial sun and can handle claylike soil. (Zones 5–9)

HOSTA 'WIDE BRIM'
This hosta has wonderful white-to-cream variegated foliage and lovely lavender flowers. Its lush mounding habit and low-light requirements (partial sun to shade) make it an especially good choice for any urban space. (Zones 3–9)

TRYCYRTIS FORMOSANA 'PURPLE BEAUTY'
With delicate rich foliage and white orchid-like blooms flecked with purple, 'Purple Beauty' is perfect for a small space, growing equally well in containers and in the garden. Trycyrtis likes rich, moist, well-drained soil and partial to full shade. (Zones 5–8)

■ **Hosta 'Wide Brim.'**

Best Bets: Shrubs for Urban Gardeners

Like everything else in the city garden, urban shrubs need to be multipurpose. At their best, they will have at least three of the following qualities: fragrance, winter interest in terms of bark or silhouette, colorful blooms or fruit, and unique leaf shape or texture. Here are some of our favorites:

CARYOPTERIS X CLANDONENSIS 'DARK KNIGHT'
With its rich dark blue flowers and silvery-green aromatic foliage, 'Dark Knight' is a great low-growing, low-maintenance shrub. These late-blooming bluebeards (August through October) do best in well-drained soil and full sun. (Zones 5–8 in the South and 5–9 in the West)

DAPHNE X BURKWOODII 'CAROL MACKIE'
Compact (three feet tall), early-blooming (May), and fragrant, 'Carol Mackie' has beautiful clusters of light pink flowers that emerge from grayish-green and gold-edged leaves. Daphnes need well-drained soil with a neutral pH, and it is preferable to keep their roots cool in the summer under a cover of mulch. 'Carol MacKie' will tolerate full sun to partial shade. (Zones: 4–7 in the South and 4–8 in the West)

HAMAMELIS X INTERMEDIA 'ARNOLD PROMISE'
After a long winter in the city, nothing is more welcome than a harbinger of spring, and this witch hazel is one of the earliest shrubs, often opening its fragrant yellow blossoms while there is still some snow on the ground. This particular hybrid will put on a dramatic display again in the fall, when it's gray-green foliage turns to fiery shades of orange and yellow. Witch hazel grows to be 12 feet tall and does well in conditions ranging from partial shade to full sun. (Zones 5–8)

HYDRANGEA SERRATA 'PRECIOSA'
Want a show-stopping shrub that flowers in July and August? Look no further. These hardy three-foot bushes have wonderful clusters of pink flowers, which become richer in color as they age. Great for partially shady sites, this hydrangea prefers slightly acidic soil. (Zones 6–8)

SYRINGA MICROPHYLLA 'SUPERBA'
This wonderfully fragrant four- to six-foot-tall, low-maintenance shrub is a joy in the garden. Remarkably, 'Superba' flowers twice: first in late May and again at the end of the summer. It's a slow-growing plant that works beautifully at the back of the perennial border. As with all lilacs, 'Superba' prefers fertile, well-drained soil with a slightly alkaline pH. (Zones 5–7 in the South and 5–8 in the West)

VIBURNUM X BURKWOODII
The most fragrant variety of all the viburnums, this tough semi-evergreen shrub produces lustrous leaves and clusters of flowers in three-inch pinkish-white balls, which are followed by berries that range from red to yellow. While *burkwoodii* can handle some shade, full sun ensures the best yield of flowers and berries. (Zones 5–8)

■ *Daphne x burkwoodii*
'Carol MacKie.'

Alternative Urban Lifestyles: Raised Beds

GARDENING IN RAISED BEDS HAS BEEN POPULAR IN urban areas ever since the first settlers reached our shores in the early 1600s. The inhabitants of Plimoth Plantation, for instance, used them almost exclusively in their backyard town gardens. These early settlers knew from experience that the sandy soil under the colony was too poor for food crops, and if they wanted to grow things quickly that would thrive, raised beds were the only way to go—a fact that still holds true for many urban gardeners.

First, though, let's talk terminology. Although today we generally consider the term "raised bed" to mean a narrow planting area held above the natural soil level by some form of containment such as stone or planks, in reality raised beds don't need to be edged with hard materials to be effec-

■ **The beginnings of urban gardening in North America: the raised beds at Plimoth Plantation.**

tive (though my personal opinion is that they almost always look much better if they are). A raised bed's principal advantage is derived entirely from the slight bit of elevation caused when mounding the soil. As a result, drainage is increased considerably; the beds warm up earlier in the spring (thereby extending the growing season); soil compaction is almost eliminated (as long as you never tread on the beds, which you should never do anyway!), and amendments are much easier to add to the soil. All of these factors mean substantial increases in productivity, often on the order of 50 percent or more.

Another benefit of raised beds is pest reduction. Insects and other infestations are easier to spot and treat when the beds are closer to eye level, and a bit of height can also do wonders in suburban areas for discouraging rabbits and other nibblers. Add to this the fact that raised beds provide easier access for those of us who have difficulty bending, and you can quickly see why they have dramatically increased in popularity in recent years, especially among senior gardeners.

Although raised beds don't *have* to be edged, some type of hard border is almost a necessity in a small urban setting, where there's no room for drifting or fuzzy visual lines. Almost any kind of material can be used to enclose a raised bed: naturally rot-resistant wood, stone, brick, even concrete block. Which you choose depends entirely upon your taste and budget. The only exception is a prohibition against chemically treated timber if you're thinking about growing edible food crops.

In terms of the size and scale of a raised bed, the sky's the limit. Just be sure to match the look and feel of your beds to that of your site, and remember that if you're building your beds for active harvesting (as opposed to raised planters for ornamental gardening), you should make them no more than four feet wide and preferably aligned on an east-west axis to maximize sun exposure. You should also make sure that your beds are easily accessible on both sides for maintenance and harvest.

Container Gardening on Decks, Balconies, and Roofs

FOR GARDENERS WHOSE ONLY OUTDOOR SPACE IS SOME form of hard surface such as a balcony, deck, or rooftop, container gardening is the way to go, and in fact can be extremely rewarding when done properly. Containers can provide a lush, almost instant garden effect to a small space where none previously existed. Granted, container gardening can be somewhat

■ **Roof decks like this one make your next weekend getaway only a few steps away.**

■ Choosing the right containers is essential to creating a beautiful container garden.

of an idiosyncratic art: it's a bit tricky to master at first, and has its own unique set of rules and guidelines for success. But that having been said, it can still be one of the most satisfying and cost effective ways to garden in the city.

The most important factor to remember about container gardening is that you are growing on top of the ground, not in it, and this fact, though obvious by definition, has some not-so-evident ramifications in terms of your plants' ability to thrive and prosper. The main culprits here are severe heat and cold. Robbed of the soil's natural insulating qualities, plants in containers are subjected to temperature extremes their earthbound cousins simply don't experience.

In the summer, container-bound plants heat up and dry out much faster than plants in the ground, not only placing much greater stress on the plants, but also increasing their watering requirements many-fold. For the gardener, this means putting into action either a vigilant watering regimen or some type of automated watering system, such as individual pot-drip irrigation. In the winter, the roots of container plants, literally surrounded by air, are subject to far more cold than earthbound plants. As a result, they often will exceed their minimum temperature tolerance, producing a quick death through winterkill. The only way to avoid this fate is to choose plants that are a full growing zone hardier than those you would ordinarily choose if you were planting directly into the ground. Of course, container size is a mitigating factor in winter and summer stress: in general, the larger the container, the less watering it will need, and the better the insulation it will provide. Large containers, however, have their own liability: weight.

If you've never picked up a large potted plant, you're probably in for a big surprise. Potted plants are *very heavy*. A midsized plant in a tub can easily weigh 60 to 70 pounds; a 10-foot tree, several hundred pounds. The main culprit, of course, is not the plant but what's in the pot: dirt weights a ton, and water, that otherwise benign substance, weighs eight pounds per gallon.

If you're planning an urban garden on top of a building, on a balcony, or on top of some other type of structure, you *must* consult with a professional engineer before placing any additional load on the structure. Fully filled planters and other garden containers can weigh thousands of pounds, making professional help a requirement when assessing whether or not your structure can bear the weight. In fact, some municipalities require a building permit before any structures can be added to a bare roof deck or balcony.

Even where decking has already been installed on a roof, it pays to double-check with a professional—roof decks are actually quite complicated mechanisms designed to distribute load evenly across the top of the building. If they are compromised at any one point, disastrous consequences can occur. Here's a true cautionary tale. Some friends of mine were about to purchase an expensive loft apartment in the TriBeCa neighborhood of Manhattan. On the day they were intending to close the deal, they drove to meet the real estate agent at their new home. As they turned the corner, they were confronted by emergency vehicles, sirens, and the sight of a half-hysterical real estate agent. It turns out their about-to-be upstairs neighbor had built an extensive rooftop garden without the requisite load-bearing studies. Arriving early to sign the deal in the loft below, the agent had been doing a final inspection of the place when the roof, along with its new garden, partially collapsed onto the floors below. Fortunately no one was seriously injured, and the damage eventually was repaired, but the misguided owners of the roof garden—who had built without permit or permission—found themselves facing years of multimillion-dollar lawsuits.

Choosing Containers

SOMEONE ONCE ASKED ME DURING A LECTURE IF designing a container garden started with the pots or with the plants, and for a moment, I was at a loss for an answer. For while the question sounds logical enough, the best response is "neither." Container gardening actually starts with an idea of what you really want to achieve: What's the purpose of the planting? Do you want to screen a window balcony from the prying views of neighbors? Add some scent to a window box? Create a rooftop hideaway? Deciding your goal will then dic-

(continued on page 264) **261**

Step by Step: Repotting a Plant

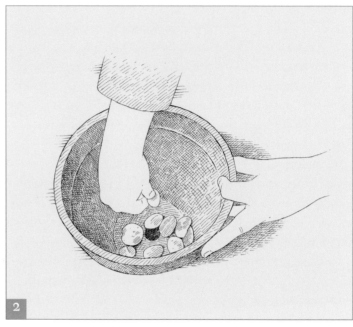

IF YOUR CONTAINER GARDENING EFFORTS HAVE BEEN successful and your plants are thriving, inevitably your charges will outgrow their pots, and you'll be faced with the prospect of finding them a larger home. When do you know it's time to re-pot? Well, often there are subtle early warning signs: pot-bound plants will start to wilt between waterings; roots may begin to protrude from the drainage hole; and the plants' leaves will often turn a lighter shade of green as nutrients in the soil are exhausted. To be absolutely sure, the best method—and one that is perfectly harmless to the plant, by the way—is to briefly remove the plant from the pot and examine the root ball.

To begin this process, bring your plant to a work area where a bit of mess won't matter. Next, water your plant thoroughly, and allow it to drain completely. (This will help to keep the soil in place during the tipping procedure.) Then place your fingers around the crown of the plant, turn the pot over, and begin to gently tap the edge of the pot against a hard surface, loosening the bond between soil and pot. (See illustration 1.) Sometimes, with heavily pot-bound plants, you may need to slide a knife or other sharp object around the side of the pot in order to free the roots. Now examine the newly exposed root ball. If the roots haven't yet completely filled the container, simply place the plant back in the old pot, and check again in three to six months. If, however, the roots have already formed a tightly interwoven mass with little or no visible soil, the plant is ready to move on to a bigger container.

Select a pot that is approximately two inches larger in all dimensions than the current one you're using. Always make sure that your choice of container provides sufficient drainage. (Pots without holes in the bottom, while often quite decorative, are death to most plants and should be avoided.) Many gardeners make the mistake of selecting too large a pot, on the presumption that if bigger is good, even bigger is better. Unfortunately this is not the case, for several reasons: large

pots are hard to handle; they are extremely heavy when wet; and they arc quite expensive. If you don't need a huge pot, don't use one (not to mention the fact that a tiny plant in a large pot looks rather silly, much like a child wearing an adult's clothes). Horticulturally speaking, using overly large pots isn't a sound practice either, because some plants, such as gardenias, clivias, and geraniums, use the process of becoming pot-bound as a trigger to flower—so if you never fill the pot, you will have few if any flowers. Also, if space is an issue, pot size matters, because smaller pots help to keep plants from growing out of bounds.

Once you've chosen your pot, place some rough materials such as stones, large bark chips, or old potsherds over the drainage hole. (See illustration 2.) Make sure that the hole is covered sufficiently to prevent soil from leaking out but is not completely blocked. Next, place about two inches of good potting soil in the bottom of the pot, and position the plant on top. (See illustration 3.) There should be an inch or so of space around all sides, and the soil surface should rest an inch or two below the level of the rim. (You may need to add or subtract soil to achieve the proper height, but be sure to leave sufficient room to prevent overflow when watering.) Then fill in the sides with soil, tamping the earth down as you go to eliminate any air pockets. (A hardy thump or two often helps this process along.) When you're done, water well, until moisture appears through the bottom drainage hole. (See illustration 4.) You may need to top off the pot with a bit of extra soil if the level has dropped after watering, and for plants that are to be placed outside or in very sunny areas you may also want to add a bit of mulch, such as river-washed gravel or bark chips. Not only does this add a pleasant decorative touch, it slows down water loss on hot days and prevents pesky weeds from sprouting around your plant.

tate what type of plants are required (tall shrubs or small trees, flowering bulbs or lush annuals), which in turn will help determine the general size and shape of the containers you'll need. After that, it becomes a question of pure aesthetics: what style and type of container do you like?

Of course, container selection can go in just about any direction, from extremely formal to extremely funky, and what's chosen will depend largely upon your taste, your budget (those planters can get pricey!), and the overall effect you're trying to achieve. It's important to remember, however, that even though a container garden is by its very definition made up of a number of distinct containers, you should try to make sure that each pot or holder relates to the other in terms of color, material, and style. A group of unrelated and discordant pots will appear to be just that, and won't ever achieve the unified garden effect you're looking for.

Material choice is again very much a matter of personal taste: some people prefer the look of wood to ceramic, for example, while others love the feel of clay or the appearance of old lead. As long as the material will stand up to the rigors of being outdoors winter and summer, in addition to keeping with the aesthetic parameters we've just discussed, the choice is up to you. Also, remember that it's you who'll be hauling all those plants, pots, and soil around, and that certain materials are considerably lighter than others!

One final consideration when creating a container garden on a deck or rooftop is the question of permanence. Most people start gardening in containers in a small way, adding pots and plants here and there until at some point the idea of permanently installed planters begins to beckon. In general, I would advise against "codifying" a container garden with permanently placed containers even if your site allows you to do so. Not only does it fix the layout of the space, thereby removing one of the container garden's chief advantages—seasonal spontaneity—but they are very costly to create and cumbersome to plant and maintain. However, if you're convinced that your garden would be enhanced by some permanent planting (or if you've inherited a garden with fixed planters), try to keep the rigidity to a minimum by supplementing the fixed planters with a changing display of movable pots.

Garden Basics:
Choosing the Right Pot

EVER SINCE THE ADVENT OF PLASTIC POTS IN THE 1970S, there has been a huge debate in the horticultural community about whether plastic is better than clay, but to my mind, much of the discussion has missed the point. While clay holds moisture better, allowing the roots to breathe, its disadvantages in terms of extra weight and cost pretty much mitigate the benefits. Far more important is whether or not the pot is appropriate for the plant, both in terms of functionality and aesthetics. The right pot meets three important criteria: (1) it has ample drainage; (2) it is the right size for the plant in terms of scale, neither dominating nor diminishing the plant, and is manageable in terms of moving and maintenance; and (3) the style and color of the pot complement the plant. If these three conditions are met, the choice of clay versus plastic really becomes one of personal taste.

■ Imagine this setting with loud, orange-colored terracotta pots, and you'll understand how well these simple white wooden planters work on this front porch.

Garden Basics:
Planting the Perfect Window Box

The Right Box for the Right Place

Window box gardening begins, appropriately enough, with the box, and finding the right one is important. In general, avoid small or poorly constructed boxes, and try to find the largest box your space (and your back—remember, you have to lift these boxes) can accommodate. The bigger the box, the more root space for your plants, and larger boxes also dry out far less quickly. In addition, make sure you choose boxes that have readily available liners (see below), are well made, and mount easily and securely. Loose window boxes can become deadly missiles if not attached properly.

Soil

For window boxes, the main concern is to find a growing medium that is both lightweight and fertile. We've found that a prefertilized soilless mix (made principally from peat moss and vermiculite) works extremely well. Adding additional fertilizer in the form of slow-release pellets at the time of planting is also a good idea. Avoid the temptation of simply top-dressing over last year's soil and old plant debris with a bit of new mix each spring. Instead, completely clean out and replace the soil in your boxes before replanting to provide the most nutritious mix possible. Replacing your soil yearly also reduces the chance of carrying over any pathogens from the previous year.

Care and Feeding

The primary maintenance issue for flower boxes is watering: window boxes need to be heavily watered once or sometimes even twice a day in the hottest summer weather. While nothing can replace a good soaking, a heavy coat of mulch laid on top of the soil will be of considerable help in decreasing water loss, as well as improving the overall appearance of the box. Here at the Victory Garden, we've experimented over the years with several automatic watering

or water-supplement devices, such as silica gel beads that absorb water. Sadly, we've found most of these lacking. If you're fortunate enough to have an automatic irrigation system, you might consider running a drip line up into your window boxes. It's a fast, efficient, and effective way to take the worry out of hot-weather watering. Finally, don't forget to use water-soluble fertilizer weekly—most annuals are such heavy feeders that they will welcome any additional food you can provide them.

Liners

You've probably seen window box liners at the garden center and thought that their only purpose was to protect the inside of your flower boxes from rot and decay. They have, however, another important use as flower box doubles and/or replacements. Provided you have a bit of extra space, you can plant up the liner just as you would a second flower box, and in so doing, use them as backup planters. The minute your flower boxes are looking a bit peaked, just pop a pre-

■ **The floral abundance of a well-tended window box.**

planted liner into the box and take the peaked plants back to your holding area for a bit of rest. Inserts also come in very handy for seasonal display changes. Just plant up your inserts ahead of time to give the plants a chance to settle in and look their best, and then pop them into the boxes when you want to change the display. Using this method, you can quickly change window boxes from early spring bulbs to summer flowering annuals, to fall annuals, and finally to winter evergreens. Planting in liners has the added convenience of allowing you to work where *you* want to work, rather than awkwardly hanging halfway out of a window frame for hours at a time.

Plant Selections

When selecting plants for your boxes, choose those with extended blooming periods, especially some of the newer and lesser-known annual varieties. Try to avoid selections that flower for only a month or so at a time or require constant deadheading. Also, when choosing your plants, be sure to select species that grow upright, as well as some that will spill over the sides. Window box gardening is very much a three-dimensional affair, and boxes situated in high locations are viewed as much from the bottom as from the top.

DIGGING DEEPER: BEHIND TROMPE L'OEIL

IN SMALL URBAN SPACES, SOMETIMES YOU NEED TO resort to a bit of visual subterfuge to achieve the effects you're seeking. The most commonly employed method is called *trompe l'oeil*, from the French, meaning "a trick of the eye." The technique uses the laws of perspective to create an impression of depth on flat surfaces. The idea isn't new; in fact it was quite popular with the ancient Greeks and Romans, and it has been commonly used in painting since the Renaissance to give the illusion of depth to two-dimensional canvases.

Perhaps the simplest use of trompe l'oeil in the landscape is to employ trellis panels to give a garden space the illusion of greater size. Hung on a wall or fence, these panels (which can be ordered pre-made or built from plans) possess strong diagonal lines that create something of a tunnel effect, thereby making the garden look bigger. These panels are especially effective when the central area is painted with a landscape scene or mirrored, giving the impression that you are looking into a window with a distant view. (The illusion can be further reinforced with a piece of statuary positioned in front of the panel.)

The same idea of diminishing perspective can also be used on a larger scale to achieve a similar effect. In the gardens of the Renaissance, long outdoor staircases were often slightly wider at the top than at the bottom. Rather than strictly parallel lines, slight diagonals were often used on walls and hedges, tapering to a single focal point. Both these alterations generate the same kind of tunnel effect as the panels do, tricking the eye into believing the space is much larger than it really is—an equally useful service in today's urban garden.

Trompe l'oeil isn't just about making spaces seem larger, though. Often the same kind of visual tricks can be used to enliven nondescript flat surfaces, such as the wall of a garage or a neighboring building. One of the cleverest applications I've ever seen was in a small New York City garden. Faced with a large, blank, uninterrupted garage wall on one side of the garden, the owners decided they needed a much more homey and inviting scene. So they created a totally convincing false facade by painting in a fake window, hanging two old shutters and a door found in a local flea market, and building a small "entrance" garden around their trompe l'oeil creation. The effect so fooled casual visitors that many inquired what the "garden cottage" was used for! This same fake facade idea can be adapted to a wide variety of applications, creating interesting spaces where none existed before—and all through the simplest trick of the eye.

■ Trompe l'oeil trellises like these are extremely effective in making small spaces appear much larger than they really are.

Creating a Small Water Feature in a Galvanized Tub

AONE OF THE BEST WAYS TO DROWN OUT CITY NOISE IS with the sound of water, and one of the easiest ways to experience the joys of water gardening is with a small portable water feature. These fountains can be made with half barrels or galvanized wash basins. They're quick to make, look great, and are a fun family project. Here's what you'll need:

- A galvanized basin or half whiskey barrel with a capacity of about 20 gallons.
- A small recirculating water pump. Pumps are rated by flow amounts, measured in gallons per minute. You'll need a pump with a registered flow of 120 gallons per hour or less.
- A small fountainhead kit (also available at hardware stores). These come with a variety of heads to make decorative fountain patterns. Make sure your kit contains a flow restrictor to adjust the water volume. (If not, these can be purchased separately.)
- Water plants. Available at most nurseries and aquarium supply houses, aquatic plants are the star of the small water garden. A variety of species are available. For a water garden of this size, two or three plants should suffice. You should try to select a single floating plant, such as a water hyacinth, as well as one or two plants that will poke up from the water, such as canna or sweet flag. Here are some possibilities:

Dwarf cyperus (*Isocladus cyperaceae*)
(Zones 9–11) A submerged plant with great fluffy texture and a bright spiky look.

Tropical water hyacinth (*Eichhornia crassipes*)
(Zones 9–11) A floater with distinct lilac-blue blooms and balloon-like leaves. (This plant is invasive in areas that stay above freezing and should never be released into the wild.)

1

Sweet flag (*Acorus calamus*)
(Zone 4) Sweet-smelling plants with two- to four-foot-tall foliage.

Canna cultivars (*Canna* species)
(Zone 7) Although many people think of cannas, with their striking colored leaves, solely as a terrestrial plant, they actually enjoy being submerged in water.

Water lilies (many different species)
Be sure to choose dwarf varieties that will remain small.

1 First, fill your basin with water and position your pump in the center of the drum. Now is the time to test the pump and adjust the flow. The cord should be run up and over whatever side you choose for the back. (If you plan to have your gar-

den viewed from all sides, you may want to drill a small hole for the cord, sealing the hole afterward with waterproof caulking.)

2 Next come the plants. Floaters are allowed to do just that. Submerged plants are potted and placed pot and all under the water's surface. When it comes to positioning, remember that taller plants work best in back; arrange the other selections in descending order of size as you continue moving forward. One handy little trick that gives greater control over the height of select plants is to use clay flowerpots (bottom side up), rocks, or bricks as staging devices to help elevate individual selections to a desired height. Pay attention to how the individual plants work together. You are attempting to produce a dynamic contrast in shape, color, and texture. When position-

ing the plants, the water may become quite dirty. To clear the water, let the basin gently overflow with a hose. You can then cover the soil with gravel to keep the earth in place, clarifying the water again if necessary.

3 Once you've arrived at an arrangement you like, plug in the pump, adjust the flow to your liking, and you're all set. Just be sure to position your water garden in full sun (most aquatic plants are sun lovers), and check the basin now and again to add water when needed. If algae or mosquitoes become a problem, the addition of a few goldfish will generally take care of both. In warmer climates with long seasons, you may want to give your plants a little boost of fertilizer.

Ask Michael:
Succulent Gardens

Dear Michael,
Once on the program I saw one of your guests make something he referred to as a "succulent pizza garden," which would be great for my deck. Can you remind me again how he did it?

The man to whom you refer is horticulturist Thomas Hobbs, owner of Southland Nursery in Vancouver, British Columbia, who created a wonderful succulent table garden (he's also the creator of the garden featured on page 126). As the name implies, his miniature landscapes are made entirely from succulent plants and resembles the color and bounty of a freshly made pizza. Not only does this tabletop garden look great, it doesn't require a lot of care, making it a great project for the busy urban gardener.

Begin with choosing an appropriate container: almost any shallow dish or trough will do. Hobbs tends to prefer 16-inch terra-cotta bowls, but you should base your selection not only on personal taste; choose a vessel that allows enough room for your creative juices to flow, while still being easily portable. The only essential here is that the container must have a hole in the bottom to allow for drainage. This may require drilling (carefully!) one yourself.

Succulents are remarkably tough and resilient, and require surprisingly little soil. They do, however, require good drainage. So instead of filling the container completely with earth, fill it three-quarters full with either styrofoam peanuts (which keeps the overall weight of the container lighter and more transportable, and is a great way to reuse that troublesome packing material) or gravel. Both serve equally well to provide effective drainage. Then cover the bottom material with an inch or so of general potting mix.

Next, it's time for the placement of the plants. Before you remove them from their containers, try arranging them on the soil surface to see how the specimens work together. The best strategy is to start with the biggest plants first and position them working from the middle (or slightly off center) out, ar-

ranging them in descending order of size. Also think about each plant's relationship to its neighbor in terms of texture and color. Take some risks: don't be afraid to position a spiky plant next to a flowering rosette, or to make startling contrasts of color or texture. Look at the overall design from several vantage points—especially from above—to insure an integrated design, keeping in mind the most important vantage point is the one from which your creation will ultimately be viewed.

When you are satisfied with your design, place each plant securely in the soil. Once all of the plants have been firmly tucked in, you should add a finishing layer of pebbles as mulch. Any neutral color stone will do fine, except white: says Hobbs, "It's far too '70s and makes the plants look bad. If you like, you can also add a few tiny trinkets in order to create the illusion of an actual landscape: small shells, bridges, paths—whatever tickles your fancy."

When you are done, water thoroughly, and place the container in full sun. Water occasionally when totally dry. Other than trimming the succulents a bit as they grow, or removing dead leaves, your landscape should thrive for several years until it outgrows its space, at which point it will be time to "rebake" your succulent pizza in a new iteration.

Here are a few of the succulents we used to give variety to our container garden:

Aeonium
Agave
Echeveria
Jovibarba
Kalanchoe
Orostachys
Sempervivum

■ **A cluster of Thomas Hobbs's marvelous miniature landscapes.**

Before

Urban

■ **The "before" shot, dark, dank, and dismal. Hardly a place in which you'd want to spend any time.**

If you're faced with a tiny urban backyard full of debris and dead plants and think you'll never be able to have a garden, take heart. Here's a makeover we did in just a few weekends on a very limited budget, following a very clever plan developed by designer Pascale Lucier.

Makeover

■ **Top:** Here's the "after" shot. Pascale Lucier's team has leveled the area slightly, and installed a small sitting terrace of flagstones. The café table and chairs are just the right size and scale for this charming space.

■ **Left:** Here's one of the best tricks in the entire garden: the old chain link fencing would have been extremely expensive to remove and replace. Additionally, it provided zero privacy. Instead, Dave Flanagan, a bamboo fencer, introduced us to a new technique, whereby pre-assembled bamboo screening is rolled out and simply attached to the fence with wire. Bamboo fencing like this provides a cool, sleek look, instant privacy, and will last 20 years or more with almost no maintenance.

273

Before

■ Above: The "before" view, looking the other direction. The entire backyard only measures 20 × 30 feet. The small raised bed was the owner's first attempt at raising a few vegetables and some salad greens.

■ Opposite: The "after" shot. The garden was replaced with a small deck of plantation-grown mahogany. The space in the center has been filled with rich soil and is intended as a small salad garden, with the idea that should the owner ever want one, a small water garden could be substituted instead.

Inspired
Gardens

The Swinnen Garden in Sint-Niklaas, Belgium

WHEN LANDSCAPE DESIGNER CHRISTOPHER SWINNEN moved into his urban town house, the small courtyard garden was a disaster. It was tiny, shady, full of debris, and cut off from the rest of the house. Despite all of these challenges, Swinnen rose to the occasion. His goal? To make this very dark space that was no bigger than the average driveway a natural extension of his house.

The first step in this process was an ingenious scheme to link house and garden together by means of a glass wall and sunken pool. These transparent elements provide the necessary physical separation between indoors and out, while still allowing viewers to experience the garden from within. Swinnen then structured the garden so that it would have several internal levels. This not only provided visual interest for the garden, but also allowed for the creation of separate garden rooms for dining, relaxing, and viewing the garden. Two of these upstairs rooms were divided using an interesting device: Swinnen clustered together a group of container plants including rosemary topiaries and boxwood shrubs that supply the required

277

separation, as well as an opportunity to change the display with plants of seasonal interest.

To counteract what had been a pervasive feeling of shade and darkness in the tiny enclosed garden, Swinnen's plan employed the use of color. The walls of the inner courtyard, which had been a dirty gray, were painted crisp white, helping both to clean up the walls and to expand the feeling of space within the garden.

One final feature worth noting in Swinnen's plan is the use of field maples as an aerial hedge—a classic European design element borrowed from gardens such as Versailles. The green foliage of the maples serves to line and soften the stone walls on the lower levels of the garden without subtracting much-needed floor space, while at the same time providing visual interest when viewed from the small balconies on the second and third stories of the house.

Fortunately for garden travelers, this little gem of a garden, along with Swinnen's attached garden shop, is open to the public. For hours and information, see the Resources section on page 283.

■ **An ever-changing collection of planters like these provides year-round interest in Swinnen's garden, as well as allowing for a dynamic use of the limited floor space. If a large party is planned, the containers simply move to the margins, to be returned to center stage once the guests leave.**

Art Credits

Abbreviations

ctr = center   rt = right   lt = left   bot = bottom

All credits with the designation "/WGBH" are © WGBH Educational Foundation.

Pages i, iv, v, vi, viii, xi, xiii, and xv: Photographs by Jeffrey Dunn/WGBH.

Page xvi: Photograph by Keller & Keller/WGBH.

Page 2: Photograph © Jessie Walker/www.jessiewalker.com. Landscape design by Kellie O'Brien.

Page 4: Photograph © Marion Brenner.

Pages 6–9: Drawings based on illustrations from *A Field Guide to American Houses* by Virginia and Lee McAlester, © 1984 by Virginia Savage and Lee McAlester. Used by permission of Alfred A. Knopf, a division of Random House, Inc.

Page 10: Original drawing by John Burgoyne, based on an illustration from *Cottage Residences* by Andrew Jackson Downing. Reprint of the 1873 edition (New York: Dover Publications, 1981).

Page 11: Photograph © Kindra Clineff/www.kindraclineff.com.

Page 12: Original drawing by John Burgoyne.

Page 14: Photograph by Jeffrey Dunn/WGBH.

Page 16 lt: Photograph courtesy of Michael Weishan.

Page 16 rt: Photograph by Keller & Keller/WGBH.

Page 17: Photograph © Jessie Walker/www.jessiewalker.com.

Page 19: Original drawing by John Burgoyne based on an illustration from *The Victory Garden Landscape Guide* by Thomas Wirth, © 1984 by WGBH Educational Foundation and Thomas Wirth (Boston, Toronto: Little, Brown and Company, 1984).

Page 20 top lt and rt: Photographs courtesy of Walpole Woodworkers.

Page 20 bot lt and page 21 lt: Photographs © Brad Simmons/Esto.

Page 21 rt: Photograph courtesy of Walpole Woodworkers.

Page 22: Photograph © Maryellen Baker/PictureArts/Botanica.

Page 23: Photograph courtesy of Laurie Donnelly/WGBH.

Page 24: Photograph © Arthur N. Orans/Horticultural Photography™.

Page 26: Photograph © Jessie Walker/www.jessiewalker.com.

Page 27: Reproduced with permission of the U.S. Department of Agriculture.

Pages 28–29: Reproduced with permission of the American Horticultural Society.

Pages 30–33: Photograph © 1997 Judith Bromley. Courtesy The Frank Lloyd Wright Archives, Taliesin West, Scottsdale, Ariz.

Page 34: Photograph by Jeffrey Dunn/WGBH.

Page 36: Photograph © Jessie Walker/www.jessiewalker.com.

Page 37: Original drawing by John Burgoyne, based on a drawing by Lea Carmichael.

Pages 38–39: Photograph courtesy of Michael Weishan.

Page 40: Photograph © Cary Hazlegrove/Esto.

Pages 42–43: Photograph by Jeffrey Dunn/WGBH.

Page 44: Design and plan © 2006 by Michael Weishan & Associates. All rights reserved. Used by permission.

Page 45: Original drawing by John Burgoyne, based on a drawing by Penny Delany.

Page 46 lt and rt: Photographs © Wally Eberhart/Visuals Unlimited.

Page 48: Photograph © Wally Eberhart/Visuals Unlimited.

Page 49: Photograph © Steve Maslowski/Visuals Unlimited.

Page 50: Photograph by Jeffrey Dunn/WGBH.

Page 53: Photograph © Jeff Daly/Visuals Unlimited.

Pages 54–57: Photographs © Louise Tanguay/www.louisetanguay.com.

Page 58: Photograph © Jessie Walker/www.jessiewalker.com.

Page 60: From *The Art of Beautifying Suburban Home Grounds* by Frank J. Scott (New York: D. Appleton & Co., 1870).

Page 61: Photograph © Mark Darley/Esto.

Page 62: Photographs courtesy of Michael Weishan.

Page 65: Original drawings by John Burgoyne, based on illustrations from *Practical Guide to Home Landscaping,* © 1972

The Reader's Digest Association, Inc., by permission of the Reader's Digest Association, Inc., New York; www.rd.com.

Page 66 top rt: Photograph © Lee Anne White/ www.leeannewhite.com. Landscape architecture by Betty Ajay.

Page 66 top lt: Photograph © Lee Anne White/ www.leeannewhite.com. Landscaping by J. C. Enterprise Services, Inc.

Page 66 bot: Photograph © Lee Anne White/ www.leeannewhite.com. Landscape design by Paula Refi. Stonework by Mark Grubaugh.

Page 67: Photograph © Lynn Karlin/ www.lynnkarlinphoto.com.

Page 68: Photograph © Roger Foley/www.foleyfoto.com. Landscape design by Tom Mannion.

Page 69: Photograph © Marion Brenner.

Page 70: Photograph © Betsy Pinover Schiff/Esto.

Page 72: Photograph © Peter Gridley/Getty Images.

Page 73: Photograph © Betsy Pinover Schiff/Esto.

Pages 74, 76, 77: Photographs © Roger Foley/www .foleyfoto.com. Landscape design by Tom Mannion.

Pages 78, 79, 80 top, 81: Photographs courtesy of Johnson's Nursery, Inc. Landscape design by Dennis Buettner FASLA. Stone provided by Halquist Stone Company. Complete site work, hardscape, plants, and installation by Johnson's Nursery, Inc. (www.johnsonsnursery.com).

Page 80 bot: Landscape design by Dennis Buettner FASLA, Buettner & Associates, Inc.

Pages 82–83: Original drawings by John Burgoyne, based on photographs by Catriona Tudor Erler.

Page 84: Photograph © Arthur N. Orans/Horticultural Photography™.

Page 88: Photograph © Betsy Pinover Schiff/Esto.

Pages 90–93: Photographs courtesy Colonial Williamsburg Foundation.

Page 94: Photograph © Elizabeth Glasgow/Esto.

Page 97: Photograph © Jessie Walker/ www.jessiewalker.com.

Page 98 top lt: Photograph © John Wang/Getty Images.

Page 98 bot: Photograph © Scott Frances/Esto.

Page 98 top rt: Photograph © Marion Brenner.

Page 99: Photograph © Steven Wooster/Garden Picture Library.

Page 100: Photograph by Jeffrey Dunn/WGBH.

Page 101: Photograph © Marion Brenner.

Page 102: Photograph © Jessie Walker/ www.jessiewalker.com. Landscape design by Kellie O'Brien.

Page 103: Photograph © Jessie Walker/ www.jessiewalker.com. Landscape architecture by Doug Hoerr.

Pages 104–105: Original drawings by John Burgoyne, based on photographs by Catriona Tudor Erler.

Page 106: Photograph © Keith Swan/Esto.

Page 107: Photograph © Mark Darley/Esto.

Page 108: Photograph by Aquascapes Designs, Inc. (www.aquascapedesigns.com).

Page 109: Photograph by Jeffrey Dunn/WGBH.

Pages 110–111: Original drawings by John Burgoyne, based in part on photographs by Aquascapes Designs, Inc. (www.aquascapesdesigns.com).

Page 113: Photograph © Jessie Walker/ www.jessiewalker.com.

Page 114: Photograph © Jessie Walker/ www.jessiewalker.com. Landscape design by Kellie O'Brien.

Page 115: Photograph © Betsy Pinover Schiff/Esto. Garden design by John Barham.

Page 116: Photograph © Jessie Walker/ www.jessiewalker.com. Design by Lee Randhava.

Page 117: Photograph © Betsy Pinover Schiff/Esto.

Page 119 lt: Photograph © Arthur N. Orans/Horticultural Photography™.

Page 119 rt: Photograph © Krischan Photography/ www.krischanphoto.com.

Page 121: Photograph © Jessie Walker/ www.jessiewalker.com.

Page 122: Photograph © Krischan Photography/ www.krischanphoto.com.

Page 124: Photograph by Keller & Keller/WGBH.

Pages 126–127, 128: Photographs © David McDonald. Garden design by Thomas Hobbs.

Page 130: Photograph © Jessie Walker/ www.jessiewalker.com.

Page 132: Photograph © Jessie Walker/ www.jessiewalker.com. Landscape artist Rocco Fiore.

Page 133: Photograph © Jessie Walker/ www.jessiewalker.com.

Page 134: Photograph © Roger Foley/www.foleyfoto.com.

Page 135: Photograph © Bill Banaszewski/Visuals Unlimited.

Page 136: Photograph © Janet Sorrell/Garden Picture Library.

Pages 138–139: Photographs courtesy of Turfgrass Producers International (TPI).

Pages 140–141: Original drawings by John Burgoyne. Illustration 2 based on a photograph courtesy of Emerald Seed & Supply (www.emeraldseedandsupply.com).

Pages 142, 143: Photographs by Jeffrey Dunn/WGBH.

Page 147: Photograph courtesy of Turfgrass Producers International (TPI).

Page 148: Photograph © Charles Melton/Visuals Unlimited.

Page 150: Photograph © John Glover/Garden Picture Library.

Page 152 top: Photograph © Sandra Ivany/ PictureArts/Botanica.

Page 152 bot: Photograph © Marion Brenner.

Page 153 top lt: Photograph © Mark Darley/Esto.

Page 153 top rt: Photograph © D. Cavagnaro/DRK PHOTO.

Page 153 bot: Photograph © Jessie Walker/ www.jessiewalker.com.

Pages 154–155, 156: Photographs by David Andersen/Courtesy of The Mount.

Page 158: Photograph by Jeffrey Dunn/WGBH.

Page 160: Photograph © Kindra Clineff/ www.kindraclineff.com.

Page 161: Photograph © Jessie Walker/ www.jessiewalker.com.

Page 162: Photograph © Jessie Walker/ www.jessiewalker.com. Landscape design by Kellie O'Brien.

Page 163: Photograph by Jeffrey Dunn/WGBH.

Page 164: This illustration, provided courtesy of The

Taunton Press, was originally published in *Fine Gardening* magazine, Issue # 78.

Page 164: Photograph © Marion Brenner.

Page 165 lt: Photograph © 2001 Darrell Gulin/DRK PHOTO.

Page 165 ctr: Photograph © 1995 Darrell Gulin/DRK PHOTO.

Page 165 rt: Photograph © Friedrich Strauss/Garden Picture Library.

Pages 166–167: Original drawing by John Burgoyne, after a plan by Kip Anderson.

Page 169 lt: Photograph courtesy of Wayside Gardens (www.waysidegardens.com).

Page 169 rt: Photograph by Keller & Keller/WGBH.

Page 171: Photograph © Jeff Drewitz/DRK PHOTO.

Pages 172, 174: Photographs by Jeffrey Dunn/WGBH.

Page 175: Photograph courtesy of W. Atlee Burpee Company.

Pages 176–177: Photograph © Kindra Clineff/www.kindra clineff.com.

Page 178: Photograph by Jeffrey Dunn/WGBH.

Page 179: Photographs courtesy of Michael Weishan.

Pages 180–181: Photographs by Jeffrey Dunn/WGBH.

Pages 182–183: Original drawings by John Burgoyne, after photographs by Jeffrey Dunn/WGBH.

Pages 184–187: Photographs © Krischan Photography/www.krischanphoto.com.

Page 188: Photograph by Keller & Keller/WGBH.

Pages 190, 191: Photographs by Jeffrey Dunn/WGBH.

Page 193: Original drawing by John Burgoyne, after a plan by Kip Anderson.

Pages 194, 195: Photographs by Jeffrey Dunn/WGBH.

Pages 196–197: Original drawings by John Burgoyne, based on illustrations from *The New Victory Garden* by Robert Thomson, © 1987 WGBH, Russell Morash, and Robert Thomson (Boston, Toronto: Little, Brown and Company, 1987).

Pages 198, 199: Photographs by Jeffrey Dunn/WGBH.

Pages 200, 207: Photographs by Keller & Keller/WGBH.

Page 208: Photograph © David Cavagnaro/DRK PHOTO.

Page 209 top: Photograph by Keller & Keller/WGBH.

Pages 209 bot, 210: Photographs by Jeffrey Dunn/WGBH.

Resources

The following "inspired gardens" are open to the public:

TALIESIN
Taliesin Visitor Center
5607 County Highway C
Spring Green, WI 53588
(608) 588-7940
www.franklloydwright.org

LES JARDINS DE MÉTIS
Reford Gardens/Les Jardins de Métis
200 route 132
Grand-Métis, Québec GoJ 1Zo
Canada
(418) 775-2222

COLONIAL WILLIAMSBURG
The Colonial Williamsburg Foundation
PO Box 1776
Williamsburg, VA 23187-1776
(757) 229-1000
www.history.org

EDITH WARTON'S THE MOUNT
The Mount Estate & Gardens
2 Plunkett Street
Box 974
Lenox, MA 01240
(413) 637-1899
www.edithwharton.org

THE BOERNER BOTANICAL GARDENS
Boerner Botanical Gardens
9400 Boerner Drive
Hales Corner, WI 53130
(414) 525-5600
www.countyparks.com/horticulture/boerner

THE VEGETABLE GARDEN OF THOMAS JEFFERSON
Monticello
PO Box 217
Charlottesville, VA 22902
(434) 984-9822
www.monticello.org

THE REDLAND FRUIT AND SPICE PARK
24801 SW 187 Avenue
Homestead, FL 33031
(305) 247-5727
fsp@miamidade.gov

Index

Page numbers in *italics* indicate illustrations.

agaves, *176*
Ageratum 'Blue Horizon,' *174*
Agrostis (bentgrasses), 138, 146, 150
ajuga, *152*
Amelanchier (serviceberry), 254
American Horticultural Society (AHS), 27–28
analagous flower schemes, 165
Anderson, Kip, *14*, 142–43, *172*, *180*, *181*, 192, 194, 199, *214*
annuals, 137, 193
    defined, 160
    flowers as, 160, 162, 163, 173–74
    grown from seed, 180–81
    rye grass as, 137, 146
    three groups of, 180
aphids, 148
apples, 240–41
    flowering crab (*Malus floribunda*), *38*, *56*, 112, *113*, 254
armyworms, 148
'Arnold Promise' (*Hamamelis x intermedia*), 256
artichokes, 218
Arts and Crafts style, 8, 10
ash trees, *114*
Asia, walkways in, 97, *98*
asparagus, 193
asphalt, *67*
    chip-sealed, 63, 64, *79*
Astilbe chinensis 'Pumila,' 255
Astrantia major 'Bo-Ann,' 255
automobiles, 60
    disembarkment space for, 64, 65
    parking for, *16*, *18*, 62, 64, 65, 253
azaleas, 76
    Exbury, 56

baby's breath, *152*
backyards, 16, 18, 94–129
    forcing branches indoors and, 121–23
    front yards compared with, 96
    Garden Conservancy and, 125
    of Hobbs, 126–29
    living area in, *see* living areas, outdoor
    planning and planting for the future in, 112
    ponds and wildlife in, 124–25
    shrubs in, 115–20
    trees in, 113–15, 118–20
    urban, 248
    water gardening in, 107–12
Bacon, Francis, 131
Bahia grass (*Paspalum notate*), 139, 146
balance vs. symmetry, 10, 11
balconies, 248, 259, 261
bamboo fencing, 273
Barbados gooseberries (*Pereskia aculeata*), 244
basil, sweet, *199*, 207
basket weave pattern, 100
beans, 199, 201, 209, 213
beech, European (*Carpinus betulus*), 62
beech hedges, 22
beets, 201, 209
begonias, *246*
Belgium, 22, 276–79, 281
bentgrasses (*Agrostis* species), 138, 146, 150
Berberis, dwarf red, *152*
Bermuda grass (*Cynodon dactylon*), 139, 146, 148, 151
berries, 220–45
    see also blueberries; raspberries; strawberries
Betts, Edwin Morris, 218
biennials:
    defined, *161*
    flowers as, 160–63
    vegetables as, 193

billbugs, 148

birches, *152*

birds, 15, 124, 141

blackberries, 220, 223

black jaboticaba (*Myrciaria cauliflora*), 242

'Black Velvet Rose' (*Geranium*), 175

blends, grass-seed, 137

blueberries, 220, 223, 235–38

    rake for, *235*

    selected, 236–38

blue gramma grass, 146

bluegrass, 137

    Kentucky (*Poa pratensis*), 138, 146, 148, 150,

      151

'Blue Horizon' (*Ageratum*), 174

'Blue Pearl' (*Vinca*), 175

Blue Poppy Glade, 57

bluestone, 100, *102*, 103

'Bo-Ann' (*Astrantia major*), 255

Boerner, Alfred L., 185, 186

Boerner Botanical Gardens, 184–86, 281

Boltania asteroides, 84

borders:

    herbaceous, 163

    shrubbery, 115–17

    see also perennial borders

boysenberries, 240

branches, indoor forcing of, 121–23

brick, 17, 71

    for driveways, 63, 64

    for outdoor living areas, *99*, 100, 103, 104–5

    for walkways, 68, *69*, *70*

Brinkley, Kent, 91–92

broccoli, 194, 195, 201

Brunnera 'Jack Frost,' 255

Brussels sprouts, 211

Budding, Edwin, 133

Buettner, Dennis, *80*

buffalo grass (*Buchloe dactyloides*), 139, 146

bushes, *see* shrubs

bush snap beans, 201

cabbage, 194, 200, 201, 211

    Chinese, 202

    red, *200*

camellias, 76

Carex siderostricta 'Variegata,' 255

'Carol MacKie' (*Daphne x burkwoodii*), 256, 257

Carpinus betulus (European beech), 62

carrots, 192, 195, 200, 202, 211

Caryopteris x clandonensis 'Dark Knight,' 256

catalogs, seed, 193–94

cauliflower, 195, 202

Cedrus atlantica 'Glauca,' *119*

celosia, 176

centipede grass, 146

Central Park, 89

Charles, Prince, 189

chemicals, 134, 192

Cheney, Mamah Borthwick, 31, 32

'Cherry Blossom' (*Salvia coccinea*), 175

children, 18, 141

chinch bugs, 149

Chionanthus virginicus (white fringe tree), 254

cilantro, 207

Civilian Conservation Corps (CCC), 185

clay, clay soil, 46–49, 135

climate, 18, 35

    grass and, 137–39

    zone maps and, 27–29

    see also microclimates

cobbles, 63, 64, *67*, 68

cold frames, 195, 196–97

collards, 202, 211

Colonial era, flowers in, 160

Colonial-style houses, 5, 6

Colonial/Tudor revival style, 8

Colonial Williamsburg, 90–93

color wheel, for flowers, 164–65, 172

complementary flower schemes, 165

compost, *46*, 47, 48, 50–52, 56, 168

    contents of, 51

    for lawns, 135, 140, 143

making, 50–51

old sod in, 182

things not to add to, 52

concrete, 63–64, *67*, 75

conifers, *26*

containers, *126*, 175–76, *176*

repotting plants in, 262–63

selection of, *260*, *261*, 264–65

for urban gardens, 259–65

Coreopsis verticillata, 185

corn, 190, 192, 206, 213

Cornus kousa (Kousa dogwood), 254

Cotoneaster, *84*

cottage style, *21*, *73*

cover crops, 213

crape myrtle (*Lagerstromia indica*), 254

crop rotation, 200

Crowley, Abraham, 95

cucumbers, 190, *191*, *198*, 199, 202, 209, 213

currants, 239

cutworms, 149

Cynodon dactylon (Bermuda grass), 139, 146, 148, 151

dahlias, 176

Daphne x burkwoodii 'Carol MacKie,' 256, *257*

'Dark Knight' (*Caryopteris x clandonensis*), 256

decks, 96–99, 248, 259, 261

Decoration of Houses, The (Wharton), 155

deer, 212

Delphinium 'Pacific Giant Hybrids,' *185*

de-thatching process, 134, 136

dewberries, 240

dill, 207

dogwood, Kousa (*Cornus kousa*), 254

dollar spots, 150

double-digging method, 183

drainage, 14, 135, 193

driveways, 16, 18, *62*, 63–68, *79*, 88, 96

paving options for, 63–64

shape, size, and direction of, 64–66

walkways compared with, 68

drought, 134, 145

ducks, 124

early Colonial style, 6, 10

early revival styles, 7

earthworms, *49*

"Echeveria pizzas," *126*

eclectic styles, 9

edible plants, *248*

eggplant, 194, 203, 208

Egyptian onions, 218

Ely, Helena Rutherfurd, 35

empowerment, 4

endive, 218

England, 35, 125

entertaining, 16, 18, 96

furniture for, 106–7

outdoor scale and, 88

Erigeron 'Profusion,' *174*

erosion, 53, 193

euonymous (*Euonymus alata*), *186*

European beech (*Carpinus betulus*), *62*

evergreens, 42, 56, 116, 127

in foundation plantings, 73, 75, 76, *78*

"evergreen spine," 116

fairy rings, 150

'Fascination' (*Veronicastrum*), *34*

'Favorita' tomatoes, *188*

feathering, 136–37

Federal-era houses, *11*

fencing, 17–21, *62*, 212, *273*

ferns, 176

Ferrabee, James, 133

fertilizer, 52–53, 168, 183

for lawns, 134, 135, 140, 142, 145

for vegetable gardens, 53, 192

fescue, 137, 138, 146, *152*

Finnie House, *91*

flagstones, *101*, 103, *273*

Flanagan, Dave, *273*

floral shears, 214

flower beds, preparation of, 182–83

flowering crab apple (*Malus floribunda*), *38*, *56*, 112, *113*, 254

flowers, 158–87

  annuals, 160, 162, 163, 173–74

  color wheel for, 164–65, 172

  in general landscape, 175–76

  in perennial border, 162, 163, 166–74

  trends and, 160, 162–63

  tulip displays and, *178–79*

  in vegetable gardens, 160, 175–76

footprint, 13

foundation plantings, 18, 63, 72–77, 96, 115

  adequate depth and, *74*

  best bets for, 85–87

  evergreens in, 73, 75, 76, *78*

  flowers for, 175

  most common mistake with, 77

  origin of, 73–75

  professional assistance with, 75

  selection of, 76–77

  stagnant water and, 14

  step-by-step instructions for, 82–83

fountains, 109

foxgloves, *161*

front yards, 16, 18, 58–93

  backyards compared with, 96

  in Colonial Williamsburg, 90–93

  importance of streetscapes and, 60–63

  Milwaukee makeover and, *78–81*

  see also driveways; foundation plantings; walkways

Fuller, Thomas, 221

furniture, outdoor, 96, 106–7, *186*, *273*

fusarium blight, 151

fuschia *Genii*, 129

Gaillardia x grandiflora 'Goblin,' *185*

Garden, The (Crowley), 95

Garden Beautiful, The (Robinson), 3

Garden Conservancy, 125

gardens:

  plant twice, cut once in, 15

  rooftop, 248, 251, 253, 259, 261

  "rooms" of, 16

  use of term, 5

  see also urban gardens; water gardens; *specific gardens*

geese, 124

Georgian/Adam/Federal style, 6, 99

Geranium 'Black Velvet Rose,' 175

'Glauca' (*Cedrus atlantica*), 119

'Goblin' (*Gaillardia x grandiflora*), 185

Goldman, Amy, 215

Gomphrena 'Woodcreek Rose,' 175

gooseberries, 220, 238, 239

  Barbados (*Pereskia aculeata*), 244

grading machines, 135

grading rakes, 136

granite, *67*, 100, 103, *116*

grass, 130–51, 176, 192

  cool-season, 137, 138, 145

  ideal mowing heights for, 146

  as mulch, 208

  right kind of, 137

  steps, 156–57

  thatch and, 136

  warm-season, 137, 139

grass seed, 134, 136–37

  blends, 137

  planting a new lawn from, 140–41

  selection of, 137

gravel, *152*, 193

  for driveways, 63, 64

  for outdoor living areas, *103*

  for walkways, 68

Great Depression, 185

greenhouses, 18, 194–95, 211

groundwater, 40

gypsum, 49

Hamamelis x intermedia 'Arnold Promise,' 256

hay, 140

heat mats, 181

hedges, 17, 18, 22–25, 115

    choosing the perfect plant for, 24–25

    for vegetable gardens, 212

Helleborus 'Pink Lady,' 255

herbaceous border, 163

herbicide, 134, 137

herbs, *152*, 207

hill raspberry (*Rubus niveus*), 244

Himalayan poppies (*Meconopsis*), *54*, 57

History of the Worthies of England (Fuller), 221

Hobbs, Thomas, 126–29, 270, *271*

holly, *24*

Hopes and Fears for Art (Morris), 59

horseradish, 193

Hosta 'Wide Brim,' 255

houses:

    fencing and, 20–21

    garden style and, 5–11, 59, *61*

    sight lines from, 16–17, *80*

    urban gardens and, 248, *250*

humus, *46*, *48*

hydrangeas, *40*

Hydrangea serrata 'Preciosa,' 256

impatiens, 160, 162

insects, 148, 149

interior design, landscape design compared with, 4

irises, 176

Italian Villas and Their Gardens (Wharton), 155

jaboticaba (*Myrciaria cauliflora* and *M. jaboticaba*), 242,
    245

'Jack Frost' (*Brunnera*), 255

Japanese garden, 251

Jefferson, Thomas, 216–19

kale, 203, 211, 218

Kentucky bluegrass (*Poa pratensis*), 138, 146, 148, 150, 151

knives, for laying sod, 142, 144

Kousa dogwood (*Cornus kousa*), 254

lady's mantle, 176

Lagerstromia indica (crape myrtle), 254

landscape design:

    checklist for, 18

    house style matched with, 5–11, 59, *61*

    interior design compared with, 4

    plans for, 11–17, *44, 45*

    scale of, 88, *133*

    symbols used for, 45

lavatera, 180

lavender, *152*

lawn mowers, 18, 70, 133

    sharpening of blades of, 146, 147

lawns, 130–57

    alternatives to, *152–53*

    amount of, 133

    assessment of, 134

    avoiding foot traffic on, 141, 144

    common problems of, 148–51

    cutting of, 133

    environmental impact of, 132

    fertilizer dos and don'ts for, 145

    grading for, 135–36

    history of, 132–33

    maintenance of, 145–47

    new, starting, 134–35

    planted from seed, 140–41

    rugs compared with, *130*

    seed vs. sod for, 136–37

    sod laying for, 142–44

    use of professionals and, 135, 136

    see also grass; grass seed

leaf spot (melting out), 150

leeks, 194, 203, 211

Les Jardins de Métis, 55–57

lettuce, 190, 192, 194, 200, 203, 211, 218

    butterhead (Sangria), *211*

Leucanthemum x superbum 'Nordlicht,' *185*

Lightfoot House, *91*

lillies, *42*, 176

    Asiatic, *160*

lime, 75, 135, 213

linoleum knives, 142

living areas, outdoor, *94*, 96–107

   design selection for, 96–99

   furniture for, 96, 106–7

   importance of, 96

   laying your own, 104–5

   paving considerations for, 99–103

   size of, 106–7

loam, 46, 47

loganberries, 240

Lolium perenne (perennial ryegrass), 138, 146, 151

Lucier, Pascale, 272, *273*

magazines, as source of ideas, 5

magnolia, lily (*Magnolia liliiflora*), 254

Malay gooseberry, *see* Otaheite gooseberry

Malus floribunda (flowering crab apple), *38, 56,* 112, *113,* 254

manure, 47–48, 51, 56, 135, 192

maple, Japanese (*Acer palmatum* species), 254

marigolds, 162–63, 175

masonry work, 104–5

Matricaria 'White Wonder,' *174*

meadows, *152*

Meconopsis (Himalayan poppies), *54,* 57

Mediterranean-style houses, 11

Mellor, David, 139*n*, 151*n*

melons, 195, 208

melting out (leaf spot), 150

Merry Hall (Nichols), 159

Michigan, gardens in, *36*

microclimates, 40, 55–57

   foundation plantings and, 75

   in urban environment, 252

Milwaukee, Wis.:

   botanical gardens in, 184–86

   makeover in, *78–81*

Mission-style houses, 11, *126*

mixtures, grass-seed, 137

modern contemporary style, 9, 11, *61*

monochromatic flower schemes, 164

Monticello vegetable garden, 216–19

Morris, William, 59

Mount, The, *154,* 155–57

mowing, of lawns, 146–47

mulch, 83, 134, 140–41, 192–93, 208–9

Myrciaria cauliflora (jaboticaba), 242, 245

Myrciaria jaboticaba (jaboticaba), 242, 245

Mysore raspberry, *see* hill raspberry

narcissus, *158*

Nichols, Beverley, 159

nitrogen, 48, 51, 52–53, 192

nomenclature, botanical, 84

nonsoluble fertilizers, 53

'Nordlicht' (*Leucanthemum x superbum*), *185*

Of Gardens (Bacon), 131

Olmsted, Frederick Law, 89

onions, 194, 200, 203

   Egyptian, 218

   Spanish, *190*

Open Days Directory, 125

Open Days Program, 125

organic matter:

   for mulch, 140–41

   in soil, 47–48, 49, 135, 183, 191

Oriental vegetables, 203

Otaheite gooseberry (*Phyllanthus acidus*), 244–45

overseeding, 134

oyster shells, as paving material, 63

'Pacific Giant Hybrids' (*Delphinium*), *185*

Palmer, Ed, 241

parking, 16, 18, 62, 64, 65, 253

parsley, 207

parsnips, 200

Paspalum notate (Bahia grass), 139, 146

paths, in vegetable gardens, 192–93

patios vs. terraces, 97

paving:

   of driveways, 63–64

of outdoor living areas, 99–103

in urban gardens, *250*

peaches, 240–41

pears, *121*, 240–41

peas, 190, 204, 213, 218

snap, 205

peat moss, 140, 141, 183, 191

peat moss spreaders, 141

peonies, 173, 176

peppers, 192, 193, 194, 204, 208, *209*

Texas bird, *219*

perennial borders, 162, 163, 166–74

in Boerner Botanical Gardens, 184–86

maintenance of, *172*

selection of plants for, 169–72

shrubs in, 115, 116

space for, 168

sun and shade and, 168–69

in Victory Garden, *163*, 166–70

perennials:

defined, 160

flowers as, 160, 162, 163, 166–74

ryegrass as, 138, 146, 151

tender, 160

time for transplanting of, 173

urban, 255

vegetable, 193

Pereskia aculeata (Barbados gooseberries), *244*

pesticides, 192, 209

pets, 141, 212

petunias, 160, 162

phlox, *171*

phosphorus, 52–53

photographs, as planting tool, 17

Phyllanthus acidus (Otaheite gooseberry), 244–45

pigeon grape (*Vitis aestivates*), 243–44

'Pink Lady' (*Helleborus*), 255

Plant Hardiness Zone Map, 27

plant heat-zone map, 27–28

planting boards, 214

plant-specific fertilizers, 53

plastic, black, 208–9

Plimoth Plantation, 258

Poa pratensis (Kentucky bluegrass), 138, 146, 148, 150, 151

pole beans, 199, 201

polychromatic flower schemes, 165

ponds, 107–12, 124–25

liner installation for, 110–12

pools:

rigid vs. lined, 109

swimming, 16, 18, 39

poppies, Himalayan (*Meconopsis*), *54*, 57

potassium, 52–53

potatoes, 193, 204, 209

'Preciosa' (*Hydrangea serrata*), 256

privacy, 17–26, 112, 251, 273

shrubs and, 115–17

'Profusion' (*Erigeron*), *174*

pruning, *241*

'Pumila' (*Astilbe chinensis*), 255

pumpkins, 205

'Purple Beauty' (*Trycyrtis formosana*), 255

pyrethrins, 192

pythium blight (grease spot), 150

rabbits, 212

radishes, 195, 209, 218

rain, 14, 35, 37, 45, 53, 193, 209

rain gauges, *147*

raised beds, 193, 258–59, *274*

rakes, 136, 144, 183, 214

blueberry, *235*

de-thatching, *134*

ranch-style house, front yard makeover for, *78–81*

raspberries, 222, 224–28, 240

canes, 225

selected, 228

trellises for, *224*, 226–27

"ratio of riser to tread," 89

Redland Fruit and Spice Park, *242*, 243–45, 281

Reford, Alexander, 55, 57

Reford, Elsie Stephen, 55–57

repotting plants, 262–63

resources, 281

rhododendrons, 76, 127

rhubarb, 193

Robinson, William, 3

rocks, 47

Rollins, Chris, 243

rooftop gardens, 248, 251, 253, 259, 261

rototilling, 135, 191–92, 213

row cover, 209–10

Rubus ideaeus, 240

Rubus niveus (hill raspberry), 244

rudbeckia, *171*

running bond pattern, 100

rust, 151

rustic style, *20*

rye, winter, 213

ryegrass:
    annual, 137, 146
    perennial (*Lolium perenne*), 138, 146, 151

St. Augustine grass (*Stenotaphrum secundatum*), 139, 146

Salvia coccinea 'Cherry Blossom,' 175

Salvia farinacea 'Sea Breeze,' *174*

sand, sandy soil, 46–49, 135

santolina, *152*

savory, summer, 207

sawdust, aged, 140

scale, outdoor, 88, *133*

Scott, Frank, 74–75

screen plantings, 17, 18, 19, 22, 25–26
    in front yard, *62*

scythes, hand, 133

'Sea Breeze' (*Salvia farinacea*), *174*

seed boxes, 194

seeds:
    annuals grown from, 180–81
    grass, *see* grass seed
    vegetable, storage of, 200
    for vegetables, 193–94, 215

serviceberry (*Amelanchier* species), 254

shade, 37, 39–41, 45, 92, 112
    full, 41
    grass and, 133–34, 137
    partial, 41, 168–69
    perennial borders and, 168–69
    perennials in, 162

shallots, 205

shears, 214

shrubs:
    in backyards, 115–20
    best bets for, 118–20
    evergreen, 72
    for urban gardens, 256–57

sight lines, 16–17, 45, *80,* 251

silt, 47

slate, 103

snap beans, 200, 201

snow mold, 151

sod, 136–37
    factors to look for in, *143*
    laying of, 142–44
    removal of, for flower beds, 182
    storage of, 144

sod cutters, 134

soil, 37, 46–53
    compost for, 47, 48, 50–52, 56
    fertilizer for, 52–53
    in flower beds, 182–83
    foundation shrub planting and, 82, 83
    for lawns, 134, 135
    manure for, 47–48, 51, 56
    nonorganic components of, 47
    organic matter in, 47–48, 49, 135, 183, 191
    pH of, 75, 135, 213
    simple test of, 46
    urban, 252–53, 265, *274*
    for vegetable gardens, 46, 53, 191–92, 193, 212–13
    worms in, 47, 49

soilless mix, 180, 181

solar power, 212

Southwest, lawns in, 132

Southwestern-style garden, 11

spades, 182

spading forks, 214

Spanish onions, *190*

spinach, 195, 200, 205, 211, 218

sports, 96

squash, 190, 208, 209

    summer, 205

    winter, 206

'Star White' (*Zinnia angustifolia*), *174, 175*

steps:

    front, 70–71

    garden, 14, 155–57

    garden, "ratio of riser to tread" for, 89

    outdoor, scale of, 88

string line, 214

stones, 17, 71, 81

    for outdoor living areas, 100–105

    for walkways, *68, 69*

straights, 137

strawberries, 220, 229–34

    clan of, 232–33

    grown in jars, 230–31

    planting times for, 233

    selected, 234

streetscapes, importance of, 60–63

string beans, *199,* 213

string line, 214

succulents, *126,* 270, *271*

Sullivan, W. Michael, 139*n*, 146*n*, 151*n*

summer patch, 151

summer savory, 207

summer squash, 205

sun, 37, 39–41, 45, 75

    full, 41, 168–69

    grass for, 137

    partial, 41, 42, *43*

    perennial borders and, 168–69

    for vegetable gardens, 190

sunflowers, 176

Sunset magazine, 28

'Superba' (*Syringa microphylla*), 256

Sweet alyssum 'Snow Crystals,' 175

swimming pools, 16, 18, 39

Swinnen, Christopher, 277–78, 281

Swinnen Garden, *276, 277, 278*

Swiss chard, *191,* 206, 209, *210*

symbols, 45

symmetry vs. balance, 10, 11

Syringa microphylla 'Superba,' 256

Taliesin, 31–33

terraces, 14, 96, 109, *113*

    furniture for, 106–7

    of Hobbs, *128,* 129

    patios vs., 97

    paving considerations for, 99–103

    step-by-step instructions for laying of,

        104–5

Texas bird pepper, *219*

thatch, 136

Thomas Jefferson's Garden Book (Betts), 218

three-dimensional plantings, 116

tilth, 191

tomatoes, 190, 193, 194, 195, 200, 206, 208, 218

    cages for, 198–99

    'Favorita,' *188*

    top, 215

    watering of, 209

tools, *see specific tools*

Tower Hill Botanical Garden, 241

trees, 15

    in backyards, 113–15, 118–20

    best bets for, 118–20

    for urban gardens, 254

trellises, 199, 224, 226–27

    trompe l'oeil, 266, *267*

triangulation, 13

trompe l'oeil, 266, *267*

tropical gardens and species, *4,* 129

Trycyrtis formosana 'Purple Beauty,' 255

tulips, 176, *178–79*

unsightly vistas, eliminating of, 17–26, 251
urban gardens, 246–79
    checklist for, 253
    concealing unsightly views in, 251
    house's relationship with, 248, *250*
    makeovers and, 272–75
    microclimates and, 252
    muffling sounds in, 251
    mystery and privacy for, 251
    nowhere to hide in, 248
    paving in, *250*
    perennials for, 255
    raised beds in, 258–59, *274*
    shrubs for, 256–57
    sight lines for, 251
    soil for, 252–53, 265, *274*
    trees for, 254
    trompe l'oeil in, 266, *267*
urban makeover, 272–75

Vancouver, Hobbs garden in, 126–29
'Variegata' (*Carex siderostricta*), 255
Vaux, Calvert, 89
vegetable gardens, 16, 18, 188–219
    in autumn, 211
    autumn soil enhancements for, 212–13
    choice of vegetables for, 201–6
    cold frames for, 195, 196–97
    fertilizer for, 53, 192
    flowers in, 160, 175–76
    hedges for, 212
    heirloom, 213
    herbs for, 207
    of Jefferson, 216–19
    laying out of, 192–93
    maintenance of, 208
    mammalian marauders in, 212
    organic vs. inorganic, 192
    pests and pestilence and, 209–10
    planning to get the most from, 200
    raised beds in, 193
    reasons for, 190
    seeds for, 193–94, 200, 215
    selection of site for, 190
    soil for, 46, 53, 193, 212–13
    soil preparation for, 191–92
    solar power in, 212
    sun and shade patterns and, 39
    top tools for, 214
    vertical growing in, 198–99
    see also specific vegetables
Veronicastrum 'Fascination,' *34*
vertical gardening, 198–99
Viburnum trilobum, 119
Victorian style, *21*, 60, 74–75
Victory Garden, 15, *114*, 121
    back terrace at, *100*
    composting at, 50–51
    driveways at, 64
    fencing for, 21
    flowers in, 42, *43, 158,* 175–78
    landscape plans for, *12, 44*
    mower blades at, 146
    orchard at, 240–41
    perennial border in, *163,* 166–72
    rain in, 35, *38*
    rear entrance of, *16*
    seed box of, *194*
    value of improving the front landscape in, *62*
    vegetable garden in, *188,* 191–95, 198–207, *210*
    water gardening at, 109
Vinca 'Blue Pearl,' 175
visual interest, year-round, 100, 116–17
Vitis aestivates (pigeon grape), 243–44

walkways, 16, 18, 22, *61, 62, 63,* 68–72, 96
    decking developed from, 97, 98
    hose planning layout for, 71–72
    size of, 70–71, 88
    straight vs. curved, 71
    weather considerations and, 68
Warner, Charles Dudley, 247

water, 18
    for growing annuals from seeds, 180–81
    for lawns, 132, 134, 137, 140, 141, 143, 144, 145
    for planting, 83
    soil type and, 47
    for vegetable gardens, 209
water-filled rollers, 140, 141, 143, 144
water gardens, 107–12
    pond liner installation for, 110–12
    urban, 252, 268–69, *274*
watering system, automatic, 137, 141, 145, *147*, 265–66
water level, 14–15
water-soluble fertilizers, 53
weather, 35–42
    walkway considerations and, 68
    wet, 81, 103
weeds, 64, 134, 136, 137
Wharton, Edith, 155–57
wheelbarrows, 18, 70, 144
white fringe tree (*Chionanthus virginicus*), 254
white grubs, 149
'Wide Brim' (*Hosta*), 255

wildlife, 124–25
wind, 15, 37, 40, 41–42, 45
windchill factor, 42
window boxes, *246*, 265–66
"winter kill," 42
winter squash, 206
Woman's Hardy Garden, A (Ely), 35
wood, in decks, 96–99
woodchucks, 212
'Woodcreek Rose' (*Gomphrena*), 175
Works Progress Administration (WPA), 185
World War II, 162
worms, 47, 49, 148, 149
Wright, Catherine, 31
Wright, Frank Lloyd, 31–32

yews, 76

Zinnia angustifolia 'Star White,' *174*, 175
zinnias, 160, 162, *174*, 176
zone maps, 27–29, *36*
zoysia grasses (*Zoysia* species), 139, 146, 148